WINE

THE WINE GUIDE FOR FUN-LOVING PEOPLE

WINE REJUVENATES

LOUIS PASTEUR

Enjoy the Magic of Wine -
Al & Sandi Putnam

ALAN R. & SANDRA L. PUTNAM

Salandi Publishers

Library of Congress Catalog Card Number: 94-92194
ISBN: 1-56044-305-7

Published by Salandi Publishers, P. O. Box 369,
Gallatin Gateway, Montana 59730, in cooperation with
SkyHouse Publishers, an imprint of Falcon Press.

Design and typesetting by Eric Heidle for SkyHouse Publishers.

Distributed by Falcon Press,
P. O. Box 1718, Helena, Montana 59624
phone toll-free 1-800-582-2665.

First Edition

Manufactured in the U. S. A.

Dedicated in memory of Dr. Anne Hartung,
who always purveyed a fun-loving spirit
and who was snatched from us
tens of thousands of glasses of wine prematurely.

Readers Rave About *Wine Magic*

"*Wine Magic* has convinced me to recommend red wine instead of aspirin for preventing heart disease. I drink it myself."

> I. B. Profen, M.D.
> Swampscott, MA

"*Wine Magic* has got to be the funniest book ever written about wine. Every time I pick it up I giggle and pee my pants."

> Melissa Merlot
> Stillwater, MT

"Like, wow! As I turned the pages of *Wine Magic*, I felt like I actually was in the heart of wine country instead of in the valley."

> Sarah Sémillon
> Sonoma, CA

"Well, gollee, it's really great to finally learn how to prenounce all of those fancy wine names."

Fred Fume (prenounced Foo-may)
Big Spring, TX

"Hurrah-Hurrah for *Wine Magic!*"

Kay Sirah-Syrah
Willbe-Willbe, Australia

"Thanks so much! With all the helpful suggestions in *Wine Magic* for good-value wines, we've been able to fill our cellar for under $1,000. Do you think it was wise to place our cellar in the ice shanty?"

Rosé Rikcowski
Manistee, MI

"After reading *Wine Magic* I developed a real nose for wine."

Cyrano DeChaunac
Paris, ID

"The flavor of wine is like delicate poetry."

Louis Pasteur

"The art of winemaking is almost a *magical* process. You start with raw grape juice and end up with an elegant beverage having superior attributes."

Doug Welsch
Fenn Valley Vineyards

Contents

Acknowledgments

Many thanks to the following people who have whetted our appetite for enological and viticultural knowledge over the past twenty-five years: Harry Agamalian, Dr. Clyde Elmore, Konstantin Frank, Joe Heitz, Dr. Stan Howell, Frank Lagomarsino, Larry Mawby, Dr. Julius Menn, Dave Miller, Jim Pedroncelli, Dr. Nelson Shaulis, Russ Smithyman, Robert Stemmler, André Tchelistcheff, Brother Timothy, and Doug Welsch.

A special note of thanks to Jim and Sandra O'Connell, Mark Barbera, and Mary Ries for reviewing the manuscript and providing helpful suggestions. We especially appreciate all the professional guidance from the folks at SkyHouse Publishing, most notably Noelle Sullivan and Eric Heidle.

Many great moments sharing wine with the following folks definitely deserve mention: Linda and Paul, Brenda and Mark, Mary and Stan, Jim and Sandra, Martha and John, Angie and Muralee, Bev and Harv, Patti and Tom, Leslie and Paul, Julie and Mark, Mark and Megan, B and Pete, Bebe and Pete, Dave and Scharry, Barbie and Ken, Jon and Susie, Amos and Evelyn, Mark and Sheila, Andy and Beth.

May the Great Spirit reserve a grand chateau in the sky for each of you.

Sal & Andi
Gallatin Gateway, Montana 1994

Preface

This book is especially intended for those people who are new to wine. Many people are eager to discover wine's magic, but realize they don't know shit[1] from Shinola.[2] If this is you, don't feel bad! Scores of folks aren't sure what wine to order with their favorite entrée at a restaurant. All too often the restaurant staff doesn't (or can't) provide much assistance. Many customers (and waiters or waitresses) are afraid they'll mispronounce the name of a wine, so they feel more comfortable pointing their choice out on a printed wine list or ordering by number. The purpose of this book is to help these people—and you—learn more about the basics of wine and wine appreciation.

There are a number of wine books on the market. In our humble, unbiased opinions, many of them have serious drawbacks. Several are so technical that they intimidate even intermediate wine lovers; many others are limited in scope to a single state or region. Some books overlook elementary (but important) discussions of wine labels or other considerations and questions, such as "How do I get the darn bottle open?" Most are poorly illustrated, some are out-of-date (since the wine business constantly changes), and almost all lack humor, an important complement to wine.

In this book, we hope to dispel two misconceptions about wine. The first is the notion that wine is a beverage intended primarily for snobs or "snottés". (Hey, watch it—we are not!) Sure there are more than a few "snottés" that drink wine, but they are rarely fun-lovers, so this book is not for them. The second notion is that wine is too expensive for the budget of the common man or woman. We'll show that people from all walks of life can afford to enjoy wine because there are many $3 to $4 bottles available for everyday drinking. There are also

---

[1] Wines named after old automobiles, rabid canines, etc.

[2] Gewürztraminer, Petite Sirah, etc.

many exceptional bottles that can be had in the $5 to $8 range. A whole chapter suggests many of the best wine values.

Many "wine experts" think all quality wines are made in either France, Italy, Germany, or California, depending on the experts' own origins. Although loyalty to local wine certainly has economic merit, having such limited horizons can cause you to miss some real treats produced in other areas. Quality wines are now produced in many areas of the world besides Europe and California and, more importantly, some very nice wines may be produced near your own backyard. Previously published wine books have missed many of the little-known domestic gems that provide both excellent quality and value.

There is some magic or mystique about wine that makes it appealing to a great variety of people. Some view wine as a treasure to be enjoyed only on special occasions or holidays. Others, like us, enjoy it every day as a complement to meals. Some people claim it as a hobby and collect certain vintages to enjoy at their prime. Still others view it as an investment for the future, and it's true that some bottles are worth a small fortune to those who have the bucks to buy them. Trips to wineries and tours of wine-producing areas (not *all* of which are prone to earthquakes) make excellent opportunities for short-term relaxation or longer vacations. Several recent studies even indicate that wine may provide important health benefits, when drunk in moderation.

And there's no denying that it's fun to drink wine with good friends; lifelong friendships can be enhanced by mutual appreciation of wine. To us, sampling a new bottle of wine is like fishing new waters, opening the pages of a new book, or listening to an album for the first time. In each of these circumstances there is an element of mystery and, hopefully, a pleasant surprise. In our travels, we've frequently encountered situations where restaurant employees were pitifully uninformed about their wine selections or the proper techniques for handling wines.[3] The information in this book will enable such employees to intelli-

---

[3]When we asked a waitress in a Montana restaurant what wine they had she retorted, "Red, white, and pink, buster."

gently guide and serve their customers. It will also provide the restaurant owner or manager with the knowledge he or she must have to stock and serve quality wines. Let's face it—properly presented wine provides greater enjoyment for the customer and can also be a big moneymaker for any restaurant.

We hope this book will set you at ease when you try wine while eating out and lead you to the bargains as well as some exceptional bottles for that special occasion. We'll offer our specific opinions from time to time, but please realize that your tastes may be different from ours. We've taken the liberty to include some other views in the book, including those of respected wine writers, vintners, relatives, friends, and even an occasional smart-ass like our special friend Luigi.

What gives us the credentials to write a wine book? Well, first and foremost, we are fun-loving people. We've had over twenty-five years of pleasant experiences with wine and consumed more than ten thousand bottles. We haven't tasted and spit hundreds of samples weekly, but we have enjoyed a hell of a bunch of wines as aperitifs, as complements to various cuisines,[4] and as desserts. We have traveled extensively to almost all of the world's wine regions, talking to many of the vintners and tasting thousands of their products. In addition to our own experience, we continue to read what other people have to say about the subject. We hope that what we've compiled and condensed will help you enjoy the magic of wine as much as we do.

---

[4] When we were younger we ate food; now we eat cuisine. Does this make us snobs?

WINE MAGIC

Chapter I
What is Wine?

To put it simply, wine is produced from fermentation of fruit juice (usually grape) by yeasts (specialized fungi). This product contains ethyl alcohol, organic acids (mostly lactic and succinic acids), numerous other chemicals (secondary metabolites) that impart flavor and taste, and sometimes a bit of residual sugar. The scientific term for winemaking is enology, and those who become experts in this trade are called enologists or vintners.

High-quality wine is made by taking grapes with a high quantity of sugar (mostly glucose and fructose) and organic acids (mostly tartaric, malic, and citric) and moving them quickly through a crushing process to remove most of the juice. Blush or pink wines are produced by leaving the juice with the skins of red grapes for a short period of time. Red wines are made by leaving the pigment-containing skins with the juice for a longer period of time. More than any other factor, the quality of the end product is determined by the quality of the grapes. Years that produce extremely high-quality grapes and ultimately high-quality wines are called "vintage" years. In addition to grape quality, the vintner's art determines the elegance of the final product.

Wines that are made from primarily one variety of grape are called "varietals." Federal and state laws specify what percentage (usually seventy-five percent or more) of juice from a variety is required to give the wine a varietal name. Many lower-priced wines are blends of two or more varieties; often these blends are pleasing and reasonably priced wines for everyday drinking. Some of the great wines from France are also blends whose components are carefully chosen to add complexity.

After juice is fermented to the desired point, it is clarified, to remove the solid particles, then bottled. Wines vary in their ability to store or age. Many of the white varietals do not store well for long periods of time and are best drunk in the first or second year after fermentation. Wines that store well or actually improve with age are often stored in oak barrels. The wine actually picks up important aromas and flavors from the oak. Oaks from different countries are known to impart special aromas or flavors and are selected specifically for each wine variety. Some red wines are aged in oak barrels for two to three years prior to bottling.

Wine has been mentioned in literature for five thousand years. It was important as a complement to meals and as a sacrament in the early history of the Mediterranean region. The Bible tells of Noah getting "blasted"[1] on wine and appearing naked in front of his boys. Apparently God was not too pissed-off[2] about this, because He later entrusted Noah with the future of all the world's creatures at the time of the great flood. We thought it was appropriate He selected a wine drinker for this task.

From the Middle East, wine was introduced to Europe, and numerous plantings were made in the river valleys of France and Germany. Grapes were brought to California by the Franciscan fathers in the early part of the nineteenth century and thrived in the accommodating habitat. Despite a series of natural and political disasters, California still contributes a major portion of the wine produced in this country.

Grape Species and Varieties

The culture of grapes, known as viticulture, encompasses numerous varieties grown throughout the world. Each region has its favorite wine types. The grapes of the Middle East, which were transplanted through-

---

[1] A slang term for over-indulgence.
[2] A slang term for God's anger.

out Europe and more recently into Australia, southern Africa, South America, and California, are the species *Vitis vinifera.* This species includes many of the famous varieties such as Cabernet Sauvignon, Pinot Noir, Chardonnay, and Riesling. The hardy native American grape is *Vitis labrusca.* Among its varieties are Concord, Delaware, and Niagara, which have been used for both grape juice and winemaking, primarily in the eastern United States. Wines made from the American grapes are often called "foxy" because of their particularly strong flavors.[3] Nonetheless, many people like these wines, most of which are made in either a sweet or sparkling style.

An exciting development for eastern growers and vintners has been the French-American crosses of grapes (*Vitis vinifera* x *Vitis rupestris* and *Vitis lincecumni*). Many of these varieties possess cold-hardiness closer to that of American grapes with wine qualities approaching those of European grapes. Among these jewels are Seyval Blanc, Vidal Blanc, and Vignoles.

The Magic of Quality

Wines produced in a particular year are known as a vintage. You might have heard someone say that 1986 was a great year for Cabernet or that 1984 was a "vintage year." In all grape-growing areas, some years produce higher quality grapes than others. These differences may be more noticeable in locations other than California because the California climate is more predictable from one year to the next.[4] Nonetheless, even California vintages vary enough that the wine expert can easily detect quality differences. This translates into a much higher price for the excellent vintages. Beginning buyers beware! That great bottle of a particular varietal you bought last year might turn out to be disappointing when purchased in a different vintage.

There are innumerable ideas about which factors separate the great wines from average wines. Most would agree that a great wine is com-

---

[3] And all this time you thought it was because they looked sexy!
[4] Yes, you can usually count on a bad fire or earthquake annually in California.

Old vines (like the ninety-year-old Zinfandel pictured here) produce grapes with special qualities.

plex in its odor and flavor components. Important aspects of quality are obviously imparted by the grapes themselves. Their chemical content (some four hundred chemicals have been identified in grapes) contribute many odors and flavors. There is a general feeling among wine experts that grapes that "suffer" contain a little something special, producing a better wine. Suffering might include environmental stresses on the grapevine from soil deficiencies (i.e., water or nutrients) or inclement weather (i.e., heat, wind, etc.) Experts also feel that older vines produce better quality fruit, and that lightening the fruit load on the vine will concentrate more goodies into fewer fruits. Having worked in plant science and natural products chemistry for much of my career, I can rationalize a scientific explanation for these observations. When

4

plants are under stress, they increase their production of secondary metabolites such as phenolics, flavonoids, and tannins, which we know are important components of the fruit. It also makes scientific sense that plants with a higher leaf-to-fruit ratio will pump more energy into the remaining fruit.

There is also a school of thought which holds that certain strains of yeast used in fermentation will impart better odors and flavors. Some vintners swear by specific strains, while others swear by mixtures of natural strains that normally inhabit the skins of the fruit.[5] The latter group worries about using any fungicides on the grapes because of potential damage to the natural yeasts. There is little doubt that part of a wine's flavor is imparted by the chemicals produced in the fermentation process, and perhaps from the yeasts themselves in cases where the wine is allowed to remain for long periods on the yeast (a procedure known as *Sur lie*). Some unwanted microbes can also produce off-flavors in wine. If you put a group of winemakers in a room to discuss this topic you will hear many different opinions.

For wines that profit by aging, there is an additional flavor aspect acquired from the barrel in which the wine is placed. Wines in extended contact with various kinds of oak will extract flavor components from the oak. Vintners carefully choose specific oaks for each kind of wine, and again, not all agree. Slow chemical changes in the bottle are the last steps in a wine's maturation process. Some of these changes, such as the softening of tannin which smooths out the wine, are good. Others, such as the loss of fruitiness or oxidation of pigments that turns a brilliant red to a dull brown, are bad. The key is to drink each bottle when it expresses its best qualities. This perfect moment will vary from one wine to another, so you will have to depend on the advice of producers, other experts, and your own expanding knowledge in making the decision.

Good winemakers are always striving for higher quality. Many set

---

[5] Actually, most vintners swear like hell about everything.

their sights high and shoot for the best wines of Burgundy or Bordeaux. These wines are expensive to produce because they involve a lot of time and costly equipment. To be financially successful, wineries must balance their desire to be world class (ego) with their need for cash flow. To achieve the latter, most must produce some good "quaffing" wines in the $5 to $10 category to sell in volume. Many wineries that depend solely on the "high-class" stuff have survived only because the owner(s) had unlimited resources to keep the ego-trip going. In other words, a winery might become a losing proposition even though its products are "Côtes du Rhône" class (one of France's premier wine-producing regions). I mention this just in case you get the idea you want to start a winery (it has occurred to us a few times). It's a very competitive and expensive venture!

Is Organic Better?

There are several wineries now offering organic wines. This means they should not use synthetic chemicals or fertilizers in the production of the grapes, although they are allowed to use sulfites in the vinification process. The rationale for the use of sulfites is that they occur naturally in fruits and vegetables. There is no scientific basis to suggest that these wines are any better for you, and our personal tasting of several organic varietals has not convinced us this wine tastes any better. Most have been average to good. Perhaps their best attribute is that they will make some people (those with chemophobia) feel safer drinking wine.[6] People who worry about ingesting infinitesimal amounts of chemical residues (which might be carcinogenic) should realize they are already ingesting massive amounts of natural carcinogens in the healthy fruits and vegetables they eat daily. And certainly there is no evidence to suggest that these are harmful in the doses we eat. When it comes to our wine, we feel more comfortable knowing the grapes were grown with proper integrated pest management practices (including minimal

---

[6] Includes movie stars and other celebrities who are pretty ignorant about science but feel compelled to utilize their visibility to speak out about it.

chemicals when necessary) and produced with clean vinification techniques (including the use of bisulfite) to remove the nasty microbes. And, personally, we enjoy wine more when we know it wasn't produced by a bunch of yahoos running through the grapes with their stinky bare feet.[7]

Wine Styles

Wines are produced in many different styles. Common terms that describe them are sweet, semisweet, off-dry, or dry, and light-, medium-, or heavy-bodied. Wines that have a sweet taste retain higher quantities of sugar. This is called residual sugar and results from incomplete fermentation of the juice. Often the vintner stops fermentation at a particular point to retain the desired amount of sugar in the wine.

Sweet dessert wines are sometimes made from grapes harvested past their normal maturity; late harvest grapes have a more raisinlike appearance. Dessert wines might contain up to forty percent residual sugar. Some of the famous European dessert wines are made from raisins that are infested with the fungus *Botrytis cinerea*, or "Noble Rot."[8] Occasionally, American vintners can also capture this rare opportunity.

Wines that contain more than two percent residual sugar will usually taste fairly sweet. Wines that contain from one to two percent sugar might be expected to be semisweet (*demi-sec*), and those with less than one percent would tend to be off-dry or dry. Wine is sometimes sweetened, but in many areas it can only be sweetened by adding back unfermented grape juice or concentrate rather than sugar. This process is controlled by state laws.

Grape to Bottle

When grapes are harvested, they are moved to the crushing area as

---

[7] And associated stinky microbes.
[8] Not pretty to look at, but often nobility isn't, e.g., Prince Charles.

rapidly as possible. This prevents oxidation, or browning, of the fruit. Grapes, like us folks, bear specific populations of microorganisms on their skins. Grape skins carry yeasts, some of which are capable of producing good wine, and a variety of fungi and bacteria, some of which are capable of spoiling wine. To prevent unwanted microbes from spoiling wine, it is common to add sulfur dioxide (as bisulfite) to stop microbial activity. Vintners then add special strains of yeast that are known to produce consistent results, batch after batch. Enology has become a rather exact science, it would seem. Not! A lot of art and individual creativity goes into the production of a particular style of wine. Some European and California vintners still use mixtures of wild yeasts because they feel they contribute more complexity to the wine. Different techniques, along with variable grapes from year to year and region to region, produce a myriad of different wine flavors that can be detected by experienced tasters.

Typical containers used in the production of white wines. The large, stainless steel tanks are used to ferment many white varietals; the oak barrels are being used to ferment and age Chardonnay.

An automated bottling line similar to that found in many wineries throughout the United States. The equipment is capable of dispersing wine, corking bottles, and affixing capsules and labels at a rapid rate.

In general, the juice from the white varieties of grapes is immediatly pressed from the crushed fruit and fermented in large stainless steel tanks. Some wineries centrifuge the juice prior to fermentation in the belief that this process produces a fresher or fruitier wine. White wine is fermented at cool temperatures for a period of several weeks. If the cellar conditions are not cool enough, cooling jackets are placed over the stainless steel tanks to maintain proper temperatures. The white grape variety Chardonnay is often fermented in smaller oak barrels so the juice can extract desired aromas and flavors from the wood.

In the production of red wines, the skins and pulp are left in the fermenting tank with the juice. The fermentation processes extract the red pigments from the grapes, making a distinctly colored product. Red wines are fermented at somewhat warmer temperatures than whites, normally in the 65-70°F range, but too warm a fermentation can produce unpleasant odors or flavors in the wine. During fermentation, chemicals called tannins are extracted from the red grapes (mostly from the skins). These compounds impart the "puckery" feel in the mouth, particularly when one drinks a young red wine. Professionals call this astringency. These chemicals also allow red wines to keep for a long time without oxidizing or browning. If stored under cool conditions, some red wines can keep for decades or even centuries.[9] As they age, the tannins soften and the wine becomes much more pleasing to the taste. Most red varieties of wine benefit from aging in wooden barrels, and there are many schools of thought regarding the best type of oak to use. Each vintner develops his/her own ideas regarding the proper type of barrel and cooperage time (time "on oak") for a particular variety of wine. This is an example of the art we mentioned earlier.

Since oak barrels are so expensive to replace, viticultural researchers are now experimenting with the addition of oak wood chips to old wine barrels. The hope is that the same flavors will be imparted at much less cost.

Before wine can be bottled, it must be clarified, or removed from the sediment which has settled to the bottom of the tank. One way to accomplish this is simply to pump the wine away from the sediment. Another method of clarification is called fining. In this technique, a material such as bentonite clay, egg whites, or gelatin is added to the tank to hasten the settling of dispersed solids. Filtration is another method of clarification, but many vintners fear that desirable taste factors can also be removed by this method.

After having been bottled for a couple of months, wines should be clear in appearance. When opening a wine, do not be disturbed to find small amounts of sediment or tartrate crystals near the cork or at the bottom of the bottle. These are natural constituents and do not reduce the quality of the wine.[10]

When wines are bottled they must be kept essentially free from air. The cork (made from the outer portions of cork oak trees) is an effective device to keep the liquid inside and almost all the air outside the

---

[9] Pretty dumb to store them longer than you might expect to live, eh?

[10] Besides, only celebrities and wimps worry about such things.

bottle. After a bottle of wine has been opened it will not keep very long unless the air is evacuated from the bottle. A number of devices are available to accomplish this task, one of which is shown. Finishing an open bottle of wine is seldom a problem at our house because of helpful neighbors and friends.

Long-term storage of wine is favored by cool temperatures (55°F is ideal). The basement or cellar is probably the best place, unless it gets too wet. If you live in an area where it is relatively warm year-round or where basements aren't normally built, you might want to consider a refrigerated storage cabinet. You can purchase these in a variety of shapes, sizes, and prices. In a pinch, try an old refrigerator set on the lowest setting to keep your wine just below 60°F. Wine should be stored at reasonably high humidity (fifty to seventy percent) to prevent excessive drying of the corks, but extremely high humidity (seventy-five percent

A small pump used to evacuate air from a partially empty wine bottle. The rubber stopper allows air to be pumped out without allowing more air to enter. This particular model is called Vacu-Vin and is produced by Vacu Products B.V., P. O. Box 498, Delft, Holland.

or more) can result in deterioration of wine labels. Oh yes, one more thing. It's best to treat your wine *somewhat* like a mushroom. Keep it in the dark—but, please, don't cover it up with horseshit.

By now we've probably told you more than you wanted to know about how grapes are handled and how wine is produced and stored. If we didn't, you can find more information in the other references we recommend.

Now let's get on to the primary purpose of this book—developing your appreciation of wine.

Chapter 2
The Wine Bottle

Wine Labels

A lot of the important information you need to know about a bottle of wine is on the label. For some reason, people have trouble interpreting labels on a variety of products. Perhaps this is because most labels spend a lot of time telling you what and what not to do. Relax, wine labels will not tell you what to do! The worst a wine label will do is hit you with some new terms. If you run into terms not covered in this chapter you'll be able to find them in the glossary. Perhaps we can

1984
WASHINGTON STATE
Chardonnay

Balcom & Moe Vineyards

PRODUCED AND BOTTLED BY BOOKWALTER WINERY, PASCO, WA USA
BW.WA.104 ALCOHOL 13.5% BY VOLUME

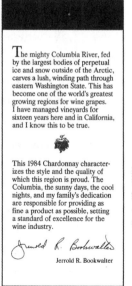

The mighty Columbia River, fed by the largest bodies of perpetual ice and snow outside of the Arctic, carves a lush, winding path through eastern Washington State. This has become one of the world's greatest growing regions for wine grapes. I have managed vineyards for sixteen years here and in California, and I know this to be true.

This 1984 Chardonnay characterizes the style and the quality of which this region is proud. The Columbia, the sunny days, the cool nights, and my family's dedication are responsible for providing as fine a product as possible, setting a standard of excellence for the wine industry.

Jerrold R. Bookwalter

A Bookwalter Chardonnay label.

better understand wine labels by looking carefully at a few different examples, the first being a domestic white wine label.

- *Bookwalter* is the name of the winery or company producing the wine.
- *1984* is the year the grapes were harvested. This is known as the vintage.
- *Washington State* means that the grapes were grown and the wine produced there.
- *Chardonnay* is the variety of grape from which the wine is produced. When a wine is primarily from one type of grape (usually seventy-five percent or more) it is known as a varietal.
- *Balcom & Moe Vineyards* indicates the exact source of the grapes. Specific vineyards, because of their soil or climatic conditions may produce grapes that yield especially flavorful wines. These grapes are fermented and bottled separately rather than being blended with grapes of the same variety from other sites.
- *B.W. WA.104* is an indication that this is bonded winery number 104 in the state of Washington, and that all agencies that can collect taxes will do so on each and every bottle.
- *Alcohol 13.5% by volume* is the alcohol content of the final product. The maximum alcohol content for an unfortified (no booze added) wine is about fifteen percent. At that point, the yeast are no longer active. Most white wines are ten to fourteen percent alcohol, while reds may go up to fifteen percent. If a wine is fifteen percent alcohol by volume, a 750 ml bottle will contain about 112 ml of alcohol, or about four ounces. If you and a companion were to consume this bottle with a meal you would each ingest about two ounces of alcohol.

Back or side labels may provide interesting information about the viticultural area or the winery. In recent years, the Bureau of Alcohol, Tobacco, and Firearms (BATF) has required health warning statements on all beverages that contain alcohol. However, this same agency (which handled the Waco Branch Davidian incident so brilliantly) will not allow any label statements regarding the health benefits of wine (see Chapter 12). Rumor has it most of these folks don't even have a sense of humor, so they probably won't read this book. Personally, I'd turn them over to the FBI![1]

Let's look at a label from a proprietary wine bottle.

- The **Konocti** winery has chosen to call this product *"PASSITO"* (a proprietary name) and has also identified it as a *late harvest Zinfandel*.
- The vintage is *1990*.
- The grapes were produced and the wine bottled in *Lake County, California*.
- The *harvest sugar* content of 41° Brix (percent by weight) tells us these were raisins at harvest. The *residual sugar* content of 12.5 percent by weight clearly shows us this is a sweet dessert wine.

---

[1] And that's just what the Government did!

A Konocti Passito Zinfandel label.

- The *alcohol content* of this wine is 14.4 percent by volume.
- The wine *contains* traces of *sulfites*. Sulfites may be added to the crushed grapes prior to fermentation to kill any bacteria or unwanted yeast. They might also be added to the wine to stop fermentation at the desired point. They are present in the wine as sulfur dioxide. Some people must be concerned about sulfites because of allergic responses to them, but they are not proven to cause other health problems (see Chapter 12).
- This label (being more recent) contains the *government health warning* statements. We hope that these statements will help prevent alcohol abuse rather than just annoy moderate consumers of wine. From time to time, they cause the authors consternation; or as Luigi so clearly phrases it, "They piss me off."

Now let's look at some imported wine labels. Foreign labels can be a bit more confusing because they contain considerable information, much of which is not in English. The example below is from a Spanish red wine label.

- The band on top indicates that the wine won a prestigious award. American wines that win awards in state and county fair competitions may also bear a band or sticker identifying the award. This obviously helps sell the wine.
- The wine is produced in *Spain*.
- *Marqués de Cáceres* is the company producing the wine.
- *1987* is the vintage.
- *RIOJA* is the region in Spain where the grapes are grown and the wine is produced.
- Since it is labeled *red wine* it is probably a blend rather than a varietal.
- The *alcohol content* is 12.5 percent.
- The wine is shipped to the United States by *Uniôn Viti-Vinicola Company* and the U.S. importer is *Vineyard Brands*.

*A Marqués de Cáceres
Rioja label.*

Our next example is a red Bordeaux wine label.

- *Mis en Bouteille au Château* translates as "Bottled at the Chateau."
- The wine is produced by *Château Les Ormes De Pez*.
- The vineyard and winery are located in the *Saint-Estèphe* district of the Médoc region in northern Bordeaux.
- *Bordeaux* wines are blends of the best grapes produced in an area and therefore do not carry a varietal name. (In Saint-Estèphe they use a lot of Cabernet Sauvignon.)
- The vintage is *1990*.
- The wine contains *13% alcohol*.

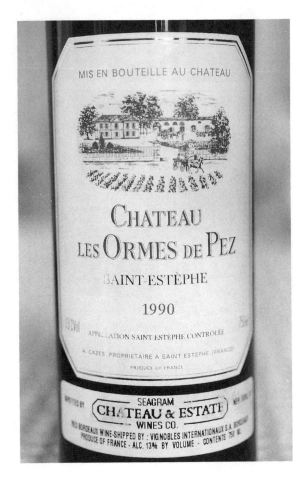

A Château Les Ormes De Pez Bordeaux label.

- The wine is shipped by *Vignobles Internationaux* and imported by *Seagram*.
- *Government warning* statements appear on a back label not shown here.

Let's look at a German wine label.

- The wine was produced for *Julius Kayser & Co.*
- The wine is termed *Piesporter Michelsberg*.
  This is a *Grosslage*, which means the grapes were received from several vineyards in the area of Piesport. The grapes were not from one specific vineyard (*Einzellage*). Usually these types of wines contain considerable Müller-Thurgau as well as Johannisberg Riesling.

A Julius Kayser Piesporter Michelsberg label.

- The grapes came from the *Mosel-Saar-Ruwer* region of Germany (see Chapter 11).
- *Qualitatswein* indicates this is not one of the two higher categories (QbA and QmP) of wine produced in Germany. Typically, *Qualitatswein* are semisweet wines that have sugar added before fermentation. They are tested for quality and distinct character.
- Interestingly, this wine was *produced for Kayser by a winery in Bingen, Germany*, which is located in another region.
- The wine is *9.5% alcohol.*
- A top label (not shown) indicates the vintage was *1992.*

Italian wine labels have become more straightforward in recent years. Let's examine one.

19

A Fontana Candida Orvieto label.

- *Fontana Candida* is the producer.
- *Orvieto* is the name of a town in the Umbria region. The grapes came from this area.
- *Denominazione Di Origine Controllata* (*DOC*) indicates the quality ranking of the wine. Under 1992 law, this wine would fall in the second highest category of ranking.
- *Classico* indicates the best lots of wine.
- *Secco* is Italian for dry.
- *1992* is the vintage.

Bottle Characteristics

You probably have noticed that wine bottles come in several different shapes and sizes. Wine is marketed most often in 750 ml (4/5 quart or 1/5 gallon) bottles, 1.5 liter (1 3/5 quart or 2/5 gallon) bottles known as magnums, and 1 gallon jugs. The bottles used for wine are different shapes and colors depending on the type of wine they contain. This is done for practical reasons (e.g., colored glass excludes light that might harm the wine) or because of tradition (i.e. Johannisberg Riesling is placed in tall-necked, brown-tinted bottles called flutes). The various sizes and shapes of bottles are shown below.

You may have noticed that wine bottles always have a decorative cover (capsule) over the top of the cork. This capsule may be a foil-like material (some of which previously contained lead) or plastic. Since there was concern about minute amounts of lead in foil covers, wineries discontinued their use at the end of 1992. Several wineries are now experimenting with new bottle-sealing techniques because cork is becoming too scarce (and expensive) and some foil capsules have caused difficulties. Perhaps we'll end up with screw caps on our premium wines, ending bottle-top snobbery for all time!

After uncorking the bottle it is a good idea to wipe the area around

Common wine bottles found in the marketplace today. From left to right: a 375 ml 'split', most often used for dessert wines; a 750 ml flute-shaped bottle, most often used for Gewürztraminer and Riesling; a 750 ml claret bottle with abrupt shoulders (which allow for better stacking), used for red wines that will be stored for long periods; a clear claret bottle used for white wine such as Sauvignon Blanc; a Burgundy bottle, most often used for Chardonnay or Pinot Noir; a 1.5 liter claret bottle.

the mouth with a damp cloth to remove any cork fragments as well as other residues (mold, etc.). This will assure that you will not pour your guest or customer a bit of cork, mold, or other material that would distract from the pleasing appearance of the wine.

Some generics (blended wines not carrying the name of the grape) are marketed in plastic-lined boxes containing three, four, or five liters. These boxes are equipped with dispenser valves that allow easy pouring without lifting the box. For example, **Almaden** sells three varietals and three generics in four liter boxes, whereas **Franzia** sells about a half-dozen of each in three or five liter boxes. These are handy wines to have around when you have a lot of riffraff[2] in the house.

Storing Wine

Wine keeps best under cool conditions that assure no entry of air into the wine bottle. The best way to keep air from getting into the bottle is to store the bottles in a position where the corks remain in contact with the wine. This means that the bottles should be stored on their sides or upside down rather than right side up. Most wine racks are designed to hold bottles on their sides. If wine is to be kept in cases, the bottles can be inserted upside down, or the cases can be positioned so the bottles lie on their sides. Another advantage of keeping your cork wet is that corks are easier to remove when they are moist. We've seen restaurant wine servers become totally embarrassed because a dry cork fell apart as they tried to open bottles at our table. We've always tried to set them at ease with a remark such as, "You handled that brilliantly!"

Not everyone has the perfect cellar for wine. The important thing is to avoid excessive heat, that is, temperatures preferably not over 70° F. The worst place to store wine is high on a rack in the kitchen or on top of the refrigerator, where heat rises and cooks your wine. The best places are in your basement or on a closet floor, where temperatures tend to be cooler.

---

[2] People who aren't necessarily friends or family but who always manage to show up when there is food or wine around.

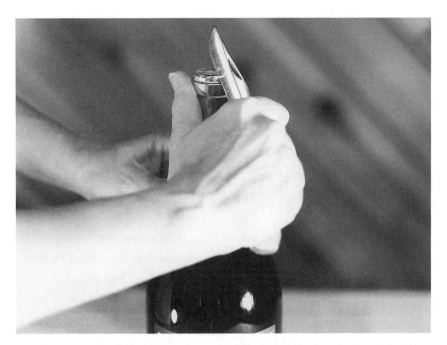

A simple way to remove the capsule top is to cut around the edge of the bottle with a sharp knife. The rest of the capsule remains intact while you remove the cork.

Wines bottled in 750 ml bottles with cork stoppers, capsules, and fancy labels are usually more expensive (and complex) than so-called jug wines. These premium wines usually have some outstanding characteristics that make them worthy of a special occasion. As you gain an appreciation for the many flavors and aromas of premium wines you will want to share these delicacies with your special friends or guests. But don't get the idea that the 1.5 liter or gallon jug wines are not worthy of your consideration. Many are good quality, consistent from year to year, and economical additions to everyday meals. You may still want to drink a pleasant $3.50 bottle of blended wine with your spaghetti or pizza when guests aren't around. And of course, pull out the jugs and/or boxes when the leeches[3] show up.

---

[3] A special breed of riffraff, i.e., those who imbibe wine like a sponge soaks up water.

Getting the Bottle Open

An old friend of mine once said, "You can tell a lot about a person's intelligence by whether he buys wines with screw-on caps or corks." While certainly not mind-boggling, the clean removal of a cork does require a bit of knowledge, the proper tools, and a little good luck. As mentioned previously, corks are easier to remove if the wine has been properly stored, either on its side or upside down, so the corks have not dried out. The tools used to remove corks are called corkscrews and pullers. Examples of inexpensive and easy-to-use devices are pictured.

Before attempting to pull a cork, you should remove the top of the capsule. Some capsules come with a pull tab that allows easy removal of their top portion and ready access to the cork. I've found the easiest/cheapest way to remove foil capsules is to cut them with a knife in a circle just outside the lip of the bottle. This allows the top to be removed while the remainder stays attached to the bottle.

Corkscrews that have a device to grip the lip of the bottle are more

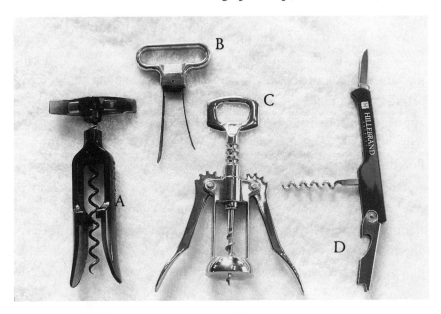

Some effective devices for removing corks from wine bottles. A is the screwpull; B is a cork puller; C is the common wing-lever corkscrew; D is a bootlever corkscrew.

foolproof than those with just a hand grip. Models A and C are examples of corkscrews with bottle grips. Notice the difference in the thickness of the screw auger on these two models. Generally, a smaller diameter auger that follows a straight path into the cork is less apt to tear the cork. Larger diameter augers tear more cork tissue and result in broken corks. Model A is known as a screwpull. It has a patented antifriction coating on the auger which slides through the cork without tearing it. If a cork does break, the portion remaining in the neck of the bottle can usually be removed with a puller (Model B). Model C is the standard wing lever corkscrew, which usually works nicely unless the cork has dried out.

The cork puller (B) is a simple tool that works effectively unless its pulling shafts become bent. To use the puller, insert the longest shaft into the area between the cork and the bottle. Then carefully insert the shorter shaft on the opposite side of the cork. Wiggle the shafts downward until the cork nearly touches the handle of the puller. Now the cork may be pulled out with a slight twisting motion. This device does not leave any holes or marks on the cork and is therefore called the butler's friend, since the butler (or our friend Luigi) can remove expensive wine, replace it with cheap wine, and recork the bottles without anyone suspecting a thing. Luigi claims it's important to have a simple tool for simple fools to use.

Any of these devices is more effective than the lever-type corkscrew (Model D) called a boot lever or waiter's friend, which is often provided to restaurant wine servers. The advantages of boot levers are that they are compact, inexpensive, and contain all the tools necessary to remove both the capsule top and cork. The main disadvantage is that the leverage is often applied at an angle and this will inevitably tear or break the cork (a recurring nightmare for cork savers like us). If the leverage is carefully applied straight up and down, the boot lever will usually work effectively on corks that have not dried out. When leverage is applied at an angle, get ready to say, "You handled that brilliantly."

If you personally have a cork break, and all else fails, clean the area

A corkscrew presented to the authors as a gift. As far as we can tell it has no practical or socially redeeming values.

around the break to remove all small particles, then push the remainder of the cork into the bottle. Do this after you have patiently listened to all the insults, of course. The wine can then be decanted into another container. (We use a more expensive wine bottle so any insulting friends will think they're getting a better wine.)

After you learn to enjoy fine wine you may really want to impress your friends. Ask Santa to bring you a fancy, wall-mounted, brass, levered cork puller.[4] These really work slick, but are more than a bit pricey for the beginner.

Chilling Wine

Many of the sweeter white wines, the sparkling wines, and the sweeter Rosé wines should be served well chilled. With these wines the objective is to get their temperature down to 40-45° F. The quickest way to do this is to immerse the bottle in a bucket of half ice and half water

---

[4] If you have big bucks you can purchase a gold-plated version for several grand.

for about twenty minutes. This is much more effective than using ice alone. If you have time, two hours in the refrigerator will accomplish the same thing. It is not a good idea to put wine in the freezer because some quality may be lost—and besides, you'll probably forget about it and let it freeze. You definitely should not put champagne in the freezer; it is just too fragile. Dry white wines should be served just a bit warmer, perhaps around 50° F. We've even had a few "powder dry" whites that have drunk well in the high-50s. This temperature also works fine for Sherry, Lambrusco, and some Roses. The lighter red wines like Beaujolais are best served at temperatures in the low- to mid-50s. Ports and Madiera are best when served in the high-50s. The low-60s would seem to be the magical serving temperature for Burgundy, Côtes du Rhône, Chianti, Merlot, and lighter-bodied Zinfandels, while the heavier-bodied red wines (Bordeaux, Cabernet Sauvignon, Petite Sirah,

Two devices used to prevent dripping of wine from the bottle: (A) a ring with absorptive liner to catch wine running down the outside of the bottle, and (B) a metal disc that can be rolled up into a spout to insert into the bottle mouth.

Syrah, and Big Zins) can be served a little warmer, perhaps 65-68° F being the ideal range. Attention to the proper serving temperature will greatly enhance your enjoyment of wine. Luigi says it will make it taste better too.

Wine Glasses

It has been said that a great wine deserves a great glass. This is probably about as accurate a statement as "Read my lips, no new taxes" or "I'm going to provide a tax cut for the middle class." Certainly we do not need to drink a $25 bottle of wine from a $25 glass. Luigi is satisfied with an old plastic beer cup. The fact of the matter is, a wineglass should allow us to view the color and clarity of a wine, and allow us to swirl and smell it. This means the glass should not be highly colored or opaque. For all but sparkling wines, the glass should be broad enough (usually ten to twelve ounces) that you can swirl the wine and get your nose into the aromas.

If you're like me, your everyday wineglasses had better not be too expensive. I manage to break more than my share, and my co-author says its mainly because I'm a left-handed klutz. The *Wine Spectator* recently rated an array of wineglasses; we were surprised to find several that were highly recommended in the $4 to $5 range. Some of these were Pottery Barn's "Epicure," Riedel's "Ouverture," and Schott's "Selection." Undoubtedly there are many others even more economically priced that will work just fine.

Recent studies show that some very expensive crystal glassware containing lead can release this lead into acid drinks. This is apparently only a problem if the liquid remains in the glass for extended periods. Luigi fondles his plastic cup and chuckles, "That's not going to be a big problem for me," and I chuckle to my co-author, "We won't have to buy any of that expensive crystal, Sweetie, because there's a chance of lead poisoning."

To make a long story short, you really only need two sets of wineglasses. One set should be either tulips or flutes, for sparkling wines,

Two basic, all-purpose wineglasses. The glass on the left is suitable for white or red wines. It has a bowl large enough to allow one to swirl the wine and smell its aromas. Some people prefer glasses with slightly larger diameters for red wines. The flute-type glass on the right is commonly used for sparkling wines. Its tall shape allows one to view the "bubbly's" ascending bubbles.

and the other can be standard ten-ouncers, which work just fine for whites or reds. If you want to get a little fancier you can get some fatter (ballon) glasses for the big red wines. A brandy snifter will also work. These fatter glasses allow you to concentrate more of the wine's aromas as you swirl it. A small Sherry or Port glass is also handy for many of the dessert wines. Hell, now you're ready for anything or anybody.

Breathing and Decanting Wine

What we're talking about here is whether we need to open and air out wines for a while prior to serving, and whether we need to decant them away from sediments that might be present on the bottom or sides of the bottles. There are really no hard and fast rules on these matters, although some gurus will tell you that a 1982 Cabernet must be decanted and allowed to breathe for fifty-eight minutes before it reaches its climax. "Horsefeathers!" I say, to that. This same dude probably boasts that it takes him and his wife that long to reach the same goal at precisely the same time.

Personal experience has told us the following: there is usually no need to breathe white wines unless they are overchilled, and the necessity then is probably more to warm the wine than to breathe it. We sometimes feel there is a slight advantage to breathing extremely dry whites like Chardonnay or white Bordeaux. This is accomplished by pouring some into wineglasses fifteen to twenty minutes ahead of drinking time. Another time you might try decanting a white wine is if you detect a slight off-aroma. We've been able to rid wine of a bit of sulfur or turnip aroma by letting it sit in a carafe for a few minutes prior to serving.[5]

Some of the heavier-bodied red wines, particularly those that have cellared for many years, may benefit from breathing and decanting. A good way to breathe a red wine that does not have visible sediment in the bottle is to simply remove one glassful from the bottle. This provides more air space over the wine. Merely removing the cork from the bottle does not provide much breathing room. If a red wine has visible sediment or has been stored ten years or more, it is safer to decant the wine. To do so, very carefully pour the wine away from the sediment into a carafe; allow it to breathe for a while in the carafe or return it to a clean bottle. We've never seen the advantage of breathing a wine for more than thirty minutes. Remember, you are going to be sipping this wine over an extended period of time, and it will be fun to experience the changes that will occur with each subsequent glass. The wine will also change when consumed with different foods. (See Chapter 13 for additional detail regarding wine and food.)

Wine Service Tips for Restaurant Employees

1) If the restaurant has a wine list, give it to the patrons along with the menu. Familiarize yourself with the wine list. Know which wines are best before dinner, with respective entrées, and with desserts (see Chapter 13). With a large party, you probably will be able to sell several bottles. If the restaurant doesn't have a formal wine list, at least

---

[5] Too bad it isn't as easy to rid an area of Luigi's sulfur odors. Just visualize him sitting inside a giant carafe!

know the specific brands and types of wine you have available, e.g., **Gallo** Hearty Burgundy, **Glen Ellen** Proprietor's White, and **Sutter Home** White Zinfandel. Never just say "red, white, and pink."

2) Make sure you deliver the wine to the table at the proper temperature. If it is to be served chilled, provide either a bucket of ice and water or an insulator sleeve to keep it chilled at the table. Bring a small towel with the bottle to wipe away any ice water that might remain on the bottle.

3) When you bring the bottle of wine to the table, show it to whomever ordered so he or she can confirm it is the proper wine and vintage.

4) Open the wine carefully, as indicated previously. If you are frequently having trouble with the corkscrew provided, request another type that grips the bottle mouth. If something goes wrong during cork removal, return that bottle and get another. (Let the sommelier or bartender do the cork repair.) Place the cork on the table beside the person who ordered the wine. Before pouring, wipe the bottle top with the towel.

5) Pour a small quantity of wine into the glass of the person who ordered, and wait for him or her to taste it. Wine should be poured slowly with a slight twist of the bottle at the end to prevent dripping, and the small towel should be wrapped around the bottle in case there is a drop or two. A main objective is to not spill anything on your customers. Ask the taster if the wine is acceptable; it almost always will be. A patron should reject a wine only if it is spoiled or terribly out of character. In any event, you shouldn't dispute a patron's rejection of a wine. Let your superior handle it if he or she chooses to do so.

Originally, the custom of pouring the host a small quantity of wine to sample had a very serious purpose. The idea was, if the wine was poisoned, the host would croak rather than his guests. Luigi always uses this as an excuse to always pour his wine first whether he is host *or* guest.

6) Fill each patron's wineglass only about half-full. This allows each person to swirl the wine and fully appreciate its aroma. When you visit

the table periodically, ask if you can pour more wine. Some parties will prefer that you pour; some will prefer to do it themselves.

7) When the wine is almost gone, ask your customers if they would like another bottle, or suggest that perhaps they would like to try another selection.

Now that we can get a wine bottle open without spewing pieces of cork in every direction, and our glasses are poured, let's find out what to look for in a good wine.

Chapter 3

How to Appreciate Wine

A wine expert's (and eventually *your*) judgment of a particular wine will depend on how it looks (appearance), how it smells (aroma/bouquet), and how it tastes (flavors, balance, finish), all of which provide an overall impression of the wine. When you first start out with wine you will not have a clear idea of what you are looking for. As you progress you will experience an array of new aromas and flavors, and these sensory experiences will be cataloged in your brain so that you'll remember them and be able to detect even subtle variations.

Components of Quality

Experienced wine tasters have developed score sheets to assign various ratings to the 1) appearance, 2) aroma/bouquet, 3) taste/flavor, 4) balance/finish, and 5) overall impressions of wines so they may be compared. Wine magazines use the numerical ratings (on a hundred-point scale) from tastings to compare and promote various wines. From the beginning, you should realize that your preferences in wine may be quite different from those of others. Your nose and taste buds may tell you that certain aromas and flavors are especially pleasing, while the same aromas and flavors may do little for your spouse or close friend. Furthermore, a wine that scores 95 in *Wine Spectator* magazine may not taste like much to you as a beginner. But as you experience more wine and develop an appreciation for new aromas and flavors, that same wine might take on new meaning.

We're making two important points here. The first is that tastes and preferences vary from person to person; the second is that your preferences may change as you experience more wines and develop an appreciation for their unique flavors and aromas.

There seems to be a pattern to wine appreciation that we experienced, as did several of our friends; from discussions with various wine experts, we suspect this might be a rather common phenomenon. When people first start to taste wine they prefer white or blush, off-dry to semisweet wines and have difficulty appreciating drier white wines and red wines in general. As their experience with wine increases they gain more appreciation for the dry whites and the reds, particularly when these are served with food. We believe this pattern represents a natural progression that beginners should expect.

Tasting Tips

Wine is a beverage to sip and savor, not guzzle. (Are you paying attention, Luigi?) When wine is poured it should first be examined to appreciate its color and clarity, then sniffed[1] to enjoy its aromas, and finally, held in the mouth to allow all its flavors to pass over the taste buds.

One of the best ways for a beginner to start is to attend a wine tasting where score sheets are provided. Wines are usually evaluated on a scale of either twenty or one hundred points. The twenty-point evaluation sheet shown is commonly used at wine tastings. Notice that the aroma/bouquet and taste/flavor categories carry more weight (six points each) than the appearance, balance/finish, and overall impression categories. Let's look more closely at each category and discuss the terms used to describe wines.

Appearance: To have the best appearance and achieve the highest score, a wine should be brilliant when viewed in good light. Hold your wineglass where you can view the wine with a light source behind it. (Not those car headlights, Luigi!) There should be no cloudiness or hazi-

---

[1] A snotty term for smelling the wine.

WINE EVALUATION SCORE SHEET

Wine # _____

Name _____

APPEARANCE (3 pts.) .... SCORE _____
AROMA/BOUQUET (6 pts.) .... SCORE _____
TASTE/FLAVOR (6 pts.) .... SCORE _____
BALANCE/FINISH (3 pts.) .... SCORE _____
OVERALL IMPRESSION (2 pts.) .... SCORE _____
                                      OVERALL .... SCORE _____

Appearance: 3 - Excellent, brilliant, good color
                       2 - Good, clear, with characteristic color
                       1 - Poor, slight haze or off color
                       0 - Objectionable, cloudy and/or off color

Aroma/bouquet: 6 - Extraordinary, characteristic aroma of grape variety or wine
                           type; outstanding, complex
                       5 - Excellent, characteristic aroma, well-balanced
                       4 - Good, distinguishable bouquet
                       3 - Pleasant, slight aroma and bouquet
                       2 - Acceptable, no perceptible aroma or bouquet, or with slight
                           off odors
                       1 - Poor, off odors, may be drinkable
                       0 - Objectionable and off odors

Taste/flavor: 6 - Extraordinary, characteristic flavors of the grape variety or wine type;
                           Well balanced, smooth, full-bodied and overwhelming
                       5 - Excellent, all of the above, but a little less
                       4 - Good, characteristic of grape variety or wine type flavor; good balance,
                           smooth, may have minor faults
                       3 - Pleasant, undistinguished but pleasant, minor faults
                       2 - Acceptable, undistinguished wine with more pronounced faults than above
                       1 - Poor, may be drinkable with strong foods
                       0 - Objectionable, undrinkable, offensive flavors

Balance/finish: 3 - Excellent, lingering outstanding aftertaste
                       2 - Good, pleasant aftertaste
                       1 - Poor, little or no distinguishable aftertaste
                       0 - Objectionable, unpleasant aftertaste

Overall Impression: 2 - Excellent
                       1 - Good
                       0 - Poor

An Example of a Wine Evaluation Score Sheet.

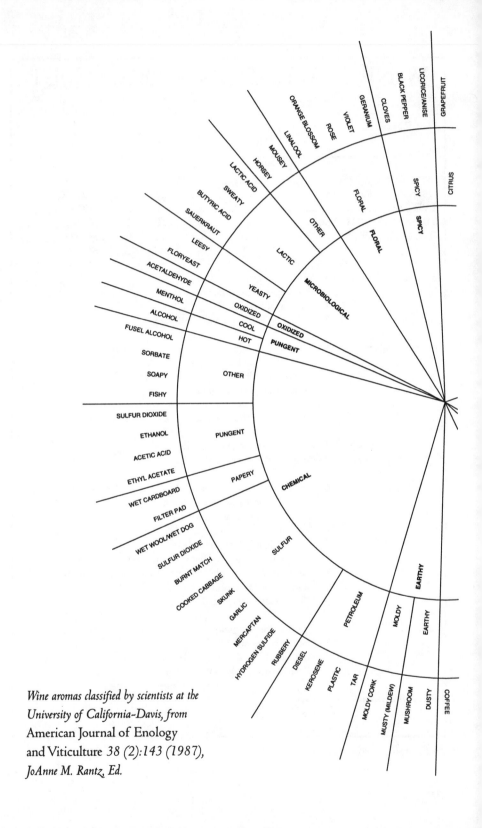

Wine aromas classified by scientists at the University of California-Davis, from American Journal of Enology and Viticulture *38 (2):143 (1987), JoAnne M. Rantz, Ed.*

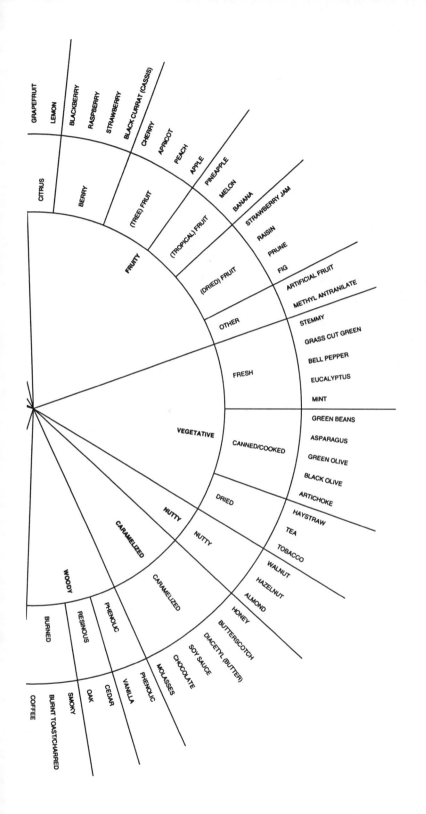

ness. Wines that appear brilliant are said to have excellent clarity and are often called clean wines. Poor clarity may indicate something wrong with the wine, or merely that the bottle was disturbed, dislodging some sediment which will not affect the wine's aroma or taste.

As you learn more about the different varieties of wine you will observe that each type has a characteristic color. For example, a Petite Sirah will be much darker than a Pinot Noir. It will take some experience to learn each wine's characteristic colors since they vary somewhat depending upon the style in which the wine is produced. To start with, judge the wine for its clarity and brilliance.

Aroma/bouquet: These terms are often used interchangeably to describe the smell of a wine. A wine that has an appealing smell is said to have a great nose. For years, whenever Luigi heard an attractive lady say that at a wine tasting, he said, "Thank you," then wondered why everyone looked at him with amusement.

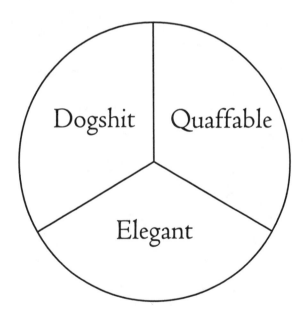

Luigi's simplified wheel for wine aroma and taste.

As one gains wine experience, it may become possible to separate the aroma from the bouquet. Traditionally, the term "aroma" was reserved for components of smell typical of the grape used to produce the wine. You probably will quickly learn to distinguish the aroma of Gewürztraminer from other white wines, and Cabernet Sauvignon from other red wines. With more experience, you will be able to identify other characteristic aromas. A few experts can actually smell a blended wine and tell which varieties went into the blend. If you want to qualify as "Master of Wine,"[2] you will have to do all that and more. As we began writing, only five Americans had passed that test.

The bouquet of a wine was originally the portion of its odor produced during fermentation and aging. These processes release a large number of volatile chemicals that our noses can identify as characteristic odors. These can be good smells, contributing to the overall great nose of the wine, or they can be objectionable.[3]

Terms used to describe the odor of wine include floral, spicy, fruity, vegetative, nutty, caramelized, woody, earthy, chemical, pungent, oxidized, and microbiological. These may seem mind-boggling to you as a beginner, but take heart; you soon will learn to recognize many of these odors. Wine experts have produced a complex aroma wheel which shows the ninety-four different aromas a wine could possibly have. These vary all the way from apricot, peach, and walnut to kerosene, skunk, and sweaty. Unless you're masochists[4], you'll probably want to stick with wines that are floral, fruity, nutty, spicy, or caramelized. The aroma wheel is overly complex for most amateur wine buffs, but it is presented here as the standardized way experts describe the smell of wine. When we showed the aroma wheel to Luigi he immediately drew a simplified version. Of course, this is from a guy who guzzles instead of sipping and savoring.

Taste/flavor: For the beginner, this will be more of an overall judgment. The wine will taste good, or perhaps be too sweet, too tart, or

---

[2] Several steps up from a Master Baiter.

[3] More often referred to as yucky.

[4] Chained-up people who make love with whips after pouring "skunky" wine on each other.

CHATEAU CHANTAL
15900 Rue de Vin, Traverse City, Ml 49684
(616) 223-4110

Tasting List Summer 1993

Our wine maker has listed our wines from dry to sweet on this list. We recommend beginning with the driest wine you wish to sample first. Please feel free to use this sheet to mark your favorites of the wines you taste for future reference.

Fair ☐☐☐☐☐☐ Great

1990 Riesling $7.00/Bottle $ 75.60/Case   Personal Opinion Rating

The vines struggled in the vintage of 1990 and reflect a steely, citrus-like flavor, mildly astringent with hints of grapefruit and green apples. We believe it will stand up well with spicy foods, pasta, and strong flavored fish.

Fair ☐☐☐☐☐☐ Great

1991 Chardonnay $12.00/Bottle $129.60/Case   Personal Opinion Rating

The Chardonnay grapes used to make this wine were the finest quality we've ever seen. The wine was partially barrel fermented giving it soft, mellow nuances of oak which carry beautifully with its intense fruit flavors. An excellent companion to shell fish and poultry.

Fair ☐☐☐☐☐☐ Great

1992 Pinot Noir $9.50/Bottle $102.60/Case   Personal Opinion Rating

To us the most interesting of all red wines; with distinct flavors and the smells of cherries and strawberries! A medium-bodied, soft red wine that won't 'knock your socks off," as do many Cabernets but will rather ease you into a silk slipper.

Fair ☐☐☐☐☐☐ Great

1992 Semi-Dry Riesling $8.50/Bottle $91.80/Case   Personal Opinion Rating

The sunny fall in 1992 with its cool nights, allowed the grapes to retain all of the acids which give this wine its fruity and delightful flavors. A strong acid structure and a hint of sweetness! Excellent with many foods fish and white meat in particular.

Fair ☐☐☐☐☐ Great

1991 Gewüztraminer $12.00/Bottle $129.60/Case   Personal Opinion Rating

A rich, fruity wine with an exotic bouquet which contains a remarkable cleanness and finesse of flavor. A sweeter Gewürztraminer with exceptional versatility. Easily paired with a variety of strong flavored foods.

Fair ☐☐☐☐☐ Great

1992 Cherry Wine $ 5.00/Bottle $54.00/Case   Personal Opinion Rating

An Old Mission tradition! We like to think of our cherry wine as fresh cherries in a glass. The wine is slightly sweet with all of the cherry character one would expect from the "Cherry Capital of the World."

A sample wine list offered in a winery tasting room. This winery has provided a simple rating system with cues at the right of each selection.

A "blind" wine tasting like this one is more often accomplished by covering wine labels than recruiting sight-impaired people as tasters—although that could work, too.

too tannic (leaving too much of a puckery feel on the tongue). As you progress in your ability to distinguish certain varietals, you will be able to judge whether the flavors are characteristic of that particular wine type. We've found that the aroma wheel can also be used to describe many wine flavors including fruity, nutty, spicy, and perhaps even floral tastes, although it may be more difficult to separate floral aromas from floral tastes. As a general rule, the better-tasting wines have a complexity of flavors presented in balance and which provide a smooth overall impression.

The taste of wine varies considerably depending on whether you are tasting it alone or with food. When sampling a series of wines, your impressions will also be influenced by the wines you tasted previously. At wine tastings, it is common to be served cheeses, crackers, or fruit as an accompaniment. These treats serve two purposes: to clear your palate between wines and to provide a food source (although limited) to help soften the alcoholic impact of the heavier-bodied red wines.

When tasting a series of different wine types it is important to start with the drier white selections, follow with the semisweet whites, blushes, and lighter reds, proceed to the heavier-bodied reds, then finish with the sweet dessert wines. Wine-tasting rooms at wineries usually list their offerings in the suggested order of tasting. The example (p. 40) is a tasting list offered by one winery.

Some wineries may limit you to four or six wine-tasting choices if they are in areas of high traffic with a large number of nonpurchasing visitors (i.e., deadbeats, cheapskates, college students, etc.).[5] This is now a fairly common practice along the main arteries of the Napa and Sonoma valleys in California.

If you find one of the wines objectionable, or just prefer not to swallow when tasting, it is not considered bad manners to spit the wine into one of the jugs provided on the tasting counter. Please be careful not to confuse these spittoons with the water pitcher! (Luigi has never been guilty of this because he's never spit out a wine.) Enjoy a cracker, if provided, to help clear your taste buds between offerings. A sip of water may also help diminish the impact of the last wine, and the water may also be used to rinse your tasting glass.

Perhaps this is a good time to raise an important issue: is it suave to swallow all of the wine you taste, or should you spit it out like the expert tasters who might have to taste hundreds of entries in a day? As TV's Frugal Gourmet says, "Certainly we amateurs do not have to comply with that silliness." We should feel free to swallow the wines that we find pleasing. The reason professional tasters sip and spit is obvious: they are trying so many samples they would be IWT[6] if they swallowed.

Since we're raising serious moral issues, remember that when you're traveling from winery to winery and tasting a lot of wine, your "designated spitter" should do the driving. Good judgment is necessary here,

---

[5] Similar to the riffraff and leeches that sometimes show up to drink wine at your home.

[6] Impaired Wine Tasters.

as it is in any other activity involving the consumption of alcohol. Also, be realistic about how many wineries you can visit in a day.

Balance/finish: Although listed as a separate category on our sample evaluation sheet, this is really a taste component and refers to the flavors remaining in the mouth after spitting or swallowing. The best scores go to wines that leave a very special lingering aftertaste. Remember the old saying "That leaves a bitter taste in my mouth"? A wine with an unpleasant aftertaste should score a fat zero. Aftertaste is the reason why previously tasted wines have such an important impact on the taste of subsequent selections. Again, if you refer to the aroma wheel you'll find some terms which also effectively describe pleasant and unpleasant aftertastes.

Overall impression: This is a relatively simple way of placing wine into one of three categories. You probably would not buy wines with a poor overall impression at any price. You might buy wines with a good overall impression for everyday drinking, if they are reasonably priced. And wines with an excellent overall impression are the ones you would buy by the carload at the right price, or buy sparingly and serve on special occasions if pricey. (Unless, of course, you happen to be wealthy, in which case you could buy a carload even if they were pricey.) This system of dividing wine into three overall categories agrees quite nicely with the system old Luigi devised to replace the aroma wheel.

When tasting wine, it is best to quietly form your own opinions and try not to be biased by the statements of others.[7] Taste is a very individual sense. You won't necessarily prefer the wines your friends or spouse like best, although married couples usually find enough common ground to enjoy similar types of wine with their meals. Those looking for a spouse can quickly discard potential candidates based on poor taste in wine or indications of excessively expensive wine preferences.[8]

---

[7] Inevitably, at every wine tasting there will be a blabbermouth who blurts out his/her impression of every wine. Not uncommonly, after tasting a large number of samples the whole group may become blabbermouths.

[8] You may not want to eliminate someone on the basis of expensive wine tastes if he/she has the financial ability to support their hobby and yours as well.

On a more serious note, food does have an important impact on your impressions of a wine, and in fact, wine might even have an impact on your impression of food. Chapter 13 deals with wine/food combinations in greater detail.

Really Getting Into It

A full appreciation of wine requires some effort to learn more about the subject. An excellent way to get started is to attend wine tastings organized by friends, colleagues, or local wineries or distributors. Membership in the Tasters Guild will offer you tasting opportunities as well as information on wine shop discounts and wine travel. For more information call (305) 776-4870.

Later comes the wine vacation; some of our most enjoyable vacations have been trips to wine-producing areas where we could combine wine tasting and buying with other sightseeing activities. Luckily, the climates and sites where grapes can be grown are usually pleasant and scenic places to visit. We've greatly enhanced our wine knowledge by visiting wineries and talking to the people actually involved with the viticultural (grape-growing) and enological (wine-making) activities. Some of the best wineries to visit are discussed in Chapters 9 and 10. In most of the larger wineries you will only get to talk with the tasting room employees. Some of these people are extremely knowledgeable and delightful to visit with, although they may not offer the insights of the winemaker or the vineyard manager. Plan to visit at least a few small wineries where you have a better chance of meeting the proprietor or the enologist. He or she may invite you to the cellar and use a "wine thief" to sample a few barrels for you. Perhaps you'll find a nugget of a wine at a reasonable price that the so-called experts have missed.

As you gain more interest in wine you may want to subscribe to magazines or newsletters that cover current topics in enology and viticulture. Some better ones are the *Wine Spectator, The Wine Advocate,* and *Wine and Spirits* (obtained by membership in Tasters Guild, International). The wine magazines all have their own rating methods. For example, the *Wine Spectator* rates wines on a hundred-point scale and describes the categories as follows:

95—100	Classic, a great wine
90—94	Outstanding, a wine of superior character and style
80—89	Good to very good, a wine with special qualities
70—79	Average, a drinkable wine that may have minor flaws
60—69	Below average, drinkable but not recommended
50—59	Poor, undrinkable, not recommended

We often use the *Wine Spectator* to look for good values in wine. Specifically, we look for wines rated over 80 that sell in the $5 to $10 range. Sometimes we'll find one rated in the 85-94 range that sells for $7 to $10 which is really an outstanding value.

Many wineries also have newsletters and will be happy to include you on their mailing lists; they occasionally offer special wine discounts as well. There are many good books that specialize in wines of a certain type or from a specific area, and many guides to the wineries within a particular region. When you really become thirsty for wine knowledge, visit the Sonoma County Wine Library in Healdsburg, California. They have more than three thousand volumes on the subject, as well as about seventy periodicals from all over the world. As with any other subject (art, basketball, music, etc.), the more knowledgeable you become about wine, the more you are bound to appreciate it.

Suggested Reading

The Wine Advocate, R. M. Parker, Jr., P. O. Box 311, 1002 Hillside View, Parkton, MD 21120.

Wine Spectator, P. O. Box 50462, Boulder, CO 80322-0462.

Wine and Spirits, One Academy Street, RD #6, Princeton, NJ 08540.

Chapter 4

White Wine Varietals

Wines made predominantly from one variety of grape are known as varietals. In the United States each state has a law indicating what percentage of a wine must be from a single variety in order to market that wine under the varietal name. Some state laws are more restrictive than the federal law governing this subject.

Depending on the variety and the style in which the wine is made, white wine may be almost clear (like water) through various shades of yellow to straw-colored, or a rich gold. Many varieties of grapes are used to make white wines, and each varietal can be made in a number of styles. Do not expect all Chardonnays, Gewürztraminers, Rieslings, Sauvignon Blancs, Vidal Blancs, Vignoles, or other varietals to taste alike; each can vary from powder dry to quite sweet. In this chapter we will present the most important white wine grape varieties so you can learn how to pronounce their names and become familiar with some of their important characteristics.

Aurore (ah-roar-ah)

A French-American hybrid that can produce a dry to semi-dry white wine. It is also used to produce sparkling wines in the eastern United States. It has a flowery aroma and a crisp, fruity taste. **Boskydel Winery** in Leelanau County, Michigan, produces a dandy with just a hint of sweetness. Aurore makes an excellent aperitif and accompanies a variety of lighter foods.

Catawba (ka-tah-bah)

This is actually a red grape, but since it is used primarily to make white and sparkling wines we've included it here. This grape was planted near Cincinnati, Ohio, in 1823 by Nicholas Longworth. His "Sparkling Catawby" soon gained fame throughout the United States and Europe, and inspired Henry Wadsworth Longfellow to write "Ode to Catawba Wine."[1] Catawba is still produced in the eastern United States and its white, sparkling, and Rosé versions have many loyal fans.

Cayuga (kay-oo-gah)

This little gem was developed by the Geneva Agricultural Experiment Station in New York, and is being widely planted in that state. It produces a floral, fruity, crisp, wine with a semisweet or sweet finish. The ones we've tasted from the Finger Lakes region have been excellent aperitif or "luncher" wines. Sweeter versions also make excellent dessert wines.

Chardonnay (shar-dun-ay)

Chardonnay is perhaps the most famous white wine grape in the world. It has been grown for centuries in the Burgundy district of France, where it produces famous Meursault, Montrachet and Pouilly Fuissé[2] wines. Many French Champagnes also contain Chardonnay grapes.

In recent years, California Chardonnays have also received worldwide acclaim. The best of these wines are relatively expensive because the vines are low-yielding, producing only about two tons per acre compared to six to ten tons for some other varieties. There are, however, some very enjoyable Chardonnays that sell in the $5 to $7 range. (See Chapter 14.)

Chardonnay is a complex and full-bodied wine whose color varies from straw yellow (sometimes with a slight greenish tinge) to pale yellow. The aromas of Chardonnay can vary from a flinty smell to that

---

[1] We have not read the poem, but a friend (no, not Luigi) told us both the poem and the wine stink.
[2] Or as Luigi once called it, "Fouilly Puisse." After splitting a gut, we promptly corrected him.

of various fruits such as apples, peaches, or figs. The wine is made in a variety of styles. Some are lighter with a reminder of citrus fruit, while others with considerable aging on oak pick up vanillin, tannins, butter (from the high glycerol content), and some spiciness along with various fruit characters. With few exceptions, Chardonnay can be characterized as a dry wine. Some of our favorites have the slight buttery aroma and taste. There are so many good to excellent Chardonnays made in so many styles that you should be able to find one to your liking. However, we would disagree with several of our California friends who proclaim that Chardonnay is the ultimate in white wine.

The lighter-style Chardonnays can be drunk immediately or held for perhaps three years. Those aged in oak might be expected to keep well for five to ten years or more.

When we first started with wine we did not particularly like Chardonnays but were crazy[3] about Rieslings and Gewürztraminers. After many moons we have learned to appreciate Chardonnay in certain styles. We mention this because when you go to a tasting room in California (or Oregon and Washington, for that matter), Chardonnay is probably the first wine you will be offered (because it is the driest). Don't be concerned if you don't appreciate it at first, and don't let such an experience sour you on wine. Incidentally, we've found that we appreciate the complexity of Chardonnay more if we drink it at a slightly warmer temperature (perhaps 50-55°F) than most of the other whites. This wine goes extremely well with a variety of fish and pasta dishes, particularly those with rich cream sauces.

Chenin Blanc (shen-in blonk)

This is another famous grape variety from the Loire Valley of France. In that area it is called *Pineau blanc de la Loire* and produces many of the famous wines of Vouvray. The wine is made in a variety of styles from very dry to slightly sweet with one to two percent residual sugar. It is usually light yellow or straw-colored and is best described as fruity in

---

[3] Not mad or insane, just exuberant.

nose and taste. Some have described its flavor as vanilla and pears. The California Chenin Blancs we have tasted are perfect lunch wines, fine by themselves or with light fare such as fruit, bread, and light cheeses. Ones we have particularly liked are **Beringer, Fetzer, Kenwood,** and **Pine Ridge,** all of which are reasonably priced. Some of the dryer French styles are hearty enough to complement a poultry or fish meal. In the Loire, some excellent dessert wines are made from Chenin Blanc. Chenin Blancs generally do not benefit from aging and should be drunk before they are three years old.

Delaware (like the state)

This native American pink-red variety is used to some extent in the eastern UnitedStates for dry table wines or sparkling wines. It makes a pleasant, fruity wine but carries some of the foxiness of the American grape. Many people think it is the best of the *Labrusca*-type grapes. It goes well alone, with lunches, or with lighter dinner entrées.

French Columbard (just like it looks)

Although most commonly used in generic blends, this grape is sometimes made as a varietal and apparently has some loyal fans. French Columbard juice contains a high amount of acid and produces a simple, light-bodied wine with low alcohol and a pleasant finish. It is sometimes described as having a citrony or metallic quality. The wine is usually a pale yellow color with perhaps a tinge of green. It is usually vinted with one to two percent residual sugar to balance out the acid. It is a good wine to drink by itself or with simple foods such as light cheeses, fruit, or lightly seasoned meats. Highly spiced or highly acid foods will overpower this wine.

Fumé Blanc (foo-may blonk)- see Sauvignon Blanc

Gewürztraminer (Gah-vurts-trah-meener)

In German, *Gewürz* means spicy, and that term best describes the wines made from this grape, which was actually selected from among clones[4] of the Traminer grape for its spiciness. This is a unique white wine that can be made in a dry (Alsatian) style or with enough residual sugar to give a semisweet taste. It also is harvested overmature (as raisins) and made into a delightful sweet dessert wine. Regardless of the style, it retains the wonderful spicy and floral aroma, which you will quickly learn to recognize. Nearly everyone (except Luigi) enjoys smelling this wine almost as much as drinking it. It makes an excellent lunch wine with light foods, and is a wonderful accompaniment to Chinese foods, poultry, and sausages or other smoked meats. Unless made in a dessert style, Gewürztraminers usually do not keep well for extended periods and should be drunk anytime after their release up to three years. Try drinking the drier versions of these wines at a slightly higher temperature (perhaps 50-55°F) than most of the other whites. Some of our favorite Gewürztraminers come from the Russian River area of Sonoma County, California.

Grey Riesling (gray rees-ling)

This grape is not a true Riesling, but actually the *Chauché gris* grape of France. It is not a major variety but a few California winemakers produce it in a dry style that makes a pleasant wine. The wines have a slight spiciness, but in other respects may resemble the White Rieslings. It is usually not considered to be on a par with the true Rieslings, but several connoisseurs and a "prique"[5] from Salt Lake City, Utah, have told us it does make an excellent complement to honeydew melon and blue cheese. Wente in Livermore, California, makes a pleasant one that is reasonably priced.

Johannisberg Riesling (yo-hahn-is-berg rees-ling) or White Riesling

This grape variety can be grown in many places throughout the world and is produced in both the western and eastern United

---

[4] Not to be confused with clowns.

[5] A slang term for prince.

States. It is the grape that makes German wines famous, and several from the Mosel and Rheingau regions have achieved global acclaim. The wine is characterized by a flowery bouquet and is made in many styles from dry to sweet. Cooler regions produce better-quality Rieslings with a superior balance of sugar and acidity. With their fragrant nose and pale yellow color, these wines are ideal when served alone, as an aperitif, or with light, luncheon-type meals. The late harvest types contain relatively high amounts of residual sugar and make excellent dessert wines. This variety is the one most often infected with the *Botrytis* fungus that produces so-called Noble Rot. Dessert wines made from these mummified raisins[6] are delicious and world renowned. Rieslings usually should be drunk young as they are not expected to improve with age, although some of the best German dessert versions will store well. Rieslings are great wines for the beginner because of their wonderful nose and flavor.

Marsanne (mar-sawn)

A variety grown primarily in the northern Rhône region of France, Marsanne produces a delightfully fragrant white wine which is fruity and full-bodied. It is also blended with some red wines of the Hermitage region to improve their complexity. A few acres are now planted in California, and the preliminary results are quite promising.

Müller Thurgau (mooler ter-gow)

This is a fruity and early ripening variety, characterized by a low acid content. It is widely planted in Germany and a few other spots around the Continent, and some plantings have been made in the Pacific Northwest and the eastern United States. It produces a pleasant but not complex wine that is a nice luncheon quaff.

---

[6] These are not grapes that were spoiled rotten by their mommies. Rather, they are raisins that carry a shroud of ugly gray mold that, yes, enhances wine flavor.

Muscat varieties (mus-cat)

The most common of these are Muscat de Frontignan and Moscato di Canelli, from France and Italy respectively. A few wineries in California and the Pacific Northwest produce Muscat Canelli, which is a fragrant and fairly sweet dessert wine. We've also tasted a few of these in a semisweet style that could be drunk as an aperitif. **Bookwalter Winery** in Pasco, Washington, produces an especially nice one. For the most part, they are a good complement to ripe fruit or sweet pastry desserts and may be used by themselves as dessert. **Chateau St. Jean Winery** in Sonoma County, California, has consistently done a great job with this grape.

Niagara (like the falls)

This native American grape has been widely used in the Great Lakes area to make sweet white wines and cream sherry. It has a distinctive foxy aroma and flavor which some people greatly enjoy. As a youth, I had one hell of a headache one morning after drinking too much of this wine the night before. But we all do a few stupid things in our youth! On the outside chance that I wasn't stupid, I haven't touched this wine since. To be fair to the grape, it has produced some award-winning cream sherries and it is enjoyed by connoisseurs of eastern United States wines. **St. Julian Winery** in Paw Paw, Michigan, makes one of the best.

Pinot Blanc (pee-no blonk)

Grown primarily in Europe, this grape produces a crisp, medium-bodied dry wine that goes well with fish and poultry dishes. Some people think that at its best it resembles Chardonnay. It is sometimes aged in oak, and in this case becomes a spicier wine. Some of the better California Chablis have Pinot Blanc included in the blend. Some good sparkling wines have also been produced using Pinot Blanc and its blends.

Pinot Grigio (pee-no gree-show) or **Pinot Gris** (pee-no gree)

The Pinot Grigio grape produces a firm white wine with a lightly floral bouquet and a dry finish. The wine should be drunk young.[7] It goes well alone or with seafood or white meat dishes. The best ones we've tasted have been produced in Italy (most are produced there) but they are beginning to exceed our acceptable price range.

Pinot Gris, as it is called in some European countries and in the United States, can be an elegant wine. It is one of our favorites with grilled trout or salmon. Some of the best we've tasted have come from **Argyle** in Willamete Valley, Oregon, and **L. Mawby** in Leelanau County, Michigan. This grape is also known as Tokay d'Alsace in France and Ruländer in Germany.

Rieslaner (rees-lan-er)

This grape was produced by crossing[8] Riesling and Sylvaner. It produces both dry and dessert wines that retain many of the Riesling-like aromas and flavors of flowers and fruit, but with more richness and acidity. This wine is produced by only a few specialists (primarily in Germany) and is almost always of exceptional quality.

Sauvignon Blanc (saw-vee-on blonk) or **Fumé Blanc** (foo-may blonk)

This grape is important in the Bordeaux region of France where it is most often blended with Sémillon to produce famous Sauternes and Graves. In Graves the blend is predominately Sauvignon Blanc, while Sauternes are predominately Sémillon. Sauvignon Blanc by itself can produce a fine, medium-bodied wine with distinctive character. (It is the Pouilly-Fumé of Loire, France.) Its flavor has been described as earthy or woody, and when made in a dry style it may have a grassy or herbal flavor. Its aroma has been described in a variety of ways, from smoke to gunmetal to figs to herbs. In California, the lighter, fruitier, more herbal wines made from Sauvignon Blanc are called Fumé Blanc

---

[7] Lest there be confusion, we mean the wine should be young, not the people drinking it.
[8] By this we mean breeding the two grapes, not making the sign of the cross.

(introduced by Robert Mondavi) and are noticeably different in style from those bearing the varietal name. These wines accompany a variety of foods, from hors d'oeuvres to seafood, chicken, veal, and pasta entreés. Well-made Sauvignon Blancs will age successfully for five to seven years in the bottle, but the majority should be drunk young. Many reasonably priced ones are now being imported from Australia and Chile.

Scheurebe (sure-ee-bee)

This variety also resulted from a cross between Riesling and Sylvaner and produces some outstanding dry wines as well as some of the most famous German dessert wines. Some of the best *auslese* (ous-lace), *beerenauslese* (beer-en-ous-lace), and *trockenbeerenauslese* (trock-en-beer-en-ous-lace) are produced from this grape. The wines have an appealing, flowery aroma and abound with grapefruit, guava, and pineapple flavors.

Sémillon (sem-ee-own)

An important grape of French origin, this is the major component of the French Sauternes. As with Gewürztraminer, you will quickly recognize the nose[9] on this one. Its bouquet is so fragrant and its taste so fruity that it's difficult to confuse with other varieties. Dry Sémillons are rare; more commonly they are sweet and go well with desserts. Because of the excellent bouquet and flavor of this wine, it is widely blended in small percentages with other white varieties to produce distinctive blends with exotic names.

Seyval Blanc (say-voll blonk)

This grape is a hybrid of French and American grapes and is hardy enough to grow in the Great Lakes area. What it lacks in aroma, it makes up for in fruity taste. It is usually produced in a crisp, dry style which provides a nice balance of acid and sugar. It can be aged in oak, and makes an excellent complement to a variety of fish and poultry

---

[9] Another Pinnocchio of a wine.

dishes as well as pasta with white sauces. This wine seems to hold up well in the bottle for several years.

Sylvaner (sil-van-er)

A variety producing excellent white wines in the Franconia and Rheinhessen regions of Germany and the Valais, Switzerland. In California, **Mirassou** has produced a version called Monterey Riesling which we've often found to be quite pleasant. This is a quaffing wine that goes nicely with fruit and vegetable platters.

Trebbiano treb-bee-ahn-o)

Widely grown in central Italy in the Tuscany and Umbria regions where it produces some of the best white wines in Italy. It is a fruity, flavorful wine usually made in a dry style. It is the same grape as the Ugni Blanc of France.

Vidal Blanc (vee-doll blonk)

Vidal Blanc is another French-American hybrid which combines a distinctive, fruity nose with a lovely,[10] fruity taste. Our favorites are produced in a reserve or *demi-sec* style that contains about one to two percent residual sugar. The drier or dessert versions are also quite pleasing to the palate. The *demi-sec* versions will nicely accompany a light lunch of fruit, cheese, and bread. They also go well with Chinese stir-fried dishes containing poultry or other white meat and with fish entrées. These wines can be found throughout the Great Lakes area. **Fenn Valley** in Fennville, Michigan, has been making an excellent reserve wine from this grape for at least the past fifteen years.

Vignoles (vin-yole)

This is without doubt the classiest of the French-American hybrid grapes now used in wine production, and little wonder—one of its

---

[10] We inadvertently used a sickening term to describe the wine's taste. For more pukey terms other people have used to describe wine, consult the glossary. Then forget them all.

parents is Pinot Noir. Let's call this one "the Chardonnay of the East." This versatile wine can be made in a Chardonnay style and aged in oak or it can be finished in a sweet or even dessert style. When made dry the aroma and taste are reminiscent of citrus fruits, and when made in a sweeter style you can detect pineapple, apricots, honey, or all of the above. It has an elegant, lingering taste. When we bring Vignoles to share with our California winemaking friends they are favorably impressed. **Good Harbor** and **L. Mawby** wineries in Leelanau County, Michigan, have turned out some dandies.

Viognier (vee-own-yay)

This is an important white variety from the northern Rhône Valley of France. The wine has a wonderful aroma reminiscent of tropical flowers, with perhaps a hint of jasmine or orange blossom. Its finish leaves a feel of cream with a hint of spice. It is recommended with spicy foods. We recently enjoyed a bottle produced by **Preston Vineyards** near Healdsburg in Sonoma County, California. It was pleasant by itself and nicely accompanied a pasta dish with cream sauce. We expect this wine will attract a large following. As with many of the whites, it should be drunk young.

Obviously, the aforementioned are not all the white wine varieties used around the world, though the great majority of varietal white wines are made from these grapes. For you, the beginner, several of these selections are good for starters. If you're in the western United States we suggest you start with off-dry Chenin Blancs, Gewürztraminers, or Johannisberg Rieslings. People starting out in the eastern U.S. could also choose from Aurore, Cayuga, Seyval Blanc, and Vidal Blanc. After you have learned to appreciate some of these *demi-sec* wines, venture into some of the drier varietals along with your fish, poultry, or pasta dinners.

Chapter 5
Red Wine Varietals

Red varietals, like the whites, can be made in a myriad of styles and will vary from light- to heavy-bodied, depending on the grape quality and vinification techniques. Many of the varietals will be blended with a small amount of another variety to soften them or to add a particular attribute. Some will benefit greatly by aging in oak barrels.

There is some confusion among newcomers to wine about the identity of European red wines. This is because they traditionally have been named after the regions or appellations where they are grown and produced rather than after their grape varieties. Adding to this confusion is the fact that California vintners have decided to name many of their blended wines after the same European regions. As we discuss the varietals we'll try to point out other names they might sometimes be given. (You can also find more detail about this in Chapter I I as well as in the glossary.) The major red wine grapes are listed below.

Baco Noir (bah-ko nwar)

This was one of the first French-American hybrid varieties to be planted extensively in the eastern United States. Named after the French hybridizer, Maurice Baco, Baco Noir is productive, disease resistant, and hardy enough to produce a crop each year. Unfortunately, the wines produced from this grape, though nicely colored, have not turned out to be widely accepted, so it is used primarily in blends. We've not tasted any varietal Baco Noir wines we could rave about. They are just too coarse for us. Perhaps longer bottle aging will calm them down.

Barbera (bar-bear-ah)

This famous Italian grape produces some of that country's best red wines, Barbera d'Asti and Barbera d'Alba. It is planted sparingly in California, where it is produced by only a few vintners (most of whom have Italian roots).[1] It produces a hearty, big-bodied wine. Barberas are usually dark red, have berrylike aromas, and are full of fruit. Some young Barberas can be a little harsh because of their high acid and tannin content, but after a few years in the bottle they mellow out and achieve a pleasant balance. Many will age ten years or more. They are great with red meat dishes and hold up well to more strongly flavored meats such as wild game. They can also accompany a variety of meat or pasta entrées that are served in highly seasoned sauces. Some exquisite American Barberas have been produced by **Preston Vineyards** in California.

Cabernet Franc (cab-er-nay fronk)

This grape is described as soft, supple, and aromatic, but it is rarely vinified as a varietal. It is one of the principle varieties used in the great red wine blends of Bordeaux. By itself, it produces a pleasant, soft wine usually without great character. For that reason it is more commonly blended, usually with Cabernet Sauvignon, to soften that wine. However, we have tasted some pleasant varietal versions of this wine from California (**Parducci Wine Cellars** in Ukiah and **Konocti** in Kelseyville). They had flavors reminiscent of raspberries and spice.

Cabernet Sauvignon (cab-er-nay saw-vee-on)

This famous wine can be the best in the world when good vintages are properly produced and aged. Unfortunately, a lot of poorer and sometimes greatly overpriced versions also flood the market,[2] giving

---

[1] Referring to their ancestry, not their anatomy.
[2] Please don't take this literally. We don't mean your next trip to the market will find you slogging through ankle-deep, cheap Cabernet.

beginners a poor impression of the wine. Some of the great French Bordeaux are made predominately from Cabernet Sauvignon, and there are many sites in California that produce excellent versions.

Cabernet probably has the most complex aroma of all the red grape varietals. It is described as spicy (sage, mint, pepper, anise, nutmeg, vanilla), berrylike (strawberry, raspberry, currant, plum, cherry), and woody (cedar, oak), with flavors of all the above plus chocolate, toast, and smoke. If you review several people's tasting notes on a series of Cabs you will honestly find all of these descriptive terms and more. (Some of these snotté descriptions might make you sick.) This broad range of response reveals the complexity of wines made from these grapes and how they can vary from winery to winery as well as vintage to vintage.

Cabs are extremely high in tannin, and for this reason require extensive aging on oak or in the bottle to achieve their highest quality. Many are released too young and will impress the beginner and wine connoisseur alike as sharp, rough wines. You can often buy these wines young at a fairly decent price and put them away for a few years, only to be rewarded with much better wines when you decide to open them for special occasions. Cabs are the wines most often purchased by investors who are betting that their value will substantially increase with storage time. They are also the wines most often associated with particular appellations or even vineyards. Nonetheless, even the vintages from these great sites vary considerably, some achieving greatness while others are rather average.

Wines made entirely from Cabernet Sauvignon can sometimes be great, but they also can run the risk of being overpowering. For this reason, it is common practice in both Bordeaux and California to blend in small amounts of other red varieties to slightly tone them down or soften them. Cabernet Franc, Malbec, and Merlot are examples of varieties commonly blended in, in amounts up to fifteen percent. These varieties may add softness and fruitiness to the wine without substantially reducing its great character.

Many of the Bordeaux and California Cabs can be cellared for long periods of time to enhance their quality. One must be careful to achieve the proper perspective on this storage issue. In our view (actually Luigi has convinced us of this), it is silly to cellar a wine past our own life expectancies. If it is a sin to drink a wine before its time, it is perhaps a greater sin to store a wine beyond our time! Wine, like wealth, should be enjoyed before we croak.

Some people are confused about Bordeaux wines and, in particular, how they relate to Cabernet Sauvignon. Bordeaux is a wine-producing area of France that includes several regions and districts. Wines produced by the hundreds of Bordeaux châteaux[3] vary greatly. In the Médoc region, for example, Bordeaux is made predominately from Cabernet Sauvignon, while in the St. Emilion or Pomerol districts the wines may be composed primarily from Merlot, Cabernet Franc, or Bouschet grapes.

Wine connoisseurs (especially those with big bucks) go for the First Growth (highest-rated Châteaux) Bordeaux wines because many of them are of excellent quality. (When you've got the money, you should be able to spend it on opulence.) Of course, many of these wines do appreciate in value.[4] Like other regional wines, not all Bordeaux are worth their asking price; some people have been disappointed, particularly with borderline vintages. Nonetheless, when we have the money, we enjoy a nice Bordeaux now and then. Actually, if you tell all your friends what a great book this is we might generate enough extra cash to buy one great bottle of Chateau Margaux.

Carignane (care-ee-nyan)

Although you rarely hear the name, Carignane is widely planted in California. The older Italian Zinfandel vineyards often contained some Carignane or Petite Sirah for blending purposes. Carignane is seldom bottled as a varietal. Rather, it is a major component of many blended wines sold as generics. Yes, it is in a lot of jug wines,

---

[3] Poetic as hell, aren't we?
[4] Just like a lawyer's Mercedes Benz.

and we've sometimes heard it described as "inoffensive and insignificant." We have tasted a few pleasant varietal versions at the **Parducci Wine Cellars.**

Chambourcin (sham-boar-seen)

Because the wines produced from some of the red varieties grown in the eastern United States have been regarded as harsh, the search is on for improved red varieties that are hardy enough for that climate. One of the more promising newer varieties is the French-American hybrid, Chambourcin. This varietal has the best ruby red color, the most delicate aroma, and the smoothest flavor of the reds that can now be grown there. We find that its intense flavor mimics cherries and raspberries. It makes a good-quality wine when vinted by itself and an exceptional wine when blended with Chancellor.

Chancellor (chance-el-ler)

This French-American hybrid was once planted heavily in France and is now becoming popular in the eastern United States. Chancellor can be reminiscent of a good Bordeaux when properly vinted and aged in oak. It is a dry, medium- to full-bodied wine that displays a smoky aroma and lots of berries in the taste. Since this wine can be relatively forward, it requires some aging or blending with another red variety such as Chambourcin to smooth it out. In France, Chancellor wine has aged well for many years. It probably has not been grown in the eastern U.S. long enough to fully ascertain its aging potential there. **Fenn Valley Vineyards** in Michigan made a 1988 and a 1991 that won many major awards. Both are still holding up well in the bottle.

Charbono (shar-bo-no)

No, this is not Sonny Bono's former wife. The grapes probably originated in Italy, and a few acres have been planted in California. This wine is only produced as a varietal by a handful of California wineries.

It is a complex, Claret-style wine that might seem average when young but will mellow into a smooth wine with age. (Someday, in some book, we'll tell you what Cher and Montana had in common in 1993.)

Concord (as in New Hampshire)

This famous grape has been grown for centuries in the eastern United States for a variety of uses, from jams and jellies to fresh juice to wine. Kosher wines, originally produced according to Jewish sacramental law, are sweetened Concord wines; those produced under the Manischewitz and Mogen David labels are widely known. The wines made from Concord grapes are sweet and flavorful and have a huge following (including my brothers). We'd be foolish to knock this wine and alienate a lot of this book's potential buyers, including our own family.[5] Rather, let's just say we don't personally crave it, as we do so many other good reds on the market. (Hey, this is the only wine Luigi sips and spits.) Seriously, the sweet wines made from Concord are produced in huge volumes, make good aperitif or dessert wines, and do appeal to the taste of millions of people who grew up with them.

DeChaunac (day-shawn-uk)

This French-American hybrid is a heavy producer of blue-hued grapes and is hardy enough to grow in the Great Lakes region. It produces a dark red wine that we've found to vary considerably in quality. It has seemed on the harsh side to us, although we have not drunk any that were aged more than three years. It does make an excellent Rosé.

Foch (foshe)

This is another hardy and early maturing variety that quickly caught the eye[6] of Eastern grape growers. When made as a red wine it has excellent bouquet, but unfortunately not much else. It is now used in blends with other reds and to make some excellent quality Rosés.

---

[5] Years ago the senior author told his brother, "If you like that crap, it's your problem, butthead."

[6] Only figuratively speaking. It did not really catch someone's eye and drag it, for heaven's sake.

Gamay (ga-may) or Napa Gamay

According to retired University of California-Davis viticulturist Dr. Austin Goheen, there is no true Gamay grape variety. Two types of grapes grown in California have been mistakenly called Gamay or Napa Gamay. Napa Gamay is undoubtedly the same grape as Valdiguie, which is grown in Europe and is now vinted under that varietal name by a few California vintners. The Gamay Noir à Jus Blanc is grown in the Beaujolais area of France where it produces a delightful, light-bodied wine ready to be drunk young. Gamay Beaujolais produced in California is probably most often made from Pinot Noir grapes. The California Gamay Beaujolais are fruity, light-bodied, and low in tannin. They are perfect wines for accompanying fruit, cheese, and bread. They are best when consumed a year or two after harvest and will not stand up to long-term storage. Beginners may find these wines a good way to start into the reds because they are seldom astringent. The best news? These are among the more reasonably priced wines on the market.

Grenache (greh-nahsh)

This grape is widely planted in Spain, where it is known as Garnacha. It has a pleasing aroma, but is seldom made as a varietal red wine. In California, it is more often vinified as a Rosé. In several areas of Spain, it is blended with Tempranillo to produce some excellent, fruity red wines. Some California vintners are also using this grape in some of their Rhône-style red blends.

Grignolino (green-o-leen-o)

This grape is widely grown in northern Italy and by a few growers in California. As a varietal, it has a spicy and fruity aroma, a light red color, and a fruity and distinctive taste. It produces both red and Rosé wines which are soft and smooth but lack a great deal of complexity. They are excellent wines to enjoy with a juicy hamburger.

Lemberger (try and screw this up)

This is another of the big reds you will not find very often, but when you do you'll be glad you did. Lemberger is an intense red, medium- to full-bodied wine produced by a few vineyards in the Pacific Northwest. The ones we've tasted have been soft and not strongly tannic on the finish, perhaps somewhere between a Merlot and a Petite Sirah. One of the best we've tasted was produced by **Kiona Vineyards** in the Yakima Valley of Washington. It is a full-bodied version full of fruit, and goes well with a big, juicy steak. A lighter version that has really impressed us is a 1989 crafted by Bill Stowe of **Indian Creek Winery** in Kuna, Idaho. **Covey Run** in Zillah, Washington, also produces a lighter version that is a great value. Lemberger holds up well to red meat and pasta entrées. Okay, smartasses, you thought we were going to say Lemberger nicely accompanies hamburger. You were right, it does!

Merlot (mare-low is correct but mer-low ain't too bad)

The popularity of this smooth and pleasing varietal has exploded in the past few years. Some of its success must be attributed to the high-quality releases from several wineries in Washington. Some excellent Merlots also are being produced in the cooler regions of northern California. Recently, some pretty nice ones with low price tags arrived from Chile.

Although not as full-bodied as Cabernets, Merlots can be full of the aromas and flavors of herbs and berries. They are fantastic wines with pizza, pasta dishes, and red meats. Merlots are relatively low in tannins compared to Cabernets or Zinfandels, and for this reason are not expected to store for as long a time. Many of the great wines from the Bordeaux region of France have Merlot in the blend. Merlots are an excellent choice for the newcomer trying to break the red wine barrier. Many excellent ones can be found in the $6 to $8 range. One of our favorites is produced by the **Columbia Crest Winery** in Paterson, Washington.

Mourvèdre (moor-ved-er)

This dark red grape is widely planted in southern France and in Spain, where it is known as Mataro. It is an important blending grape in the wines of the Rhône valley, Provence, and Chateauneuf du Pape. Only limited acreage occurs in California, where it is being blended into Rhône look-alikes. Wines that contain this grape can be described as big, both in color and body.

Nebbiolo (neb-bee-o-lo)

Nebbiolo is one of the great red grape varieties of Italy. It is currently in limited production in California. It produces a dark, robust wine that presents a lot of fruit in the nose and ages to a beautiful smooth finish. The famous Barbaresco and Barolo wines of Italy (their best reds) are produced from this grape. We recently enjoyed a pleasant, lighter-bodied one produced by **Viansa Winery** in St. Helena, California.

Petite Sirah (pe-teet sir-ah)

Just mention this wine and we get excited. For us, this is the biggest of the reds. It's got the color (purple ink), the aroma (spice, pepper, berries), and a complex flavor of balanced fruit and tannin. Like Zinfandel, these wines get little publicity compared to Cabernets and Pinot Noirs. They are hard to beat when accompanying a spicy bowl of chili, pasta dishes in highly-spiced tomato sauces, or juicy venison steaks. Full-bodied Petite Sirahs that are full of tannin will cellar for many years, and we've enjoyed some dandies in the ten- to fifteen-year-old range. Some of our favorite versions of this wine are produced by **Parducci Wine Cellars** in Ukiah, California, and **Fieldstone Winery** in Healdsburg, California. They are reasonably priced. When I had my Concord-loving brother taste this wine, he said, "If you like that crap, it's your problem, butthead."

Pinot Noir (pee-no nwar)

This is the famous red wine of the Burgundy region of France where

65

it often achieves superior quality. At its best, Pinot Noir is a soft, full-bodied, and even velvety wine with excellent fruit (cherries) in the nose and taste. It is a temperamental wine that requires the best of sites, climates, and viticultural techniques to bring it to perfection. It performs well in cooler regions, including some sites in the northwestern and eastern United States. A lot of the Pinot Noirs produced in California and Oregon seem to be lighter either in color or taste, although every now and then exceptional ones are produced. We've had some excellent vintages from **Robert Stemmler, Rochioli,** and **Williams Selyem** of the Russian River area of California, but they are quite pricey ($18 to $30). A more reasonably priced ($7), tasty Pinot Noir is produced by **Parducci Wine Cellars** in Ukiah, California. After a recent visit to Oregon, we were impressed by Pinot Noirs produced by **Bridgeview** in the Rogue River area and by **Eyrie Vineyards, and Knudsen Erath, Lange,** and **Sokol Blosser** wineries in the north Willamette region. Some of these were good values, under $10 per bottle. Pinot Noirs vary considerably in their aging potential, the best of which will keep five years or more. They are excellent complements to a variety of foods including veal, turkey, scallops, beef, and salmon. Pinot Noir grapes are also used extensively in the production of sparkling wines.

Sangiovese (san-jee-o-vay-zeh)

This is another of Italy's best red wine varieties. It is the main ingredient of most wines produced in the Chianti region of Tuscany. It produces a medium-bodied, fruity wine that nicely accompanies many pasta dishes. We recently enjoyed a reasonably priced one from **Brolio** which we consumed with a delicious chicken cacciatore. Interest in this grape is increasing in California, where it is now being released as a varietal by a few wineries.

Syrah (sir-ah) or Shiraz (sure-as)

Syrah from the Rhône River valley of France, or Shiraz as it is called in Australia, produces an elegant, full-bodied wine. Its aroma gives hints of smoke and plummy fruit, and its flavor is a mouthful of berries. This wine finishes so smoothly that vintners often blend in a little Petite Sirah to add additional tannin and spicy flavors. This is one of our favorites with an elk roast, venison steaks, and other red meats. It will also accompany pasta dishes prepared with lots of garlic in their sauces. These wines drink well after a couple of years in the bottle and many will keep for eight to ten years. We have really enjoyed Syrah-Sirah produced by **Preston Vineyards** in California. These wines are typically eighty to eighty-five percent Syrah and fifteen to twenty percent Petite Sirah. An excellent Shiraz is produced by **Rosemount Winery** in southeastern Australia. The 1990 vintage was rated among the top ten wines in the world (by the *Wine Spectator*) and sold for around $8.50 per bottle. To put this in perspective, the average price of the other nine wines in that group was about $65 per bottle. The 1991 and 1992 vintages have also been very good and comparably priced.

Zinfandel (zin-fun-del)

This is thought by many to be the same grape as the Primitivo of Italy. It has adapted well to several areas of California, especially Amador and Sonoma counties. Like other reds, Zinfandel often has been hidden in the shadow of Cabernet and not given the acclaim it deserves. This wine is produced in a variety of styles from light and fruity to big-bodied, inky black, and full of tannin. Some is also made into Port-style dessert wine. The wine is characterized by a big nose full of spice and fruit, with similar flavors. It goes well with all red meats, pasta dishes with tomato sauces, and even roast or smoked turkey. There are a lot of good Zins available in the $6 to $10 range and the 1990-1992 vintages will be good ones to put away in the cellar. The good vintages will cellar perhaps for ten years or more. Some of the classiest Zins come from old vineyards that are pushing the century mark. We've had some dandies from **Ravenswood, Dry Creek**, and **Lytton Springs** wineries in Sonoma County, California, and a memorable few from **Boeger, Karly**, and **Montevina** over in the Sierra foothills of California.

Around 1980, the **Sutter Home Winery** pursued the idea of producing a light pink wine from Zinfandel by leaving the juice with the skins for a short period of time. This wine, called White Zinfandel, turned out to be a big hit. We'll talk more about it in the blush wine section (Chapter 6).

As with the white varietals, we did not mention every variety of red grape grown in the world. However, we did cover the major red wine varieties you will encounter in the marketplace. When you look at the label of a blended red wine and see some of these varieties, they will no longer be a mystery. Instead of that blank stare you can manage a little smile, knowing full well what's in your red wine.

Chapter 6
Blushes and Blends—The Quaffs

And I'm all yours in blushes and blends. Or is it buttons and bows? Damn, I'm sorry! My mind started wandering back to songs of my youth.[1]
Actually there is no logical reason to put blushes and blends together in the same chapter except that they have two things in common: many of them are blended generic wines, and almost all of them are reasonably priced. Anyway, blushes and blends sounds a little catchier than Rosés and blends which doesn't bring back memories of anything. The bottom line here is it's our book and we'll put stuff anyplace we want to.

Blush or Rosé Wines

Some of the wine gurus have viewed Rosé as a "blush bastard wine" somewhere between red and white. In reality, these are extremely popular wines, accounting for about twenty-five percent of the wine sold in the United States, and are excellent choices for wine newcomers. Pleasant and flavorful but not complex, they can be produced quickly and inexpensively and released immediately—they are the ultimate cash flow for a winery. You can bet that a winery like **Sutter Home** has found a better name than "bastard" for these wines.

Rosés or vin Rosés can be produced as blends of red and white wines or, increasingly, as varietals. They range from light pink to light

---

[1] Since ninety-eight percent of you, including my co-author, don't remember "Buttons and Bows" (sung by the late Dinah Shore), I must be getting pretty old. In fact, when Bill Haley's "Rock Around the Clock" hit number one on the charts, I hit sweet sixteen.

red; in recent years, more have been made in a light pink (hence the term blush). The color of wine is related to the amount of time the juice is on the skins, since many of the flavor components are also in the skins, the light pink Rosés are less flavorful, the medium-colored ones may have more flavors, and the light red ones are the most complex. After the skins are removed from the juice, Rosé wines are handled essentially like white wines. They are cool-fermented, clarified, bottled, and drunk at a young age.

Perhaps the biggest impact on the blush wine market was the introduction of White Zinfandel in 1980 by **Sutter Home Winery**. This is a pleasant lunch and dinner wine with none of the body or tannin of its red counterpart. It was an immediate hit with the yuppies and has now brought financial success to several wineries. The only bad thing we can say about it is that it has led many people to think Zinfandel is a white grape; as lovers of big red Zins, that pisses us off.[2]

Excellent Rosés are also made from DeChaunac and Foch in the eastern United States, from Cabernet Sauvignon, Gamay, Grenache, and Pinot Noir in the western U.S., and from a variety of grapes in Europe. Each has a particular color, aroma, and flavor. Because of the increasing popularity of these light wines, almost every winery now has a blush or Rosé wine in its repertory. Some common names given to these releases are: Cabernet Rosé, Rosé of Cabernet, Foch Rosé, Gamay Rosé, Rosé of DeChaunac, Grenache Rosé, White Grenache, Rosé of Pinot Noir, Pinot Noir Blanc, White Zinfandel, Zinfandel Blanc, and vin Rosé. Some European versions are Bandol Rosé, Castel del Monte, Chiaretto del Garda, Côtes-de-Provence Rosé, Sancerre Rosé, and Tavel. No wonder the poor consumer is confused.

One of our favorite Rosé wines is Grenache. It has a flowery fragrance typical of the grape, usually more of a pink-orange or salmon color, and a dry finish. The drier Rosés will accompany a variety of foods from pasta salads to Chinese dishes to hams and turkeys. The

---

[2] When we were younger, things like this caused us considerable consternation. Now we just get irritated.

sweeter ones make excellent aperitif or 'luncher' wines. A really "classy" Rosé, called Grenache Rosé California Vin du Mistral 1992, was recently released by **Joseph Phelps**. Some good-value Blush wines (and approximate prices) recommended for everyday consumption are:

Bel Arbors White Zinfandel 1991 Founders Selection (CA) $8/1.5 l

Blossom Hill White Grenache NV (CA) $7/1.5 l

Blossom Hill White Zinfandel 1992 (CA) $7/1.5 l

Corbett Canyon Coastal Classic White Zinfandel NV (CA) $8/1.5 l

E & J Gallo White Grenache 1992 (CA) $7/1.5 l

E & J Gallo White Zinfandel 1993 (CA) $7/1.5 l

Franzia White Zinfandel NV (CA) $13.50/5 l

Glen Ellen Proprietor's Reserve White Grenache NV (CA) $7/1.5 l

Hogue Cellars Harvest Blush NV (WA) $8/1.5 l

Saddle Mountain Columbia Valley Cascade Blush NV (WA) $6/1.5 l

Sebastiani Proprietor's White Zinfandel 1993 $7/1.5 l

Sutter Home White Zinfandel 1992 (CA) $4/750 ml

Vendage White Zinfandel Autumn Harvest 1993 (CA) $7.50/1.5 l

Washington Hills Columbia Valley Blush NV (WA) $6/1.5 l

Woodbridge White Zinfandel 1992 (CA) $8.50/1.5 l

Why Blend?

Doug Welsch, winemaker for **Fenn Valley Vineyards** in Michigan, recently wrote an article entitled "Blending for Perfection," which appeared in the *Michigan Wine Country Magazine* 3 (3):1993. This is the best brief we've read on wine blending and we'll try to relay the important points.

Welsch outlines the various reasons for blending wines. The first reason is to achieve a specific goal or correct a certain defect. This is called "mechanical" blending. One obvious goal might be to extend a very good wine that is in short supply. This can be done by adding some neutral wine (wine with little character), taking care not to exceed the level where it appreciably affects the good wine's character. Remember, if the wine is to remain a varietal, the blended portion cannot exceed twenty-five percent (stipulated by law). Another reason wine is mechanically blended is to balance its acidity. This can be accomplished by blending low-acid wine with high-acid wine. In many regions, wines produced in southern districts are lower in acid than those produced farther north. Those from northern districts may contribute more fruitiness to the blend. Vintners also blend wines from different years to minimize differences in non-vintage products (whites, blushes, or reds). This is a common practice with popular proprietary products that must remain uniform from one year to the next.

A second approach to blending is "artistic." Artistic blends are designed to combine varietal characteristics that complement or synergize one another. Welsch uses as examples the blends of Seyval, Vidal, and Vignoles used in producing several elegant white proprietary blends. In his view, Seyval offers light fruit and a vinous character, Vignoles adds a fruity nose and lingering finish, and Vidal contributes a youthful, fresh fruit character. These crisp wine blends are enjoyable when young or aged for several years. Another example of an artistic blend is the combination of two red varietals, Chancellor and Chambourcin. Again, the aim is to combine the strengths of each variety. Chancellor provides a complex, up-front character of tobacco, raspberries, and smoke, while Chambourcin is added for its cherry and raspberry character as well as its lingering finish. Welsch will also often add Chambourcin to improve the flavor and color of his Pinot Noirs.

Blending is a tedious task that involves mixing many combinations in small measured quantities and tasting each one meticulously. After deciding on a few blends, a handful of sample bottles are prepared for additional tasting by the winemaker and a chosen few (with and without food). At this point the winemaker gains some confidence as to how the proper blend can be put together in the cellar. Welsch believes that the blending process sets wineries apart, since it is the skillful execution of this art that allows the winemaker to add his or her personal signature to a wine. The fact that many European vintners have been practicing this art for centuries certainly should provide a different perspective for those who frown on blended wines.

Generic White Wines

Good-quality, inexpensive wines are made in all of the major wine-producing countries. For the locals in wine regions, these are as much a part of life as are coffee and tea to ordinary Americans. Each area of the world has white grape varieties that are blended in proper proportions to provide pleasing wines. This *vin ordinaire* is also produced in great quantity in California, and to some extent in the eastern United States. Much of this wine is bottled in 1.5 liter or gallon jugs or in plastic-lined dispenser boxes. Many of the grapes for such wine are grown in the large interior valleys of California rather than the choice sites where the grapes "suffer." In California, varieties such as French Columbard, Emerald Riesling, Chenin Blanc, Palomino, and Sémillon are widely used in blended white wines. At one time the table and raisin grape Thompson Seedless found its way into many jug wines; some may still sneak into bottles today.[3] Blended white wines can be produced cheaply because their grape varieties may produce five to ten times the tonnage and sell for one-tenth the cost of the varietals struggling on the hillsides of California's Napa, Sonoma, or Mendocino counties. The wineries in the interior valleys are large, totally automated facilities where lots of science and little art enters the winemaking process. Companies like **Gallo** and **Franzia** are geared to crank out millions of gallons with good reproducibility from batch to batch.

Confusion arises from the fact that many California white blends are named for wine-producing regions of Europe, such as Chablis, Moselle, Rhine, and Sauternes. Holy Liebfraumilch![4] They bear no resemblance to wines produced in these areas. California Chablis, for

---

[3] Actually, grapes are not able to sneak into a product on their own. People like Luigi's Uncle Guiseppe dump them into each batch.

[4] First retorted by Robin, Batman's little buddy. (See Glossary for translation.)

example, will contain several varieties, each of which contributes its own flavor and aroma components. Muscat and Sémillon are often used in small quantity to contribute a flowery character. Chenin Blanc and French Columbard will contribute a good balance of fruit, acid, and dryness. Of the generic whites, Chablis is usually the driest, followed by Rhine and Sauternes.

Personally, we feel it is a mistake to use these European names to market American wines, even though the labels must indicate they are American products. Fortunately, many wineries now "hook" consumers on consistently good wines with catchy proprietary names. They trust consumers will remember names like Renaissance, Sandpiper, Thousand Flowers, or Trillium.

Foreign wineries also produce large amounts of blended wine for everyday consumption by the natives; in Europe particularly, everyday consumption is considerably higher than here. The Europeans prefer to export their higher quality (and priced) wines, but nonetheless, one can find a fair number of German blends (e.g., Liebfraumilch, Piesporter Michelsberg) and French white table wines (*vin de Table*) on the U.S. market. The Australians and South Americans are also exporting some reasonably nice blended wines. We have more to say about these imports in Chapter 11 and present an extensive list of good-value, blended, proprietary wines in Chapter 14.

Some blended white wines available in magnums or boxes that we feel are good values include:

Fetzer Premium White 1992 (CA) $7.80/1.5 l
Franzia Mountain Chablis NV (CA) $13.50/5 l
Geyser Peak Premium Vintage White NV (CA) $7/1.5 l
Glen Ellen Proprietor's Reserve White NV (CA) $7/1.5 l
Hogue Harvest Dry White NV (WA) $8/1.5 l
Parducci Vintage White 1991 (CA) $6.25/1.5 l
Saddle Mountain Columbia Valley Blanc de Blanc NV (WA) $6/1.5 l

Sebastiani Proprietor's White 1992 (CA) $7/1.5 l
Washington Hills Premium Dry NV (WA) $6/1.5 l

Generic Red Wines

There are many good-quality blended red wines on the market. As with the whites, many American producers have chosen to "genericize" the European regional names, so we have a plethora of American Beaujolais, Burgundies, Chiantis, etc. Again, we are not thrilled with this naming system, mainly because it is so confusing for the beginner and gives the consumer little indication of what may be expected. For example, Gallo's Hearty Burgundy, a reasonably good product, bears no resemblance to a Burgundy from France. Please, folks, just give these wines a good proprietary name and quit implying that they have a European flair.

Generic reds are often blends of several vintages and varieties such as Cabernet Sauvignon, Carignane, Charbono, Merlot, Ruby Cabernet, and Zinfandel. Many of these blends are quite pleasing and should be drunk immediately since they will not improve with age. Two of our favorite red blends, Glen Ellen's Proprietors Reserve Red and Parducci's Vintage Red, can often be found on sale in wine shops for less than $6 per magnum. Another good value is the old standby, Gallo's Hearty Burgundy, which usually can be found in the $6 to $7-per-magnum range. So in essence here gang, we're talking about decent, everyday red wine for $3 per bottle. Other values worthy of mention include:

Blossom Hill Premium Red NV (CA) $7/1.5 l
Corbett Canyon Coastal Classic Proprietors Red NV (CA) $7/1.5 l
Farron Ridge (Chateau Ste. Michelle) Columbia Valley Premium Red NV (WA) $8/1.5 l
Fetzer Premium Red NV (CA) $7.80/1.5 L
Geyser Peak Premium Vintage Red NV (CA) $7/1.5 l
Sebastiani Proprietor's Red NV (CA) $8.50/1.5 l

Chapter 6

Truly Snooty Generics

We first heard this term used by Dr. Richard Peterson (**Monterey Vineyards**) on a California wine video we saw several years ago. Earlier in this chapter we mentioned that blended wines are not necessarily lower in quality. In fact, many of the great European wines owe their greatness to the fact that the vintner has carefully combined the strengths of several grape varieties into one. Recently, California winemakers have tried to craft Bordeaux-style wines by blending their better-quality, first-class varieties into wines that might compete with the better French offerings. These wines are given fancy proprietary names. Thirty-eight American vintners have formed the Meritage Association, a group that is attempting to have this name officially designated as the name for premier American blends. While Meritage wines must contain only certain varieties, they cannot be more than ninety percent of any one variety. The association hopes to reserve this name for the highest quality blended wines produced in America and prevent other wineries from using it on lower-end blends.

Red wines can be designated Meritage if they are made from a blend of two or more of the following Bordeaux varieties: Cabernet Sauvignon, Merlot, Cabernet Franc, Malbec, Petit Verdot, St. Macaire, Gros Verdot, or Carmenere. For example, one might blend sixty percent Cabernet Sauvignon, twenty-five percent Merlot, and fifteen percent Cabernet Franc to produce a smooth and very pleasing wine that could fetch $20 to $50. White wines can be designated Meritage if they contain at least two of the following varieties: Sauvignon Blanc, Sémillon, or Sauvignon Vert. Although some Meritage blends are very nice, and may appeal to yuppies or snottés, we often find them too pricey. We know we can find great varietals such as Zinfandel and Petite Sirah that will knock our socks off for about half the price.

Less Snooty Generics

Another factor weighing against the acceptance of expensive Meritage wines is the availability of some well-crafted, imported blends at much lower prices. In recent years, several Australian wineries have produced Cabernet Sauvignon/Shiraz blends showing excellent balance and selling in the $8 to $10 range. The Spanish blends from Rioja are also quite competitive in quality and price. Many imported blends of excellent value are listed in Chapter 14.

We do believe the California vintners will have success with some of their premium generics, but they may have to become a bit less snooty and drop prices to compete with the excellent imports. Some of these less-snooty California generics available under proprietary names and at reasonable prices include **Parducci's** Bono-Sirah, **Preston's** Faux, **Signorello's** Il Taglio Napa Valley, **Cline's** Côtes d'Oakley, **Hop Kiln's** Marty Griffin's Big Red, **Pellegrini Family's** Côtes de Sonoma Deux Cepages, and **R. H. Phillips's** Night Harvest Cuvée Rouge.

Chapter 7
The Sparklers

parkling wines (mostly Champagne) have achieved wide popularity for special occasions such as wedding dinners and New Year's brunches. Legend says the blind French monk Dom Perignon,[1] who was cellarmaster of the Benedictine Abbey, discovered the process for making Champagne late in the seventeenth century. The French must take this legend seriously because they have erected several statues commemorating the event in the Champagne region, and they market a fine Champagne named for him. His original method for making Champagne, slightly refined, is still used by the best vintners today. The process is known as Mèthode champenoise (me-toad shamp-en-wahs) and is extremely labor intensive, which explains why these Champagnes are so expensive.

Mèthode Champenoise

Champagne begins like many other white wines, with fermentation in stainless steel tanks. The most commonly used blend (*cuvée*) is a mixture of Chardonnay and Pinot Noir, although many other varieties are successfully used throughout the world. Pinot Noir contributes great character and richness to the French Champagnes. The major requirement for a Champagne grape is high acid content. If the grape varieties used are all white, the product will be labeled Blanc de Blancs. After the wine (still wine) is made, several lots (varieties or vintages)

---

[1] As far as we can determine, he conducted the first blind tasting.

may be blended to provide the cuvée. A mixture of sugar, yeast, and wine (*liqueur de tiriage*) is then added to the cuvée. This mixture is then bottled and capped with metal beer caps so that the secondary fermentation can take place in the bottles.

Secondary fermentation may take several months as the yeast slowly converts the added sugar to alcohol and carbon dioxide bubbles. Most Champagnes are fermented for a minimum of nine months and many for periods of two to three years. The slow decomposition of yeast cells is believed to contribute much of the desirable flavor and richness of the final product. This fermentation and aging process occurs with the bottles resting in a horizontal position.

In the ensuing weeks, after secondary fermentation is complete, workers make several rounds through all of these bottles, shake them carefully to loosen the yeast residues, and gradually move them to an inverted position. This technique is known as "riddling," and when it is complete all of the yeast sediment rests in the neck of the bottles, where it can be disgorged. Disgorging is accomplished by a neat little trick.[2] The wine and yeast mixture in the bottle necks is quickly frozen by dipping the bottles in a super-cooled brine solution. The bottles are then turned upright, the caps quickly removed, and the pressure in the bottles forces out the frozen yeast sediment and wine mixture. The bottles are then topped off with a mixture of wine and brandy containing enough sugar to provide the desired amount of sweetness in the final product. The bottles are now ready to be fitted with their special corks, restraining wire hoods, and decorative foil covers. After a month or two of rest, the bottles are ready for your pleasure.

Throughout the world, Champagnes (like people) are produced in varying degrees of sweetness. This is achieved through the cuvée that is selected to start with and/or the final addition of sugar and brandy at the end. If no sugar is added at the end, the Champagne is known as *Natur* or Natural. This is the driest version and requires a special palate to appreciate. *Brut* Champagne has a small amount of sugar added

---

[2] Not to be confused with a clean-cut prostitute.

prior to bottling and is off-dry in taste. Extra Dry versions contain 1.5 to 3.0 percent residual sugar and are noticeably sweet, while *Sec* and *Demi-sec* selections may contain up to 6 percent sugar, and *Doux*[3] (sweet) versions up to 10 percent.

Any sparkling wine made by this labor-intensive technique will be labeled "naturally fermented in this bottle." Although some wineries have been able to partially automate the riddling and disgorging processes, making wine by this method is still an art, and the final result is worth the extra cash.

More Economical Sparklers

Now that we've outlined how the classy stuff is made, we should let you know there are two other methods widely used to produce sparkling wines. In the first, called the "transfer method," the riddling and disgorging processes are not used. Instead, the contents of each bottle are transferred under pressure to a tank where the yeast residue is filtered out and the final blending mix added in. The sparkling wine is then put into new bottles. The label of a wine produced by this technique will say "naturally fermented in *the* bottle" instead of in *this* bottle, which is a very minor label change. Sparkling wines produced by this method may, in fact, be very good, though traditionalists will argue that some quality is lost in the handling and filtering processes. We've not been able to tell a great deal of difference between these two types of products, but we do not pretend to be Champagne connoisseurs. The important aspect of both of these processes is that the wine has had an opportunity to age with the yeast in the bottle for an extended period of time.

A totally different approach that can produce a noticeably different end result is the "Charmat" (named after its inventor) or bulk process. In this technique, the secondary fermentation occurs in large five-hundred- to fifteen-hundred-gallon, stainless steel tanks. The tank becomes a giant bottle, trapping the carbon dioxide bubbles in this large volume

---

[3] When I really want to impress my co-author, I refer to her as "Douxy." (Co-author's note: NOT!)

of wine. This process takes only two to three weeks, after which the wine is clarified, adjusted to the proper sugar content, and bottled under pressure. The whole procedure from crush to bottling rarely takes more than a few months, compared to several years for the traditional process. For this reason, the sparkling wines produced by this method are inexpensive. Although some of the wines produced in this way are acceptable, none have the complexity of those produced by the other two processes.

Other Offerings

If you like sweet wines, you will probably like Asti Spumante, a sparkler from Italy crafted from Moscato di Canelli grapes. The Germans produce sparkling wine called Sekt, most often from a cuvée of Riesling and Sylvaner grapes. In the good old U.S. of A. a number of sparklers, with loyal followings, are produced from eastern and western grape varieties. The name "Cold Duck" (from the German *Kalte Ente*) was applied to a sparkling wine developed in Michigan in the mid-1960s. A variety of other cold fowls[4] were introduced soon after. These are pink blends of white Champagne and sparkling Burgundy, most of which are produced by the bulk process. Concord wine may be added for sweetness or fruitiness. Of better quality, in our view, are eastern varietal sparkling wines made from Catawba and Delaware grapes, or sparklers made from blends of *vinifera* varieties similar to those used in France.

Most of the California sparkling wines are Blanc de Blancs, and a few are even varietals. Some of the better ones are made from blends of Chardonnay and Pinot Blanc grapes, while others may contain Sémillon or Riesling. Almost all are made in a *Brut* style. One of the more interesting versions we have tasted is produced from Gewürztraminer by **Navarro Vineyards** in the Anderson Valley. Many California sparkling wines are excellent values. In general, they are fresh and fruity in character, lacking the mustiness of many French Champagnes.

---

[4] Turkeys, swans, and just about all other birds except chickens. We certainly do not mean to imply the wine is foul.

Chapter 7

How to Pop a Cork

Since sparkling wines are under about six atmospheres of pressure in their uniquely designed bottles, things obviously can go wrong if they are handled improperly. Douxy says you should open champagne as if you are disarming a bomb. Actually, the most common problem is releasing the cork too rapidly and disgorging precious wine where you did not intend to—perhaps all over your undeserving mother-in-law.[5]

Sparklers should be well chilled prior to serving.[6] The quickest way to do this is to place the bottle in a mixture of half ice and half water for about twenty minutes. When the wine is thoroughly chilled, wipe the bottle dry with a towel and keep the towel handy for insurance later on. The proper steps for opening the bottle are:

1. Remove the foil cover.
2. Untwist the wire hood that covers the cork and set it aside.
3. Point the bottle at a forty-five degree angle away from you— and your mother-in-law. Do this over a sink or in an area where you can tolerate a spill until you become an expert.
4. Grasp the cork firmly with one hand and slowly turn the bottle with the other. This is much more effective than trying to turn the cork.
5. Once the bottle turns freely on the cork, carefully pull the bottle away from the cork as you turn. You should see just a bit more cork with each turn; the idea is to ease it out rather than pull it out quickly, which forces a lot of wine out of the bottle.

The best way to pour sparkling wine is to hold the glass at an angle so the wine hits the side of the glass instead of the bottom. Otherwise, you will pour a glassful of bubbles. The glass should be filled only about two-thirds full. The wine presents itself best in a tulip- or flute-type glass.

---

[5] Undeserving of good wine, but perhaps deserving of being spilled upon.

[6] More importantly, they should be well chilled prior to *opening*. We once opened a warm bottle to take some pictures of the process. As soon as the wire hood came off, she blew!

Proper steps in opening a bottle of sparkling wine. After removing the foil cover, (A) loosen the wire hood by twisting its handle, and (B) carefully twist the bottle while firmly gripping the cork.

Budget Bubbly

Some of those vintage-dated Mèthode champenoise French Champagnes can set you back $50 to $150 a bottle. If you're one of those people who dread spending that much on the entire wedding reception, here are some sparkling wines that could fit your budget. These wines have received high ratings and are priced at $10 or less per bottle.

Bodegas Jaume Serra Seco Dry Cava Spain Cristalino NV $8
Castellblanch Brut Cava Extra Spain NV $6
Cordorniu Brut Blanc de Blanc Cava 1988 (Spain) $10
Domaine De Martinolles Brut France Blanquette de Limoux 1989 and 1990 $9 and $10
Domaine Ste. Michelle Brut Washington Columbia Valley NV $9
Freixenet Brut Cava Spain Cordon Negro NV $9
Gancia Brut Castello Gancia NV (Italy) $7
Gratien & Meyer Brut Saumur NV (France) $9.25

Hardy's Brut Australia Grand Reserve NV $8
Korbel Brut California NV $10
Lembey Brut Cava Spain 1988 $9
Navarro Gewürztraminer Brut California Anderson Valley 1989 $8.50
Seaview Brut South Australia 1988 $9
Segura Viudas Brut Cava Spain Aria Estate NV $10
M. Tribaut Blanc de Noirs Monterey County NV (CA) $10
Varichon & Clerc Blanc de Blancs France 1989 $9
Veuve Du Vernay Brut Blanc de Blancs France NV $7

A Few Nice Ones For That Special Occasion
S. Anderson Brut Napa Valley 1986 (CA) $18
Argyle Brut Oregon Willamete Valley Cuvee Limited 1988 $18
Bouche Pere & Fils Brut Champagne Cuvee Reserve NV (France) $20
Domaine Ste. Michelle Blanc de Blancs Washington Columbia Valley 1986 $14
Piper Sonoma Blanc de Noirs Sonoma County 1988 (CA) $13.50
Piper Sonoma Brut Sonoma County 1988 (CA) $13.50
Scharfenberger Brut Mendocino County NV (CA) $16.60
Zonin Brut Blanc de Blancs Italy Chardonnay NV $12

Chapter 8

Dessert Wines

I n recent years we've paid less attention to dessert wines, mainly because calorie counting has forced us to pay less attention to dessert. Nevertheless, on a special occasion[1] the dessert wine comes out of the cellar. On our visits to wineries we're continually impressed with the fine selections being produced by a large number of vintners. Many dessert wines are sweet, no question about it; some boast residual sugar above forty percent. We've found that many of our favorites are nectars themselves, and certainly do not need to be served with a calorie-laden dish of pastry covered with whipped cream. Some of the fruit and berry wines come in either a sweet or *demi-sec* style, and all are pleasant for sipping alone after a meal. Oftentimes, a saucer of almonds or a few wedges of fruit and cheese are all that are needed to accompany a delicate dessert wine. These wines come in a variety of shapes, colors, and—oh, yes—prices. Many dessert wines are expensive because they are costly to produce—either the fruit needed is in limited supply, the vinification techniques are labor intensive, or the cellaring time is of long duration. Let's take a look at the various types of dessert wine.

---

[1] Onset of menopause, full moon, circumcision of grandsons, etc.

Late Harvest Dessert Wines

Great dessert wines can be made from many white wine varieties: Gewürztraminer, Johannisberg Riesling, Sauvignon Blanc, Scheurebe, Sémillon, and in the Loire, even Chenin Blanc. European vintners have developed the art of making these delicacies over centuries, and now some of the American winemakers are doing a remarkable job with these wines as well. The key to late harvest dessert wine is a grape with a very high sugar content. This elevated sweetness can occur through luck of nature or through the clever manipulations by the winemaker.

Many of the great German and French dessert wines owe their success to Noble Rot, the fungus *Botrytis cinerae*, which infects the grape and turns it into an ugly mass of gray mold. This ugly mass contains a dehydrated grape[2] with a highly elevated sugar content. Winemakers have not been able to duplicate wine made with *Botrytis*ed grapes by substituting raisins. No one quite understands what the fungus does, but it somehow adds a great complexity of aromas and flavors that cannot be achieved in any other way.

Two of the great Sauternes of France, **Château d'Yquem** and **Château Riessec** are examples of wines made from *Botrytis*ed grapes, yet they are very different. **Yquem** is often described as cream and caramel, while **Riessec** is reminiscent of fruit and honey. Recent vintages of **Yquem** have fetched $130 to $310 per 750 ml bottle. **Riessec** comes in a bit cheaper at $38 to $74. The *Wine Spectator* has highly recommended the 1986 and 1988 **Château Les Justices** Sauternes, which can be found for a mere $15 per split (325 ml). These are obviously wines for very special occasions, and are to be sipped and savored.[3] They have excellent keeping quality and may continue to improve over a fifteen to twenty year period.

Other famous *Botrytis*ed dessert wines are the German *Beerenauslese* (BA) and *Trockenbeerenauslese* (TBA). These are most often made from Riesling and Scheurebe grapes. We are quite partial to dessert wines

---

[2] Luigi insists the grapes are pretty dried out, too.
[3] We don't even hint to Luigi that we might have any of these in the cellar.

made from Gewürztraminer, which display the nose of a flower and spice garden and the taste of apricots, honey, and caramel. **The Hugel Family** and **Domaine Ostertag** make excellent dessert-style Gewürztraminers near the Rhine River in Alsace, France.

Three of the more famous producers of Riesling dessert wines are **Langwerth von Simmern, Egon Müller,** and **J. J. Prüm.** Some of their recent BAs and TBAs (1988-1990) have sold in the range of $35 to $450 per bottle. Although it seems incredible, they are probably a steal at anything under $100, assuming you are a dessert wine nut. Those who aren't too eager to throw a century note at a bottle of anything might want to just taste one of these gems sometime when celebrating a special occasion at a restaurant. Some restaurants with extensive wine lists would be happy to pour you a fine dessert wine for perhaps $6 to $8 per glass.[4] Put this in perspective: you've probably paid $4.50 at the airport for a watered-down Bloody Mary.

Other late harvest or selected harvest dessert wines are produced by processes involving lower levels of *Botrytis* (German *Auslese*), allowing the grapes to freeze in the field prior to harvest (German *eiswein*), hanging grapes on the barn rafters to dry (Italian *vin santo*), or blending some *Botrytis*ed grapes with other wine and allowing it to ferment again (Hungarian *Tokaji Aszu*). Some excellent dessert wines are produced by these various methods, but none are raved about like the heavily *Botrytis*ed wines.

The *Wine Spectator* recently proclaimed two German dessert wines as exceptional buys. They are the 1990 **Reichstrat von Buhl** Riesling Auslese Rheinfalz Forster Freundstruck and the 1990 **Heribert Kerpen** Riesling Auslese Mosel-Saar-Ruwer Graacher Himmelreich, which sell for $14 and $17, respectively.

In California, there are only certain sites and years where *Botrytis* will successfully attack the grapes. **Freemark Abbey** and **Chateau St. Jean** have done exceptional jobs with late harvest Rieslings, though in recent years it has only been possible to produce the wines in about half

---

[4] Don't expect the glass to be full, Luigi. This is liquid gold we're talking about here.

the vintages. These wines sell for about $20 to $25 per split.

Several California vintners have attempted to produce quality dessert wines from Sémillon and Sauvignon Blanc, and their efforts are beginning to bear fruit. Definitely worth a try are **Beringer's** Nightingale, **Bonny Doon's** Malvasia Bianca Vin de Glaciere, **Chalk Hill's** Late Harvest Sémillon, **Chateau St. Jean's** Sémillon d'Or, and **Far Niente's** Dolce. Nightingale is produced by spraying *Botrytis* over freshly harvested grapes and allowing the fungus to grow in a temperature- and humidity-controlled room. At this point it's a relatively small operation, resulting in only one hundred to two hundred cases of wine.

A few California wineries also produce a nice late harvest Gewürztraminer from year to year. Among these are **Arrowwood**, **Chateau St. Jean**, **Mark West**, and **Navarro**. The wines are priced at $17 to $25 per split. Some eastern winemakers are also achieving good success with late harvest dessert wines. If you're in the Great Lakes Region, try a late harvest Vidal Blanc or Vignoles.

The Muscat varieties, most notably Muscat de Frontignan from France and Muscat di Canelli from Italy, can produce some especially fragrant dessert wines. Two of our favorite American Muscats are the 1989 **Chateau St. Jean** Sonoma Valley Muscat Canelli and the 1990 **Bookwalter** Washington State Muscat Blanc. In addition, the *Wine Spectator* recently highly recommended the French **Prosper Maufoux** Muscat de Beaumes-de-Venise NV and the 1992 Italian **Guissepe Rivetti & Figle** Moscato d'Asti La Spinette Vigneto Biancospino.

Fruit Wines

From our point of view, a dessert wine does not necessarily need to be made from grapes. As you travel to the grape-producing areas you will find that many of these places are also suited to growing other species of fruits and berries. Put a winemaker in the area and he/she cannot resist the temptation to ferment some of these babies as well. A skilled winemaker can produce some semisweet delights from blackberries, blueberries, cherries, peaches, pears, raspberries, strawberries, or even rhubarb. We've had superb cherry wines (like cherry pie in a glass) from the Leelanau and Old Mission peninsulas of Michigan and found a delicious raspberry wine crafted by Doug Welsch of **Fenn Valley Vineyards** in southwestern Michigan. His raspberry wine recently received the highest award ever given at the Michigan Wine Show. Our friends in the Pacific Northwest tell us that great berry wines can be found at the **Hoodsport Winery** on the Olympic Peninsula of Washington; the **Bjelland Vineyards** in Umpqua Valley, Oregon; **Henry Endres** and **Wasson Brothers** wineries in Clackamas County, Oregon; and the **Hood River** and **Mt. Hood** wineries in the Columbia Gorge area of Oregon. The secret to enjoying these wines with dessert is to be sure the accompanying dessert does not overpower the wine. These wines will usually accompany fresh or cooked fruit or nuts, but beware of fancy tarts.[5] Remember, many of these wines are fine desserts by themselves.

Fortified Dessert Wines - Sherries, Ports, and Nectars of Berries

The authentic versions of these well-known dessert wines have been produced for several centuries in southern Spain (Sherry), northwestern Portugal (Port), and on the Isle of Madeira (Madeira), located about four hundred miles west of Morocco. Several imitations are being produced now in California, Australia, and various other places, and both the originals and the imitations vary considerably in quality and price. All of these wines, plus what we're calling Nectars of Berries, are fortified with additional alcohol from wine spirits or brandy (distilled wine). Their alcohol contents vary from sixteen to twenty-five percent.

Sherry

Sherries are produced from white grape varieties and may be sweet or dry depending upon when the fermentation is stopped. When fermentation has reached the desired point, the wine is fortified with

---

[5] When I was a boy my father warned me about those tarts. I'm passing along the advice.

brandy. This mixture is then aged in barrels for several years, and the final product will be light to dark amber color. The Sherries that might be available at your wineshop are:

Cream Sherry: An amber, sweet sherry that traditionally is made by sweetening a blend of well-aged Olorosos, which are heavy, rich sherries.

Fino: A completely dry and pale-colored sherry, considered to be one of the finest. It is often drunk as an aperitif, at a cool temperature.

Manzanilla: Normally a Fino Sherry that acquires a salty character by being cellared near the coast.

Oloroso: A style of sherry with a heavier-body and darker color than Fino. It ages to a great richness.

Pale Cream: A popular style of pale Sherry made by sweetening Fino.

Solera: A procedure used to make Sherries. Briefly, it entails adding younger wine progressively to more mature barrels, the object being a uniformity in the final wine.

When used as dessert wines, Sherries go well with desserts that contain nuts. Think about Sherry with pecan pie or an almond croissant. Too bad we're counting calories—damn!

Some drier sherries that are fairly good buys include: **Emilio Lustau** Fino, **Gonzales Byass** Tio Pepe Fino, **Pedro Domecq** La Ina Fino, and **Vinicola Hildalgo** La Gitana Manzanilla. Good values in the off-drys are **Emilio Lustau** Palo Cortado and **Sandeman** Character Oloroso. In the sweet Cream Sherries, we suggest you try **Emilio Lustau** Cream Sherry, **Pedro Domecq** Celebration Cream, or **Sandeman** Armada Cream.

Port

Are you ready for the $64,000 question? Where are authentic Ports made? Portugal, of course!

Ports are almost always made from red grape varieties. They are fortified, and almost always sweet. Like Sherries, they are made in a variety of styles, which translates into a range of prices. The types of Port are:

Ruby: The youngest and most economical style of Port, described as simple, sweet, and red. Some are flavorful, while others can be strong without a great deal of character.

Tawny: A style of Port which has several years of barrel aging and which becomes tawny in color. Some of the best are aged up to twenty years. Cheap imitations are made by blending red and white Ports.

Vintage Character: Ports that are aged in casks for four to five years, cold stabilized, and filtered prior to bottling. They contain no sediment and will keep for a week or two after opening. They are an excellent choice for restaurant stock.

Vintage: The highest quality Ports of only special vintages are bottled after two years in wood, then aged in the bottle for twenty years or more. These bottles contain a heavy deposit, and the wine must be decanted prior to drinking. A simple way to do this is to pour it into the decanter through a paper coffee filter.

White: A Port occasionally made from white grapes, which turns out to be a golden color. It is now more often made dry than sweet.

Ports recommended for beginners are **Churchill's** Special Reserve, **Cockburn's** Special Reserve, **Fonseca** Bin 27, **Sandeman's** Founder's Reserve, and **Warre's** Warrior. If you develop a taste for Port you can try nice Vintage Ports by **Dow, Fonseca Guimaraens, Taylor,** or **Warre.** The *Wine Spectator* recently listed four Vintage Ports as exceptional values. They are **Château Reynella** Port, South Australia 1981 ($11.50), **Dow** Vintage Port 1980 ($28), **Fonseca** Bin 27 Port 1988 ($17), and **Quinta De La Rosa** Vintage Port 1988 ($18).

Madeira

This is probably the least-known fortified dessert wine, although it has been produced for centuries and was prized by the early American colonists. Madeira is known to cellar exceptionally well, with reports of great bottles that are well over one hundred years old. This staying power may be achieved through an unusually high acid content. Madeira fans rave about the balance of sweetness and acidity, which is absent in Sherries and Ports. As with the other dessert wines, there are several styles of Madeira.

Bual or Boal: A sweet and dark-colored dessert Madeira produced from a grape of the same name, often described as soft and smoky.

Malmsey: The sweetest style of Madeira, with a dark amber color and a rich honey flavor. A true dessert by itself.

Rainwater: A fairly light-colored Madeira which may be finished with a touch of sweetness. It is produced from the Verdelho grape. This wine makes an excellent aperitif.

Sercial: A dry Madeira produced from the Sercial grape and used as an aperitif.

Verdelho: A rich and off-dry style of Madeira produced from the grape of the same name.

It is a mistake to pair a dessert Madeira with an overpowering dessert such as heavily frosted cake. To savor all the flavors of an excellent Bual or Malmsey, we recommend drinking them by themselves or with lightly flavored pastry.

Beginners to Madeira might want to try a relatively inexpensive **Blandy** (Duke series), **Cossart Gordon**, or **Leacock** selection. Excellent quality but more expensive selections are also available from these shippers and from **Barbeito**, **Henriques and Henriques**, **Lomelino Tarquinio**, and **Rutherford & Miles**.

Nectar of Berries - (Whidbey's)

Realizing this product is not wine but a liqueur, we still have chosen to include it here. As the Mouseketeers used to say, "Why? Because we like you!" One of our favorite dessert beverages, Whidbey's is made by extracting (with alcohol) all the goodies out of loganberries. The end result is a fragrant and flavorful product that is about twenty-two percent alcohol. We're continually amazed at how many people have never heard of Whidbey's. This exquisite beverage is produced by **M. W. Whidbey's, Ltd.** in Greenbank, Washington, located on Whidbey's Island near Seattle. They have managed to capture the entire essence of the loganberry in this elegant after-dinner drink. Its distribution is pretty well limited to the state of Washington and a few border towns, and it sells for around $18 per 750 ml. Whenever your friends or neighbors travel to Washington, offer to watch their house in exchange for a bottle of this nectar. Try Whidbey's alone, with a sliver of fudge, or over a dish of ice cream. Luigi enjoys it over pancakes. At the Whidbey's Greenbank Berry Farm they also produce a loganberry wine as well as a Port made from Cabernet Sauvignon and Grenache grapes. Both are definitely worth a try.

Chapter 9

A Look at Domestic Wines and Wineries,
Western United States

"Kiss French, Drink American!" said the poster in a California wine shop. So what should one do? Be loyal Americans and drink only wines made in the good old U. S. of A.? If you chose to do this, you certainly would have a great array of wines to choose from. We personally drink about ninety percent American, not just from loyalty, but because we truly enjoy the variety of products available domestically. We think most of our readers will spend a lot more time in American wineries than they will skipping about Bordeaux. Every now and then we do sample the imports to keep abreast of what other regions offer. In our view there are only a few instances where imports are superior, and these exceptions tend to be considerably more expensive.

America is blessed with several areas where soil and climate allow the production of quality wine grapes. The largest and best-known production areas are California's interior and coastal valleys, where good climatic conditions usually prevail year after year. California is by far the most important wine-producing state. After World War II, California was blessed with a strong Department of Enology and Viticulture at the University of California-Davis. There, Drs. Amerine and Winkler and others guided the California wine industry to a level of excellence previously unseen in the United States.

California enjoys another great advantage over many other grape-producing areas since its mild winters do not annually threaten the death of the very vines that produce the fruit. The cold winter temperatures that periodically strike many regions can kill grapevines down to ground level; occasional spring frosts will wipe out or greatly reduce that year's crop. This is particularly true with the *vinifera* grapes, a major portion of the better wine varieties—we've occasionally witnessed these catastrophes in Michigan, New York, Oregon, and Washington. However, some wine-producing regions of Europe, particularly northern France and Germany, suffer rather severe winters but still produce great wine. The fact is, some of the *vinifera* varieties are better suited than others for production in these marginal climates. Growers in these areas have determined which varieties are best adapted, which is why we commonly find Gewürztraminer, Johannisberg Riesling, Pinot Gris, and Pinot Noir in the cooler Pacific Northwest and Great Lakes areas as well as northern France and Germany. A large number of French-American hybrid grapes also have proven to be hardy enough for the eastern U.S. production areas.

Excessive heat and humidity in the southern United States are limiting factors in the cultivation of quality grapes in much of that region. It is difficult to maintain proper levels and balances of sugars and acids in the fruit when temperatures regularly exceed 95°F. In addition, fungus diseases run rampant under warm, humid conditions. Nonetheless, a few varieties grow there and produce a decent, albeit not great, wine. Today, we think that good wine is being produced in about thirty states. For convenience, we're dividing America into six regions and two chapters: California, the Pacific Northwest (ID, MT, OR, WA), and the Southwest (AZ, CO, HA, NM, TX) are presented in this chapter, and the Great Lakes (IN, MI, MN, NY, OH, PA, WI), Eastern (CT, MD, NJ, NC, RI, TN, VA), and Southern (AR, FL, GA, MS, MO) regions are covered in Chapter 10.

CALIFORNIA

In spite of all the excitement in other states, California still contributes nearly ninety percent of the wine produced in the United States.

1. South Coast
2. Central Coast
   a. Southern
   b. Northern
   c. Central Valley
3. North Coast
   a. Bay area
   b. Napa
   c. Sonoma
   d. Mendocino & Lake
4. Sierra Foothills

The general wine regions of California. Consult Winery Guide to Northern and Central California *for specific appellations and viticultural areas.*

Although we've made one or two trips each year to California wine country over the past fifteen years, we've still only visited about sixty percent of the wineries. In fact, new ones start and older ones change hands faster than greased lightning. Today there are at least 610 California wineries from San Diego County in the south to Humboldt County in the north. The wineries vary in size from extremely large corporations such as **Gallo**, with megaton production, to small family operations that produce a few hundred cases annually. California grape-producing areas are generally divided into four regions which are, in turn, subdivided into numerous viticultural areas. In our view, the best guide to these regions is the *Winery Guide to Northern & Central California* produced by Compass Maps, Inc., P.O. Box 4369, Modesto, CA 95352 ($2.95). This guide provides a complete list of wineries, addresses, phone numbers, and tasting room hours. Their maps are much easier to use than many of the free regional guides that are published monthly in the wine country. Unfortunately, this guide does not include some forty wineries located in Los Angeles, Orange, Riverside, San Bernadino, and San Diego counties in southern California, or the handful of wineries located in Humboldt County in the northernmost corner of the state. Few of the wineries in these excluded counties are world famous, but they do have a loyal following of local people and provide good-value wine every year.

The four major California regions are: South Coast, Central Coast, Sierra Foothills, and North Coast. Most famous of these is the North Coast, which includes the renowned Napa and Sonoma valleys and additional areas in Mendocino and Lake counties. In this chapter we will give you an overview of the highlights of each area rather than a complete listing of all the wineries.

South Coast

This area includes everything south of Santa Barbara and represents about forty smaller wineries that serve the greater metropolitan areas around Los Angeles and San Diego. These wineries seldom receive much publicity from wine gurus, which leads us to conclude that those folks would rather spend their time amid the beauty and reduced smog conditions of northern California than in the L.A. jungle. We really can't understand why they would prefer to be up there rather than fighting earthquakes, traffic, fires, and riots. We've visited a few of the wineries in Riverside and Los Angeles counties and find their wines to be well-made and quaffable. We did not taste any great wines in this area but there may be some we didn't discover. The wines are obviously good enough to attract a local following and to keep these wineries in business. Most were reasonably priced.

Central Coast (Southern Portion)

To start, the **Santa Barbara Winery** deserves mention for its 1991 Zinfandel, rated as one of the top values in the state. This light-style Zin is loaded with fruit and berry aromas and flavors, and is light enough to accompany a turkey sandwich lunch as well as much heavier fare.

Leaving Santa Barbara and moving north on U.S. Highway 101, one first passes through the viticultural area known as the Santa Ynez Valley. There are currently about twenty wineries in this area, some of which are starting to gain national attention. For example, **Sanford Winery** near Solvang recently produced a highly acclaimed Chardonnay (1990), as did **Zaca Mesa** near Los Olivos. **Firestone**, just down the highway, released a highly acclaimed Gewürztraminer the next year. Also in 1991, **The Gainey Vineyard** produced one of the best values in Johannisberg Riesling and a great limited-selection Chardonnay. Obviously, something in this little Southern California valley allows the production of some remarkable wines.

The next viticultural area to the north is the Santa Maria Valley, located southeast of the city of Santa Maria. There are only about a half-dozen wineries here. One of these, **Cambria**, produced a highly touted 1990 Chardonnay from their Katherine's Vineyard. A bit further north are the Arroyo Grande and Edna valleys, located just south of San Luis Obispo and home to about ten wineries. One of these is **Corbett Canyon,** a high-volume producer of pleasant, reasonably priced generic and proprietary wines. The smaller wineries here produce some nice, clean, reasonably priced varietals. For example, **Claiborne & Churchill** received acclaim for their 1991 Alsatian-style dry Riesling.

Further north in San Luis Obispo County is the increasingly famous Paso Robles viticultural district. Each year, more wines from this and the adjacent York Mountain area are receiving national acclaim. For example, a Cabernet Sauvignon from **Castoro Cellars** (1989) was cited recently as a *W.S.*[1] Best Buy, as were **Arciero's** 1988 Estate-bottled Chardonnay, J. Lohr's Cypress Merlot, and **Chestnut Hill's** 1989 Zinfandel. **Meridian** gained fame for their 1990 Chardonnay (made from grapes grown in Santa Barbara County) and their 1988 Cabernet Sauvignon (from Paso Robles grapes). **Meridian** is located east of Paso Robles and is definitely worth a visit. Some of the more famous wineries to the north now also draw upon the quality grapes from the Paso Robles area.

Central Coast (Northern Portion)

This large area starts at the southern Monterey County line and extends northward into Contra Costa County. There are about one hundred wineries scattered throughout the several viticultural districts in the area. From south to north one passes through the districts of Arroyo Seco, Monterey, Carmel Valley, Chalone, Lime Kiln Valley, Paicines, Mount Harlan, Cienega Valley, San Benito, Pacheco Pass, San Ysidro, Ben Lomond Mountains, Santa Clara Valley, Santa Cruz Mountains, and Livermore Valley. Some of these isolated valley and mountain areas lend special attributes to the grapes produced there. For example, **Ridge Vineyard's** famous Monte Bello Cabernet vineyard is located in the Santa Cruz Mountains east of Sunnyvale. **Ridge** is also acclaimed for its Zinfandels, for which grapes are selected from several different areas of the state.

The **Concannon** and **Wente Brothers** wineries are famous landmarks in the Livermore area, having produced quality wines for many decades. Both have produced some elegant Chardonnays in recent years, and **Concannon's** 1990 Sauvignon Blanc was rated as a *W.S.* Best Buy. **Mirassou**, with wineries in Soledad and San Jose, is a famous family operation known for producing wines in California through several generations. **Almaden** and **Paul Masson**, both large-volume produc-

---

[1] Abbreviation for the *Wine Spectator*. Pretty clever, eh?

99

ers, have wineries at Paicines and Saratoga respectively. **Paul Masson's** 1989 Vintner's Selection Merlot was widely recognized as one of the best buys in everyday red wine. Another famous name in this area is **Weibel Champagne Vineyards** at Mission San Jose.

There are several up-and-coming wineries in this area that will deserve close scrutiny in the future. For example, one of the very nicest 1990 Zinfandels was produced by **David Bruce** in Los Gatos. This monster Zin contains about twenty percent Petite Sirah; although it's drinkable now, it should have excellent cellaring potential. **Bonny Doon Vineyard** in Santa Cruz has made headlines with several recent releases including a 1991 Pacific Rim Riesling and a 1993 Clos de Gilroy Grenache. **Chalone Vineyard's** 1991 Pinot Blanc received one of the W.S.'s all-time highest ratings for this varietal. They had received similar accolades for their 1991 Chardonnay. This winery is located in the southern part of the region, near Soledad, and definitely deserves a visit.

Perhaps you are beginning to see that not all of the action is in Napa Valley. Before we head up that way, let's move into the northern San Joaquin Valley and look at a few of the important wineries in this fruit and vegetable smorgasbord.

There are about seventeen wineries in an area near U.S. Highway 99, from Manteca in the south to Lodi in the north. There are some biggies here, including **E & J Gallo** and **Franzia**, which together account for a high percentage of the jug wines produced in the United States. **Robert Mondavi** and **Sebastiani** both have facilities located near Woodbridge, where they produce some of their less expensive wines. In fact, Mondavi's second label bears the name of this interior valley town. Though this area is known more for quantity than quality, many good-value wines for everyday drinking are produced here. (See Chapter 14.)

North Coast

This famous wine-producing area stretches from San Rafael and Vallejo in the south all the way to Fort Bragg and Willits in the north. There are about 340 wineries scattered throughout the twenty-four-odd viticultural districts in this region. Included are the world-famous Napa and Sonoma valleys as well as several other smaller valleys and districts. We've visited a high percentage of these wineries and particularly enjoy Sonoma and Mendocino counties as vacation sites. If you spent two weeks intently visiting wineries in those places, you still wouldn't get to see more than ten percent of them.

Napa Valley

Without doubt, this is the wine-producing area in the United States that has received the most publicity. It probably has as many wineries per mile as any other region in the world, except perhaps Bordeaux. The relatively wide (five to ten miles) valley has about 175 wineries scattered over its thirty-five-mile length. Two major highways that serve this area, California 29 to the west and Silverado Trail to the east, come together at the northern end of the valley near Calistoga.

In the old days, we used to drive through here and sing, "I'm the most happy fella in the whole Napa walley." Now we drive through and cuss about all the traffic and all the people and how some of the folks in the tasting rooms don't seem to treat us like human beings anymore. To be fair about this, if you go in midweek off-season (winter) you can still enjoy a quality learning experience, particularly in many of the smaller wineries.

Frankly, the issue of what type of tasting experience one will receive revolves around the "people skills" of tasting room personnel. Luigi (who is a damn good salesman) wonders why some wineries have hired the Wicked Witch of the West as their public relations person. Certainly there is little to be gained by snubbing the very people you hope to cultivate as customers, since what the wine industry needs more than anything right now is new customers. We don't mean to get persnickety here, but Napa needs to watch its image; a hell of a lot of high-quality wine is being produced in other parts of California and in other states, and by emerging competitors from abroad.

Now that we've badmouthed[2] Napa just a little, let's try to get back in its good graces. The area has some neat wineries that you must see and some superb wines that you should taste. There are so many good wineries here that there just isn't enough time to see them all. Let's assume you will only have time to visit about twenty. We are also going to assume you want a sampling of large and small wineries, beautiful buildings, great scenery, a few gift shops, and of course, some good wine values as well as a few great wines.

The following are places we would highly recommend on your first visit. As you travel north out of the town of Napa check out **Pine Ridge Winery, Silverado Vineyards, Stag's Leap Wine Cellars**, and **Trefethen Vineyards**. Moving north toward Yountville, be on the lookout for **Domaine Chandon**, unless you are not crazy about Champagne. Their Champagne is of high quality and a bit pricey.

Near Oakville you will have the opportunity to contrast two great wineries, a very large one and a tiny one. The tiny one is **Robert Pepi Winery,** where you will be treated to an array of superbly made white wines. We hope they'll still have a split or two of their delicate dessert Sauvignon Blanc for your pleasure. **Robert Mondavi** is a must because of the buildings, grounds, and quality wines. You'll want to pay homage to the guy who has probably done more for the California wine industry than any other living person.[3] Mondavi has been an innovator and a stalwart supporter of research, which always impresses us academic types.

Continuing north to the Rutherford area, we recommend stops at **Beaulieu Vineyard, Cakebread Cellars, Caymus Vineyards, Grgich Hills, Rutherford Hill Winery**, and **Sequoia Grove Vineyards**. Expect some remarkable wines (especially reds) from these people. They've racked up their share of awards from the wine critics.

In the St. Helena area, take a look at **Beringer Vineyards** (great old mansion and grounds), **Burgess Cellars, Dunnewood Vineyards, Heitz**

---

[2] An honest term for constructive criticism.
[3] For that matter, we can't think of any dead person who did more for that industry.

Wine Cellars, Louis Martini, Markham Vineyards, Sutter Home Winery, and V. Sattui Winery. These stops will demonstrate the contrasts between volume producers (with good values) and boutique-type wineries that aim some higher class (and higher-priced) wines at the connoisseurs. In addition to wine, V. Sattui offers a unique gift shop with one of the nicest collections of cheeses and sausages we've ever seen. One of the world's most celebrated Cabernet Sauvignons (Martha's Vineyard) is produced at **Heitz Wine Cellars**. On my first trip to Napa Valley (1968, with several other young professors) I met Joe Heitz in his little tasting room, where we chatted about the future of California wine. His tasting room is a bit larger now, but don't be surprised if you see him there still, with the same zeal for winemaking and wine talk that he had twenty-five years ago.

No trip to the Napa Valley would be complete without a visit to the beautiful **Sterling Vineyards** at the valley's north end near Calistoga. You'll ride a tram up the hill to the winery, which offers a breathtaking view of the valley to the south. Sunny days in the fall or early spring are especially beautiful. There are some excellent wines to be tasted, too. They may seem a bit pricey, but such fine visitor accommodations entail a lot of overhead; be sure to do your share.

In making the trip from south to north you'll have passed through the Los Carneros, Mt. Veeder, Stag's Leap, and Howell Mountain viticultural districts, which are some of the choicest areas of the state. You will often see these district names printed on wine labels. Keep in mind that we have given only a sampling of the fine wineries available in this area. You've got to start somewhere, hey Luigi? Once you've whetted your appetite on these, we're convinced you will want to come back for more.

Sonoma Valley

It'll probably be hard for us to hide our biases, because some of our favorite wineries are in this area and a bit further north. Once again, we're assuming you're coming here for the first time and have time to look at twenty to twenty-five wineries.

The southernmost wineries in Sonoma County begin to appear in the western portion of the Los Carneros district, just north of San Pablo Bay. We'll start our tour with **Buena Vista,** near the small city of Sonoma in the southern end of the valley. This magnificent old stone building is believed to be the oldest standing winery in California. The winery's history includes Agoston Haraszthy, who had a major impact on the California wine scene when he introduced about 100,000 vines of some four hundred varieties into the state in the mid-1800s. You'll find some pleasant wines to taste at **Buena Vista.**

While you're in the neighborhood, zip over to **Ravenswood,** which in our view is one of the finest producers of Zinfandel in California. The bad news (for us, not them) is that their wines are so popular the best vintages sell out early; the only hope is to get on their list for new releases. They produce many different Zinfandels with different vineyard or appellation designations. Even their Vintner's Blend, which they refer to as "Château Cash Flow," is a pretty darn good Zinfandel.

Also in Sonoma (the town) is **Sebastiani Vineyards,** which offers a large variety and some excellent values, particularly in red wines. Their tours are extremely popular. Other nearby wineries worthy of a visit are **Gundlach-Bundschu** and **Viansa,** the latter having an exceptionally fine gift shop.

The Glen Ellen and Kenwood areas are next. We highly recommend a visit to **Glen Ellen Winery** for the beauty of the site, the buildings, and the unique opportunity to taste a series of wines targeted for three different price ranges under three different labels. Their premium Estate wines bear the **Benziger** label, while the everyday drinking wines bear the **Glen Ellen** and **M. G. Vallejo** labels. Many of the **Glen Ellen** wines are excellent values. As we wrote this book, the **Glen Ellen** and **M. G. Vallejo** wine brands were sold to Heublein, Inc.

A little further north on California 12 you'll find the **St. Francis Winery and Vineyards,** home of some of the best California Gewürztraminers and sometimes an exceptional Chardonnay or Merlot.

Some fun-loving wineophiles leaving Ravenswood Winery with their big Zins. Guess which one is Luigi?

We've always found friendly employees and good wine values here. Across the street is **Chateau St. Jean,** which offers some exceptional white and dessert wines. Don't miss **Kenwood Vineyards,** just down the road, where you'll always find good values in their Chenin Blancs, Chardonnays, and some of their Jack London Series robust reds. These are fun-loving folks who make your visit enjoyable.

As you move out of the Sonoma Valley and Sonoma Mountains districts and proceed north through Santa Rosa toward Healdsburg you enter the Russian River Valley viticultural area, west of U.S. Highway 101; the Chalk Hill area lies to the east. Further north, the Dry Creek Valley is to the west and the Alexander Valley to the east. We highly recommend visiting a few wineries in each of these areas.

You can begin a neat trip by exiting U.S. Highway 101 north of Santa Rosa on River Road and heading west toward Forestville. Just north of River Road on Trenton-Healdsburg Road is the **Mark West Vineyard.** They consistently produce pleasant Gewürztraminers made in a variety of styles, and every now and then will surprise you with a big Zinfandel. You can either proceed north up East Side Road or, if you like sparkling wines, get back on River Road and head toward Guerneville. **Korbel Champagne Cellars** is on the right-hand side of River Road; their sparkling wines are always good values.

On your way back east, watch for Westside Road headed north (Whew! Are you lost yet?). This winding little road will take you all the way up through the Dry Creek Valley north of Healdsburg. There are many interesting wineries along this narrow road—but there are also lots of bikers, so be careful.[4] Definitely visit **Rochioli Vineyards** and **Hop Kiln,** which are within a stone's throw of one another. At the former you'll find some lovely Gewürztraminer and Pinot Noir. Some of the best Pinot Noir grapes in California are grown in the Rochioli vineyards. At **Hop Kiln** there are good values in Johannisburg Riesling and a white blend named Thousand Flowers, as well as their Primitivo and Marty Griffin's Big Red Zinfandels. The winery building, formerly a hop kiln, is in itself worth the visit.

As you continue heading north, look for Lambert Bridge Road; before you know it you'll be at **Robert Stemmler's,** where German shorthaired pointers provide a friendly welcome (They request that you make an appointment for tasting.) Expect some elegant Pinot Noir and Chardonnay at this stop. Proceed a few hundred yards east and you will see **Dry Creek Vineyard.** These folks have produced some excellent Zinfandels and Cabernets over the years.

Proceed north on West Dry Creek Road to two highly recommended stops: **Quivera,** which is producing some quality full-bodied Zinfandels, and **Preston Vineyards,** one of our favorites for the big reds. Preston does a superb job with Barbera and Syrah and is experimenting with a number of other exotic varietals. Its blended red, Faux, is an extremely good value. The owners strike us as being innovative.

Head north to Dutcher Creek Road and take a short jaunt to **J. Fritz Winery.** This winery has an unusual layout that uses only gravity

---

[4] These are bicyclists, not Hell's Angels. Just take it easy and don't hit them—or let them hit you.

Hop Kiln Winery near Healdsburg, California, offers a rustic tasting room with an array of fine wines. Courtesy of Brenda Eickelberg.

feed to move its wine downhill from crush to bottling. The beautifully designed tasting room features an array of clean and pleasing wines. We were particularly impressed with the Sauvignon Blanc, Barrel Select Chardonnay, Cabernet, and a Late Harvest Zinfandel. Everything here sparkles, including the service.

Before we cross the superslab (U.S. Highway 101) to get a look at the east side, let's visit **J. Pedroncelli Winery** on Canyon Road. This family operation always provides good-quality wine at a reasonable price as well as an enjoyable tasting room experience. Another highly recommended stop is **Lytton Springs Winery**, which is located a few miles to the south on—guess what?—Lytton Springs Road. This winery is now owned by **Ridge**, a development which interests us since we consider Zinfandel to be the strength of both. Both parties appreciate the value of old vines and good vineyard locations. We hope that this partnership will continue to provide diverse Zinfandel styles from its numerous viticultural areas. The **Lytton Springs** tastings have always been among our favorites because this winery takes its wines, but not itself, seriously.

Before you leave Sonoma County, you must get a look at the Alexander Valley. which lies east and mostly north of Healdsburg. There are three wineries off California 128 that definitely deserve a look. **Sausal** has one of the more scenic little tasting rooms, surrounded by vineyards and a great view of the valley. They have quality Zinfandel at a reasonable price. Further south you will find **Alexander Valley Vineyards**, the home of a fine array of high-quality but reasonably priced wines. We recently found a 1990 Cabernet there that really rang our bell.[5] Just down the road, you'll find the quaint stone structures of the **Field Stone Winery**, much of which is underground; it cellars some of our favorite Petite Sirah.

On your way back into Healdsburg stop at **Simi Winery**, which is nestled in a stand of redwoods just north of town. We still talk to these people even though they quit making one of our favorite Gewürztraminers several years ago. They are doing a splendid job with Cabernet and Chardonnay and offer a great picnic area in the redwoods. We always picnic there with a bottle of **St. Francis** Gewürztraminer, the closest thing we can find to what **Simi** used to make. (That'll teach 'em.[6]) If time allows, swing by **Clos Du Bois** (Clo-Doo-Bwah) **Winery** in downtown Healdsburg where you'll find an impressive array of fresh, clean wines, including Gewürztraminer, Merlot, and Cabernet. It's been a long trip; better rest your palate for a day or two before our jaunt into Mendocino and Lake Counties.

Mendocino and Lake Counties

Get ready to leave the beaten path to head for the boondocks, where you will not be able to visit as many wineries per day since there are a lot more miles between them. North of Cloverdale on U.S. Highway 101 is the small town of Hopland. There are a half-dozen wineries

---

[5] Which is quite a feat as we get older and harder of hearing.
[6] One of those resentful and childish little things people do to try to get even with others, even though it has absolutely no impact.

near Hopland, but we highly recommend a stop at **Fetzer Vineyards,** where you'll always find excellent values in many different varietals. You'll also find a large assortment of "Barrel Select" older vintage Zinfandels and Cabernets, some of which will knock your socks off.[7] The tasting room folks at **Fetzer** are always in good humor, even when they are busy; they always make you feel you're important, not a pain in the ass. In addition, they have a fantastic gift shop. (A note to the new owners: please don't change a thing!)

You will want to stop just across the street at **McDowell Valley Vineyards.** We give several of their red selections high marks(try their Syrah). Moving north to California 175, snake over the mountain and visit the folks at **Konocti Winery** located near Clear Lake, north of Kelseyville. Again, you will find friendly people and an array of excellent wines. We were impressed with their Fumé Blanc, Merlot, and Cabernet Franc, which are made in a variety of styles.

If you don't want to return over the winding mountain road, you can proceed north on California 29 to California 20, which passes Lake Mendocino. CA Highway 20 will take you back to U.S. Highway 101, where you'll turn north to Ukiah.

If you don't accomplish anything else in the Ukiah area, be sure to visit **Parducci Wine Cellars** just north of town. This is the home of friendly people (look for Shirley, Jim, and Larry on the weekends) and a wine list as long as your leg.[8] For sixty years, **Parducci** has emphasized value as well as quality. They typically offer a six-pack of assorted reds or whites in the neighborhood of $25. It doesn't get much better than that! **Parducci's** philosophy is that wine is an honest, natural product that should never be over-produced. They certainly practice what they preach.

You'll find **Hidden Cellars Winery** just east of Ukiah. It's definitely worthwhile to stop here for some very flavorful Gewürztraminer and Riesling.

---

[7] This can be prevented by wearing shoes, although we just like to kick back and let it happen.
[8] Okay, we may have exaggerated. Would you believe as long as your arm? Believe it!

Navarro Winery in the Anderson Valley near Philo, California, offers great wines, great scenery, and a quality tasting-room experience.

If you're beginning to like mountain driving you'll enjoy taking the Boonville Road over to Anderson Valley. We think you'll really relish this isolated little valley. Why? It's off the beaten trail, so it's not unusual to be the only party in a tasting room.[9] More importantly, there are some pleasant surprises in wine here. We strongly recommend the small group of wineries north of Philo. First and foremost is **Navarro Winery,** which has always done a magnificent job with Gewürztraminer and Riesling and now offers some delicious Chardonnay and Pinot Noir as well. This is one of our favorite tasting rooms because of the beauty of the building and patio, the surrounding scenery, and, of course, the friendly personnel. You will find **Greenwood Ridge Vineyards** next door, with a pleasant array of wines, including a few nice surprises in reds. Other nearby wineries that are definitely worth a visit include **Brutacao, Handley Cellars,** and **Husch Vineyards.** We've enjoyed

---

[9] It has been said that by ourselves we are a crowd, and always a party.

Sauvignon Blancs, Gewürztraminers, and Rieslings at these stops. If you're a sparkling wine fan don't miss **Scharffenberger Cellars.**

The northern end of this wine area is very near the Pacific Ocean. Be sure to drive over to take a look; perhaps you'll see a whale emerge not too far offshore. There are several excellent lodging choices along the coast.

Sierra Foothills

This viticultural area stretches from the Ione-Jackson area in the south to the Placerville area in the north, covering Amador and El Dorado counties; it's accessible from California Highway 49. The scenic foothills have a rich gold mining history.

The greatest concentration of wineries is in the Shenandoah Valley near Plymouth. Our main reason for visiting this area has been the Zinfandels, which have a reputation for being "massive." This area exemplifies the rapid changes in the California wine industry. We had not visited this area for several years; during this brief period two of our favorite Zinfandel producers had changed hands and wine styles as well.

Just northwest of Plymouth you will find about a dozen wineries in close proximity to Shenandoah Road. We're happy to report that you can still find some big Zins here. We found many star wines—and supporting casts of big reds—at **Karly** and **Santino** wineries. We definitely recommend a stop at **Boeger Winery**, further north in El Dorado County, another fine maker of Zinfandel and other red wines. **Boeger's** tasting room is the old Lombardo winery building, constructed in 1872. We were also impressed with the **Madroña Vineyards** which offered a superb Cabernet Franc, a fine El Dorado Estate Claret, and a delicious 1992 Gewürztraminer. If you appreciate artistic wine labels, **Madroña's** are among the most beautiful we've seen. The wineries in the Sierra Foothills offer excellent values. Check 'em out.

We've offered you only a brief sampling of the California wine country. However, just doing what we've outlined here would take a good month, especially if you participate in other sightseeing activities as well. Remember, don't try to do too much in one day. After visiting these areas, you'll want to return again and again.

THE PACIFIC NORTHWEST

OREGON

Currently, western Oregon supports more than sixty wineries. These fall mostly in four viticultural regions stretching from the California border to the Washington border. If you plan to visit the Oregon wineries, you should obtain the brochure entitled "Discover Oregon Wineries" by writing to the Oregon Winegrowers' Association, 1200 N.W. Front Avenue, Suite 400, Portland, OR 97209, or telephoning (503) 228-8403. This handy guide provides excellent maps and a descriptive paragraph about every winery in the state.

Although Oregon winemaking dates back to the 1800s, the majority of today's wineries were established in the 1970s and 1980s. Some say this is too short a time to judge, but we think Oregon has definitely proven itself with some of its varietals. There have been outstanding vintages of Pinot Noir, Pinot Gris, Johannisberg Riesling (and a related variety, Müller-Thurgau), and Gewürztraminer produced by a number of wineries throughout the state. We enjoy visiting Oregon wineries in the early spring when there are no crowds and we're able to visit with many of the proprietors and winemakers.

If you come into Oregon from California, the southernmost wine area is the Rogue River region, located in proximity to the cities of Ashland and Medford. **Ashland Vineyards**, just east of Ashland, offers some pleasant selections of white varietals including a Chardonnay and Müller-Thurgau. Nearby is **Weisingers** of Ashland whose popular Italian-style blend called Mescolare is featured along with some nice clean white wines.

It is certainly worth your time to visit the **Bridgeview Vineyards** which is off the beaten path and tucked into a small valley in the Siskiyou Mountains near Oregon Caves National Monument. We have had the pleasure of visiting with **Bridgeview** winemaker Laurent Montalieu, who

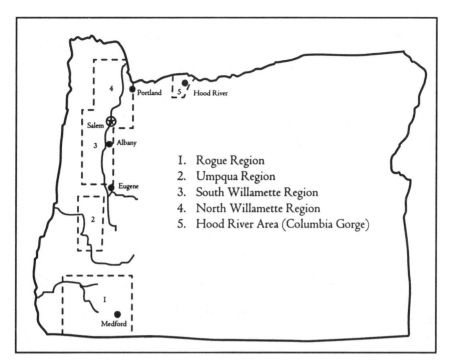

1. Rogue Region
2. Umpqua Region
3. South Willamette Region
4. North Willamette Region
5. Hood River Area (Columbia Gorge)

Oregon's four official wine-producing regions and a fifth production area, all of which are located along major rivers.

does a superb job with Pinot Noir, Chardonnay, Pinot Gris, Gewürztraminer and Riesling. This winery offers some special vintages and selections of Pinot Noir, as well as a reasonably priced quaffing version. Their white wines are also excellent values. Nearby **Foris Vineyards Winery** is a relatively new and small operation which appears to have a bright future. We found its Gewürztraminer especially good.

As you travel north along Interstate 5 near the city of Roseburg you enter the Umpqua viticultural region, named after the Umpqua River. There are eight wineries in this region. Most are open only seasonally, so plan your visit accordingly. Of particular interest is **La Garza Cellars,** which operates a gourmet kitchen and sells a variety of wines in addition to their own. **Girardet Wine Cellars** produces quality white wines and the occasional outstanding vintage Pinot Noir. **Lookingglass Winery** produces some very unusual Pinot Noir and Cabernet

Laurent Montalieu, winemaker for Bridgeview Winery in Oregon, prepares a tasting at the Rogue River location.

Sauvignon bearing the **Rizza Cellars** label. Also highly recommended are several white varietals and Pinot Noirs from the **Henry Estate Winery.** We've found the **Henry Estate** Pinot Noir in many fine restaurants in the Pacific Northwest. It is delicious.

The bulk of Oregon's wineries are located in the north and south viticultural regions of the Willamette River Valley. The south Willamette region begins near Eugene and extends northward to Salem. There are about two dozen wineries in this area, several of which are definitely worth a visit. If your time is limited, give highest priority to the **Tyee Wine Cellars** south of Corvallis, **Airlie Winery** northwest of Corvallis, and **Eola Hills Wine Cellars** and **Chateau Bianca Winery** west of Salem.

You're in prime Pinot country now.[10] **Tyee Wine Cellars** does a great job with both Pinots, Chardonnay, and Gewürztraminer. **Airlie Winery** features good versions of these varietals as well as a no-

---

[10] Noir and Gris, that is.

table Müller-Thurgau and a delicious late-harvest Gewürztraminer. The Pinot Noir and Cabernet Sauvignon from **Eola Hills Wine Cellars** are very impressive. They also offer a fine array of white wines, and their dining room puts forth some great gourmet feasts. **Chateau Bianca** stocks its remarkable tasting room with such an enormous selection of good-value wines that you're bound to find something you like.

The north Willamette region west of Interstate 5 between Salem and Portland contains the largest concentration of wineries in the state. Many award-winning Pinot Noirs have come from this area. A number of fine white wines such as Pinot Gris, Riesling, Gewürztraminer, Müller-Thurgau, and Chardonnay also are produced here. Several of our favorite wineries are located in the Dundee-McMinnville area. McMinnville hosts the annual International Pinot Noir Celebration on the last full weekend in July. Unlike a lot of wine events, this celebration is attended primarily by fun-loving people.[11] It features great roast salmon and a potpourri of wines. (You do have to get on the invitation list to attend.)

We recently found a 1991 Pinot Gris from **Argyle** (**The Dundee Wine Company**) to be as elegant as any we have ever tasted. Others which have received high acclaim come from **Eyrie, Ponzi,** and **Rex Hill.** This wonderful, dry white wine is often overshadowed by the publicity given to Pinot Noir. While at **Argyle,** be sure to sample their Chardonnays and traditional-style Champagnes.

West of Dundee, **Knudsen Erath** and **Lange** wineries are definitely must stops. **Knudsen Erath** is most famous for its Pinot Noir; some of its vintages are world class (and pricey). It also produces a quaffing Pinot Noir for us fun-loving, common folk. **Lange** also does a great job with Pinot Noir as well as Pinot Gris and Chardonnay. Nearby, **Rex Hill** and **Sokol Blosser** wineries both offer pleasant tasting rooms and good-quality wines, some of which are good values. Although **Adelsheim Vineyard** has no tasting room, you should definitely try its

---

[11] People who are not wearing tuxedos and paying thousands of dollars for a bottle of wine.

Pinots (Noir and Gris) at the **Elk Cove** tasting room in Dundee. You can easily spend a day or two visiting the wineries between Newberg and McMinnville and you won't be disappointed in any of them.

Perhaps the most famous winery in this area is **Eyrie Vineyards,** whose 1975 Pinot Noir shocked the French in international wine competitions held in Paris and Burgundy in 1979 and 1980 by placing second and third respectively. This success showed vintners throughout the world that Pinot Noir from Oregon could be as good as that produced anywhere. The Lett family, which owns **Eyrie,** pioneered plantings of *vinifera* grapes in Yamhill County in the mid 1960s; they have seen their experiment pay off handsomely. Now, even French vintners are pumping money into this area, which has proven potential for Burgundian-class Pinot Noirs.

Elk Cove Vineyards near Gaston boasts one of the most scenic tasting room settings and presents a fine array of white wines, Pinot Noir, and Cabernet Sauvignon. If time permits, a trip further north to **Laurel Ridge Winery** and **Tualatin Vineyards** will provide you with as nice a collection of white wines as you'll find in the Pacific Northwest. The wineries of Oregon continue to produce new treasures for our discovery.

WASHINGTON

Washington now ranks third in the United States in number of wineries (about eighty), but if it continues its rapid expansion it could catch up with New York (currently number two). The state is divided into three viticultural regions: Columbia Valley, Yakima Valley, and Walla Walla Valley appellations. We suggest you obtain the brochure *Touring the Washington Wine Country* by sending $1.50 to the Washington Wine Commission, P.O. Box 61217, Seattle, WA 98121, or calling (206)728-2252. You can spend several weeks covering the Washington wine scene because its many wineries are scattered over a wide expanse of geography.

The Yakima Valley, Washington's first approved viticultural region, extends from the foothills of the Cascades in the west to the Kiona

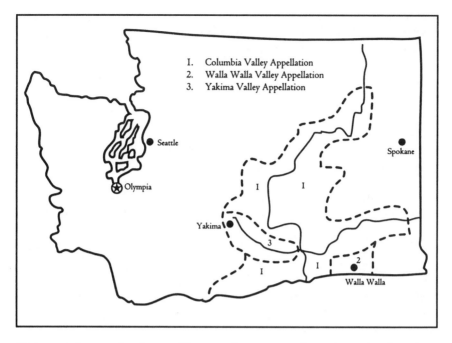

Washington's three viticultural regions. Wineries and tasting rooms also can be found in the Spokane, Seattle, Puget Sound, Olympic Peninsula, and Columbia Gorge areas.

Hills near Richland in the east. This intensively cultivated fruit area requires irrigation, primarily from the Yakima River. There are about twenty wineries located in the area between Richland and Zillah. One favorite, the **Kiona Winery** near Benton City, produces superior quality red wines, particularly Cabernet Sauvignon, Lemberger, and Merlot. Their Lemberger is the richest and most full-bodied version of the varietal that we've tasted. They also produce a big, buttery Chardonnay.

Another winery that warrants your time is **Hogue Cellars** near Prosser. This relatively large producer turns out some excellent values in both white and red wines, especially Rieslings and Merlots. They have an elegantly furnished tasting room, although the outside looks like a Butler building.[12] You'll want to sample the pickled vegetables, including asparagus, snap peas, snap beans, and sweet peppers, as well as the fine array of wines available in their tasting room.

[12] This is not a building where the butler lives; it is a type of metal building, some of which were manufactured by Butler.

Hogue Cellars in Prosser, Washington, is home to many fine wines, as well as pickled vegetable treats.

Chateau Ste. Michelle (part of the Stimson Lane conglomerate) has a red wine facility near Grandview. This high-volume winery produces good-value Cabernet and Merlot at this facility as well as good white varietals at other locations. Some of their library selection reds will pleasantly surprise you. Another must visit is **Covey Run Winery** near Zillah, which has received numerous plaudits for their recent vintages of Chardonnay and offers a broad range of values in both white and red wines. Usually you can put together a mixed case for under $50. The **Covey Run** tasting room offers great views of Yakima Valley vineyards and orchards and their gift shop is extremely well outfitted. (If you're into quail, you'll go wild in here.)

In the Columbia Valley, we recommend a stop at **Columbia Crest Winery** near Paterson. This winery is producing some especially good values in Chardonnay and Merlot. Their 1989 and 1990 Merlots stack up to anybody's.[13] Near Pasco, **Bookwalter Winery** and **Preston Wine**

---

[13] The wines are as good as anybody's and the bottles stack just like other bottles.

Cellars both offer exceptional values in white wine. Try Jerry Bookwalter's Chenin Blanc, Chardonnay, Muscat, and Riesling. **Preston Wine Cellars** offers a scenic tasting area perched high over the vineyards. Here you can taste a large selection of varietals. We were partial to their Gewürztraminers; the Rieslings were also especially enjoyable.

Two wineries in the Walla Walla region have established outstanding reputations for quality. **Woodward Canyon Winery** has been lauded for its Cabernet Sauvignon and Chardonnay and quickly sells out of its outstanding vintages, albeit at handsome prices. **Leonetti's Wine Cellars** specialize in Cabernet and Merlot with outstanding results nearly every year. You will probably need to make an appointment to visit them.

Some of the larger Washington wineries also operate tasting rooms in the greater Seattle area. You will also find many smaller wineries along the Olympic Peninsula and in the Puget Sound area and sur-

Chateau Ste. Michelle's red wine facility in Grandview, Washington. Look for some fine Cabernet Sauvignon and Merlot here.

119

rounding suburbs. The Washington wine industry is expanding rapidly with the addition of about twelve new wineries each year. Since Washington's vineyards are located at about the same latitude as some of the great wine regions of Europe, outstanding viticultural areas will probably emerge as the vintners gain more experience. In the western part of the state, excellent Pinot Noir, Chardonnay, Riesling, Müller-Thurgau, and Gewürztraminer can be grown without irrigation in the cooler climate. In central and eastern Washington, red varieties thrive on the slopes overlooking the Columbia and Yakima rivers, where warm days and cool nights build the proper balance of sugar and acids.

IDAHO AND MONTANA

These states are perhaps better known for scenic mountains and blue-ribbon trout streams than they are for grapes; nonetheless, there is wine in "them thar hills." Idaho is home to twelve wineries, the

Ste. Chappelle, one of Idaho's best wineries, also offers a spectacular view and horticultural splendor around their elegant tasting room and gift shop.

Some fun-loving tasters at the Weston Winery, Idaho, enjoy a visit with winemaker Cheyne Weston.

majority of which are located along the Snake River between Twin Falls and the Oregon border west of Boise. Particularly impressive are the excellent, clean, and flavorful wines presented by **Ste. Chappelle Winery** and **Pintler Cellars** at Caldwell and Nampa respectively. Nearby **Indian Creek** and **Weston** offer consistent values in white wine. Bill Stowe at **Indian Creek** also offers an extremely rich Lemberger. Cheyne Weston at **Weston Winery** exemplifies what fun-loving people are all about and offers an exceptional Riesling sold under the "River Runner" label. (He is also a river guide.) **Carmela Vineyards** near Glenns Ferry and **Hells Canyon Winery** near Caldwell are also recommended. To better enjoy your tour, we suggest you obtain "Idaho Wine Country," a brochure that briefly describes the state's wineries and how to find them. It is available from the Idaho Grape Growers and Wine

Producers Commission, P.O. Box 790, Boise, ID 83701; (208)334-2227.

Montana is home to more than a million cattle, fewer than a million people (including us powder-hounds and wine-sucking dogs), hundreds of thousands of deer and elk, and—you guessed it—one winery. **Mission Mountain** is located on Flathead Lake near Dayton. Because Montana weather is not particularly hospitable to grape production,[14] its owners struggle to keep enough grapevines alive for tourists to look at. Nonetheless, with the help of Idaho and Washington grapes they produce some fine Riesling, a nice sparkling wine, and a quaffing blush wine called Sundown.

The Pacific Northwest wineries have made great strides over the past two decades. Many of their creations have won international acclaim. More importantly, you and I can depend on this region for many good-value wines for everyday drinking and an occasional varietal that turns out to be as nice as anything we've ever tasted. These vintners can give California a run for its money with several varietals and blends because their land is not yet priced out of sight, and their overhead is considerably lower.

THE SOUTHWEST

TEXAS

In the early 1980s, Texas wines looked like a bonanza[15] about to happen; the realization that quality is the name of the game brought people back to their senses. It appears that the survivors of this modern boom-bust cycle will make names for themselves through a few Texas wines now gaining national attention. For example, **Bell Mountain**, in the Texas Hill Country, produced a celebrated 1989 Cabernet Sauvignon. **Fall Creek**, a lovely chateau on the shores of Lake Buchanan, recently has released some very tasty Chardonnays and Sauvignon Blancs. **Ste.**

---

[14] Luigi says they don't grow worth a shit here, either.
[15] Not to be confused with the steakhouse or the old TV series.

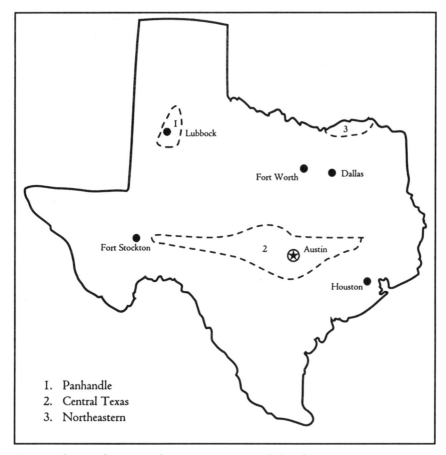

Texas now has several wineries and wine regions, many of which produce wines from vinifera grapes.

1. Panhandle
2. Central Texas
3. Northeastern

Genevieve Winery now produces about 200,000 cases annually from a planting made by the Univeristy of Texas. Most of these are reasonably priced and average- to good-quality white wines. Its Sauvignon Blancs and Chardonnays are the best offerings.

Another large winery is **Llano Estacado**, which probably has done the best job among the Texas wineries at generating nationwide publicity. Its strengths have been Chardonnay, Sauvignon Blanc, and Riesling. The **Teysha Winery** initially went bankrupt, but with the help of Plains National Bank it now appears that some excellent wines will be available, starting with 1991 releases. A few other small wineries worthy of mention are **Messina Hof**, which makes a lovely Late Harvest Riesling;

Pheasant Ridge, which has released some excellent Cabernets and Sauvignon Blancs; **Schoppaul Hill**, which does a nice job with Chenin Blanc, Muscat Canelli, and Sauvignon Blanc; and **Slaughter Leftwich**, whose forte is Sauvignon Blanc.

NEW MEXICO

The oldest winemaking region in the United States may well have been the Rio Grande Valley of New Mexico. Certainly, vines were planted there by early Spanish settlers long before they were brought to other regions. **Anderson Valley Vineyards** near Albuquerque produces some excellent Cabernet Sauvignon, along with several other *vinifera* wines of average quality. **Domaine Cheurlin** is a tiny winery in Truth or Consequences[16] that specializes in sparkling wines, and now and then kicks out a nice one. A few years ago we visited the **Sun Winery** near Las Cruces. Their wines were only average, but the wineglasses they sold us are tough as nails. Over the years we've broken numerous glasses from other sources, but those from **Sun Wines** live on and on. According to a recent article in *W.S.*, there are now nineteen wineries in New Mexico. This appears to be an excellent reason for us to make another trip south, perhaps in the dead of a Montana winter.

COLORADO

Colorado Cellars concentrate on the local and tourist trade on the western edge of the Rockies. They make a popular Rosé wine called Alpenglo by blending a tiny amount of Lemberger with Riesling. They also do well with White Zinfandel, Cabernet, and Chardonnay. The winery has expanded rapidly since 1985, when the Turleys assumed ownership.

ARIZONA

Winemaking is as difficult in Arizona as it is in Montana, but **Soñoita**

---

[16] Who in their right mind would name a town after a game show?

Vineyards, in the mountains southeast of Tucson, is giving it the old college try.[17] Some Cabernets and Pinot Noirs from this location look promising.

HAWAII

On our first trip to Hawaii, we were surprised to find the **Tedeschi Vineyards** of Ulupalakua, Maui. The big seller here is their pineapple wine, Maui Blanc, which reaches the Japanese market primarily. Pineapple wine is certainly a different experience; it is only slightly sweet and very tasty. These folks also present a nice array of grape wines, including some from the variety Carnelian, which is adapted to warm climates. Incidentally, did you know the grapevines on Maui have to be fooled into thinking it's winter? This is the reverse of the situation in Montana, where grapes have to be fooled into thinking there's a summer.

Suggested Reading

Adams, L. D. *The Wine of America.* 4th ed. New York: McGraw-Hill, 1990. 528 pp.

Clarke, O. *The Essential Wine Book.* New York: Simon & Schuster, 1988. 300 pp.

Hill, C. *The Northwest Winery Guide: Tasting and Touring.* Seattle: Speed Graphics, 1989. 384 pp.

Thompson, B. *The Wine Atlas of California and the Pacific Northwest.* New York: Simon & Schuster, 1993. 240 pp.

---

[17] The owner is actually a former college professor, so he's familiar with this technique.

Chapter 10

A Look at Domestic Wines and Wineries, Eastern United States

Plantation owners and small farmers planted vineyards in the eastern United States as early as the 1700s. Some, like Thomas Jefferson, appreciated wine's contribution to the quality of life[1]; many farmers raised grapes for juice and jellies. The native American grapes (*Vitis labrusca*) were adapted to the northeast, and several varieties thrived along the Great Lakes and the coastal areas of the eastern United States, where the airflow from the large lakes or the Atlantic Ocean prevented spring freezes and severe winter damage. Perhaps the first eastern commercial wine venture was that of Nicholas Longworth, who planted vineyards of Catawba near Cincinnati, Ohio, and marketed his Sparkling Catawba wine to a receptive audience.

A development in the late 1800s had a profound influence on the eastern wine industry. An amateur grape breeder from Missouri named Herman Jaeger collected and crossed many grape varieties (mostly *Vitis lincecumni* and *Vitis rupestris*) from the southcentral U.S. and sent cuttings to a French grape researcher named Contassot. Contassot crossed many of these cuttings with European *Vitis vinifera* and fostered hybrid plants that showed good attributes. French researchers Couderc and Seibel also worked with these French-American hybrids and named many of their outstanding selections. Current researchers continue to improve the genetic material. To make a long story short, many of these hybrids

---

[1] The only problem was T. J. could never make a decent wine from his own grapes.

126

are now prominent varieties in the major wine-producing areas of France, as well as in the eastern United States. The varieties Aurore, Baco Noir, Chancellor, Chambourcin, DeChaunac, Foch, Seyval Blanc, Vidal Blanc, and Vignoles (Ravat 51) all sprang from this effort. Many California wine "experts" (and even a few individuals from New York) scoff at these varieties and claim the only great wine "genes" are in the pure *vinifera* varieties. They forget that a lot of other attributes (such as *Phylloxera* resistance) might be gained from the hybrid approach. In fact, the variations within any given *vinifera* variety (i.e., different clones) are so great that it is doubtful that one grower's Pinot Noir is the same as his or her neighbor's. In any event, some very good wines from French-American hybrid grapes are being made in the eastern United States. Are they ever as good as *viniferas*? We personally think several of the white varieties are. The debate will go on; meanwhile, let your own palate decide.

Eastern wine production also changed with the discovery that several *vinifera* varieties (e.g., Chardonnay, Gewürztraminer, Pinot Noir, and Riesling) can be successfully grown on choice sites along the Great Lakes, in the Finger Lakes region, and on Long Island, where moderating influences from the large bodies of water apparently prevent their demise. Some excellent *vinifera* wines are being produced today in these areas. Some people (mostly Minnesotans) want to grow these grapes so badly that they are willing to cover the vines in the winter to assure their survival. (Keep in mind, these are the same masochists who fish through the ice!) Eastern production of *vinifera* varieties will undoubtedly be limited by the scarcity of appropriate cultivation sites and the devastation from the occasional severe freeze. Nonetheless, many *vinifera* producers are as confident as those who tout hybrids; both groups see their varieties as hope for the future.

Most of the wineries in the East are relatively small, and only a handful market nationally. Because the smaller wineries focus on local markets, their products may be unfamiliar to people from other states. You may be pleasantly surprised at these wineries; some can offer you a wide choice of tastes, particularly when they offer selections from American, hybrid, and *vinifera* grapes all under one roof. Our overview of wineries in the eastern United States is arbitrarily divided into three areas: Great Lakes (New York, Michigan, Ohio, Pennsylvania, Minnesota, Indiana, Wisconsin), Eastern (Connecticut, Maryland, New Jersey, North Carolina, Rhode Island, Tennessee, Virginia), and Southern (Arkansas, Florida, Georgia, Mississippi, Missouri). Obviously a state like New York could fit into the Eastern category as easily as the Great Lakes category, and probably North Carolina could go Southern as well as Eastern. Some people really worry about this, but not us!

GREAT LAKES REGION

NEW YORK

"Uncork New York!" is the slogan of The New York Wine and Grape Foundation, and their brochure of the same name is a helpful guide for touring the four wine regions of the state. New York is the second largest wine producer in the United States; its one hundred-odd wineries produce approximately thirty million gallons of wine annually. New York's commercial wine production began in the mid-1800s in Chatauqua County and the Finger Lakes region. The history of wine development there tells of all sorts of disputes about who did what first, who fired whom and why, what kinds of grapes to plant, and who lost his last name to the Coca Cola Company. You really must visit to learn all the fascinating details.

Many New York wineries still use native American grapes; others make some excellent wine from French-American hybrids and from *vinifera* varieties—in the selected locations they'll survive. Our recent family visit to New York proved there is a marketing niche for all of these types. Just imagine—Concord drinkers, hybrid lovers, and *vinifera* freaks all in one family. What in the hell went wrong with our genes? When I posed this question to Luigi he replied, "If your jeans are messed up, it's probably 'cause you spilt wine on 'em."

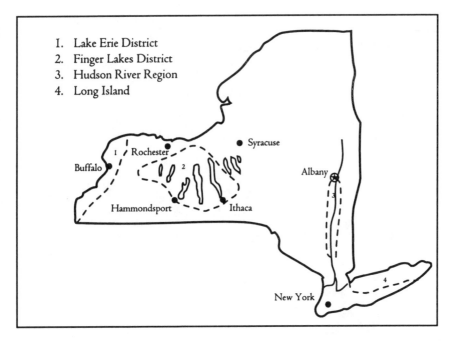

1. Lake Erie District
2. Finger Lakes District
3. Hudson River Region
4. Long Island

New York's four viticultural regions. The largest, the Finger Lakes area, contains about fifty wineries.

The four grape-growing districts in New York are: Long Island, the Hudson River, the Finger Lakes, and Lake Erie. Long Island's unique climate makes it a prime spot for *vinifera* production because it boasts a growing season that lasts fifteen to thirty days longer than the other areas'. Long Island also experiences cool ocean breezes that moderate summer temperatures. The island currently has more than one thousand acres of vineyards and seventeen wineries. These numbers are sure to grow with the district's reputation for fine Chardonnay, Merlot, and Cabernet wines.

The Hudson River district also has about one thousand acres of vineyards. These border both sides of the river, which extends about sixty miles north of The Big Apple.[2] The river valley serves as a conduit for moderating maritime air. The twenty-odd wineries in this region enjoy a long history of winemaking. Although we've not yet had a

---

[2] Much too nice a nickname for a city that seems to have lost its civility. It's a more appropriate name for Wenatchee, Washington.

A group of visitors at the Taylor and Great Western Visitor Center near Hammondsport. Rumor has it some of these people enjoy a glass of "happy juice" for breakfast.

chance to visit the Long Island or Hudson River wineries, we've read some impressive reports and sampled a few of their Chardonnays. **Rivendell Winery**'s 1990 Chardonnay excited wine critics, confirming the potential of this region.

The Finger Lakes district contains about fourteen thousand acres of *vinifera*, hybrid, and American grapes. The fifty wineries in this region produce most of the state's wine. The wines here will satisfy every taste; they range from traditional sweet wines made from Concord, Catawba, Niagara, etc., to *demi-sec* and dry versions of the hybrid varieties. Perhaps the best place to start is the **Taylor Wine Company**'s visitor center near Hammondsport. This large conglomerate includes the **Great Western** and **Gold Seal** wine labels as well as the **Henri Marchant** sparkling wines. Would you believe you can taste about eighty different wines here? Believe it! They represent all of the grape types mentioned above, and for the most part are reasonably priced. You will want to try Cayuga, from a grape of that name developed at the Geneva Agricultural Experiment Station, Cornell University. (Incidentally, the New York wine industry owes a great debt to researchers at Geneva who have contributed considerable knowledge on appropriate varieties and cultural techniques for grapes of this area.[3]) You will find some excellent Seyval Blanc, Vidal Blanc, and Vignoles in a number of wineries in the Finger Lakes region. Perhaps the biggest advocate for these hybrids has been Walter S. Taylor, whose family winery (and name) was sold to the Coca Cola Company in the 1960s. After losing his last name, Walter S.——— started the **Bully Hill Winery** near Hammondsport, overlooking scenic Keuka Lake. Walter S.——— has cleverly exploited the loss of his name to market **Bully Hill** wines, using nameless humor and numerous words of wisdom on his wine labels. You will get to taste a variety of pleasant white and blush wines here; many red wines also are available, but none of them really im-

---

[3] Spoken like a true academic.

A must visit for fun-lovers in New York's Finger Lakes district, Bully Hill is near Hammondsport.

pressed us. Some of these reds might be better with food.

The late Dr. Konstantin Frank pioneered *vinifera* in the Finger Lakes area, growing and vinting these varieties for decades at his **Vinifera Wine Cellars** near Hammondsport. Over the years he produced some excellent Riesling, Chardonnay, and Gewürztraminer; his work is now being continued by his son. Another *vinifera* advocate is **Hermann Wiemer**, whose small winery near Dundee is making a reputation with dry Riesling, Chardonnay, and Pinot Noir as well as sparkling wines from the latter two varieties.

A number of wineries in the Finger Lakes district are using both hybrids and *vinifera* to produce an impressive array of pleasant wines. Among these are **Glenora Wine Cellars** on a bluff above Seneca Lake, **McGregor Vineyards** east of Keuka Lake, and **Wagner Vineyards** east of Seneca Lake and south of Lodi. Trips to the wineries in this extremely scenic area certainly would be worthwhile.

No visit to New York would be complete without a stop at the beautiful Sonnenberg Gardens, home of the tasting room for the famous **Canandaigua Wine Company**. With the planned purchase of Vintners International, it will become the second largest wine company in the nation. This conglomerate now includes these famous labels: **Widmer, Manischewitz, Sun Country Cooler, J. Rojet** Champagne, and **Wild Irish Rose** wine; with the acquisition they will add **Paul Masson, Taylor California Cellars, Taylor New York, Deer Valley, St. Regis,** and **Great Western** labels. This facility is open daily from mid-May to mid-October and features an enormous selection of area wines. It is located in the city of Canandaigua, north of the lake.[4]

Further west, the Lake Erie district grows about twenty thousand acres of grapes; almost ninety percent are Concord, grown primarily for juice. There are seven wineries near the New York Thruway and Lake Erie. You'll find a few pleasant selections at these stops.

---

[4] What lake, you ask? Canandaigua Lake, of course.

MICHIGAN

The "Pleasant Peninsula" state is home to some older wineries and some promising upstarts; it ranks right up there with New York in the quality of its wines. We had the pleasure of working in Michigan during the modern era of winery development, and have had the opportunity to taste many commercial products as well as experimental selections from **Spartan Cellars**, Michigan State University's program in enology and viticulture. Our youngest son pursues graduate work in this program at present. How he ever got interested in this field is beyond us, though we suspect the time he spent as our designated driver in the California wine country during his teen years had an impact.[5]

There are currently eighteen wineries in Michigan. For assistance touring here, pick up a complimentary copy of *Michigan Wine Country* at a tourist information center or your first winery stop. The majority of vineyards and wineries are located in the western part of the state, all the way from southwestern Michigan to the Leelanau Peninsula northwest of Traverse City, where successful grape culture depends on moderating influences from Lake Michigan. The two oldest wineries, **St. Julian Wine Cellars** and **Warner Vineyards**, near Paw Paw, originally concentrated on sweeter wines, sparkling wines, and cream sherries, all from American grapes. **St. Julian** still receives acclaim for its cream sherries, but both wineries now present a nice array of wines made from hybrid grapes. The newer wineries have given more attention to hybrid and *vinifera* varieties, and some premium-quality, good-value wines are available from a number of them.

One of the best wineries in southwestern Michigan is **Fenn Valley Vineyards**, where winemaker Doug Welsch turns out a fine collection of *vinifera*, hybrid, and fruit wines. You will always find a pleasant Riesling, Seyval, or Vidal here, and sometimes a great Gewürztraminer; don't leave without begging a taste of the raspberry wine. Doug has also crafted some fine Chancellor—a pleasant surprise for us, since

---

[5] We still wonder if he used the Butler's Friend when he was growing up.

133

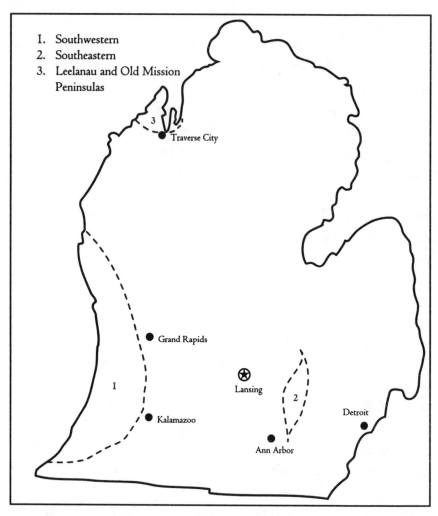

1. Southwestern
2. Southeastern
3. Leelanau and Old Mission Peninsulas

Traverse City

Grand Rapids

Lansing

1

Kalamazoo

2

Detroit

Ann Arbor

Wine-producing areas of Michigan. The major grape-growing areas are located close to Lake Michigan.

we've been harsh critics of eastern red wines.

Also in southwestern Michigan, **Tabor Hill** has been producing some fine hybrid and *vinifera* wines for several years, and now **Lemon Creek Winery** and **Madron Lake Hills Estate** are getting into the act. **Peterson and Son Winery** presents an impressive array of fruit and grape wines, several of which are quite nice.

The Traverse City area boasts beautiful Lake Michigan views, Sleeping Bear Dunes National Park, the National Cherry Festival, and yes, some

Doug Welsch, Fenn Valley Vineyards (left) and Russ Smithyman, Michigan State University researcher, check grape vine survival after a harsh Michigan winter.

really fine wines! The wineries here are located on two peninsulas,[6] Leelanau to the west and Old Mission to the east. There are some unique personalities in the Michigan wine business, and meeting these people is an experience in itself. Two of them, Bernie Rink and Larry Mawby, do business on the Leelanau Peninsula at **Boskydel Vineyards** and **L. Mawby Vineyard,** respectively. Bernie's philosophy of life, which he is more than happy to share via his wall hangings and conversation, is precious; as a bonus he produces one of the nicest Aurore wines we've ever tasted. Larry Mawby's humor is more subtle; he's the only winemaker we know who has successfully marketed commemorative empty bottles (at the regular price) to celebrate a lost vintage. **L. Mawby** produces high-quality sparkling wine, superb Pinot Gris and Vignoles, and some of the best hybrid blends available anywhere.

Good Harbor Vineyards near Leland produces excellent Riesling

---

[6] Or as the locals say, "peninsuli."

and Vignoles, a primo cherry wine, and a delicious white blend called Trillium, which in our opinion ranks as one of the five best white wine values in America. **Leelanau Wine Cellars** at Omena presents a wide array of quaffable wines and the occasional Chardonnay that could be described as outstanding.

Old Mission Peninsula offers gorgeous views of Grand Traverse Bay and a few choice *vinifera* wines at **Chateau Grand Traverse** and **Bowers Harbor Vineyards**. Chardonnay and Riesling are the gems here, some have been highly touted at local and national wine competitions. The recently completed **Chateau Chantal** definitely has the classiest architecture of all the Michigan wine facilities, and if the first vintage is a true indication it may soon produce wines to match its physical appearance and panoramic views. You can taste wines here and stay overnight as well, since part of the winery is a bed-and-breakfast.

Some folks in the wine business believe there is something special about being located on the forty-fifth parallel. The Old Mission and Leelanau peninsulas of Michigan fit into this scheme, as do the northern Willamette Valley of Oregon, the Bordeaux region of France, and the Piedmont and Veneto regions of Italy. There's gotta be more to it, since this theory doesn't work worth a damn in the Southern Hemisphere! We've noticed that those who really believe in the magic of the forty-fifth parallel are those who happen to be located there. It's a great marketing gimmick!

OHIO

Areas adjacent to Lake Erie are hospitable to grapes, but even more hospitable is Isle St. George, an island about twenty-five miles from Sandusky and just a stone's throw from the Canadian border (which is clearly defined on maps by a dotted line running through the lake).[7] **Firelands Winery** (a subsidiary of **Meier's Wine Cellars**) has a seventy-acre vineyard of *vinifera* grapes (mostly Chardonnay and Cabernet) on the island. Their 1990 Chardonnay was highly acclaimed by the

---

[7] We've spent years looking for these dotted lines on the water while fishing the Great Lakes.

wine critics. Most of the other **Meier** wines had previously been made from American grape varieties. **Markko Vineyard** was a pioneer in *vinifera* grapes, with plantings on the Lake Erie shore as early as 1968. They produce several varietals including Cabernet and Pinot Noir. **Debonne Vineyards** at Madison grows both hybrids and *vinifera*, and has turned out some good Chambourcin as well as a number of good white wines.

PENNSYLVANIA

Perhaps the two best-known Pennsylvania wineries are **Chaddsford**, a few miles west of Philadelphia, and **Naylor**, near Harrisburg. **Chaddsford** specializes in top quality *vinifera*, with a smattering of hybrid wines. They are best known for their Chardonnays but also produce some lively Pinot Noirs and Chambourcins. Their wines command top dollar. **Naylor** also produces wines from hybrid and *vinifera* grapes. Their Chardonnays are quite nice, and they produce an excellent aperitif wine called Ekem, which is made from Vignoles.

MINNESOTA

Minnesota doesn't have a very hospitable climate for grapes, but sure enough, those who vant to vint vill find a vay to do it. In Hastings, Minnesota, there is a winery named after the town founder, **Alexis Bailly**. Five generations after that founding, David Bailly planted his vineyard of hybrid grape varieties and started the winery; today it is operated by David's daughter Nan. The winery offers primarily dry red wines, some of which are fairly nice. In recent travels, we followed our nose to another Minnesota winery, **Chateau Devenois**, near Rice. Obtaining grapes from a variety of sources, they blend wines that are quite pleasing. Their reasonably priced Montier Blush and Montier Rouge are particularly enjoyable. Both of these wineries have to bury some of their grapevines to get them through the harsh winters.

INDIANA

Oliver Winery in Bloomington makes award-winning wines from *vinifera* grapes imported from the West Coast; some of their best have been Sauvignon Blanc and Merlot. There is nothing wrong with this practice, although there are a hell of a lot of great wines produced from similar grapes that have traveled a much shorter distance. But if wine made in Indiana sells better in Indiana, more power to 'em.

WISCONSIN

Wollersheim and the recently purchased Cedar Creek are making wine from their own hybrids and some Michigan fruit. Some of these grapes grow on the same property where Agoston Haraszthy first tried to grow grapes prior to his move to California in 1840. None of their wines could be considered great, but several are pleasant enough for an enjoyable luncheon quaff.

EASTERN REGION

VIRGINIA

Virginia's wine industry has grown rapidly since the early 1970s and now boasts about fifteen hundred acres of vines, the great majority being *vinifera*. There are about fifty wineries in the state; ten of these can be considered major. White wines have gained more of a reputation than reds, although a few of the latter are becoming popular. Chardonnays are perhaps the most successful varietals released to date.

Larger wineries are located in the northcentral region and along the eastern shore, while smaller wineries are scattered throughout the state. About ninety percent of Virginia's production (some 200,000 cases) is sold within state borders, which proves that an area with a strong tourist industry can develop strong local markets for wine, both at the winery and in local inns and restaurants.

There are a cluster of wineries in northern Virginia within a stone's

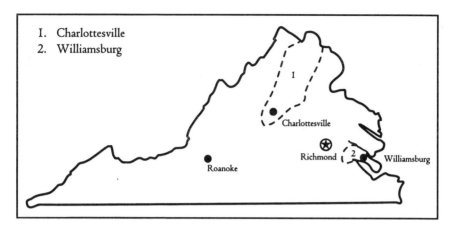

1. Charlottesville
2. Williamsburg

Charlottesville

Roanoke

Richmond

Williamsburg

The two major wine producing areas of Virginia:(1) Northeast of Charlottesville toward Washington, D.C., and (2) the Williamsburg area.

throw[8] of the Washington, D.C., area. **Linden Vineyards** is the epitome of the American dream: a young couple planned, bought, planted, and built their own winery, complete with log cabin. Anything including a log cabin brings a tear to our eyes, since we've built two ourselves. All sentiment aside, these folks are now producing a nice array of *vinifera* and hybrid wines including Cabernet Sauvignon, Chardonnay, and Seyval Blanc. The owners of **Meredyth Vineyards** near Middleburg were modern pioneers who got the Virginia wine industry moving. They started with five acres of hybrids in 1972; by 1979 their wine had been served at the White House.[9] They now produce about 35,000 cases per year and do a wonderful job with Seyval Blanc (the wine that got to the White House), some red *vinifera* varieties, and some American grapes as well. **Piedmont Winery** also pioneered *vinifera* grapes in Virginia in the early 1970s. It now produces some particularly nice Chardonnay and Sémillon. **Tarara Winery** is also expanding rapidly and has already released some high-quality Chardonnay and Cabernet.

A bit further south are **Prince Michel** and sister winery **Rapidan River**,

---

[8] Actually, it would have to be a pretty tiny stone and you would have to have one hell of an arm.
[9] We're pretty sure this was the one at 1600 Pennsylvania Avenue, not the white house just down the road from the winery.

Virginia's largest producers by far. Many of their grapes are purchased out-of-state, and their wine quality seems to be on the rise. Many of their offerings are pricey. Nearby is **Misty Mountain Winery**, which has developed a reputation for some of the best red wines in the state. This winery specializes in *vinifera* grapes and produces some excellent Cabernets and Merlots.

Near Charlottesville, **Barboursville Vineyards** (owned by the Italian **Zonin Company**) is producing high-quality white wines that have received international acclaim. Their 1989 Monticello Reserve Chardonnay was particularly elegant, and some of their Sauvignon Blancs have turned out to be quite nice. **Montdomaine** has specialized in Bordeaux-style red wines. Their 1988 Heritage blend and 1987 Merlot Monticello Reserve are examples of recent successes.

Over on the eastern shore of Virginia, **Williamsburg Winery** has undergone rapid growth since 1987. They are one of the state's best and largest producers of Chardonnay and release it in a variety of styles. Several of their 1990 Chardonnays received ratings in the high-80s from American wine critics.

NORTH CAROLINA

The best-known winery in North Carolina is **Biltmore Estate**, where George Washington Vanderbilt erected a 250-room mansion in 1880. There are about eighty acres of grapes on the eight thousand-acre estate. Their North Carolina Chardonnays and Cabernets, labeled **Chateau Biltmore** or **Biltmore Estate**, are excellent wines. The 1990 Chardonnays were particularly flavorful.

TENNESSEE

We have information on only two Tennessee wineries, although we expect there are more hidden somewhere in the hills. **Tennessee Valley Winery**, founded in 1984, has about thirty acres of grapes and produces wines that are pleasant but not outstanding. **Mountain Valley**, in east Tennessee, released its first wines in 1991, so it's a bit early to make judgments. Though on the sweet side, its Mountain Valley White has attracted some local attention.

MARYLAND

Again, only a couple of wineries surfaced in our search of Maryland. **Boordy Vineyards**, established in 1945, produces wines primarily from hybrid varieties. They have produced some very nice, reasonably priced Vidal Blanc and Seyval Blanc. **Catoctin Winery** produces very fine Cabernet Sauvignon and Chardonnay at reasonable prices. Two of its recent offerings were rated *Wine Spectator* Best Buys.

NEW JERSEY

The Garden State's **Tewksbury Winery**, founded in 1979, is a small winery producing a variety of *vinifera* and hybrid wines and an outstanding cherry wine. Their Rosé, called Sunset, is a quaffing wine, as are some of their hybrid offerings. All of their wines are reasonably priced.

CONNECTICUT

Crosswoods Winery, developed in the mid-1980s, produces wines from its own grapes and those grown on Long Island. Its 1987 Merlot North Fork Long Island Ressler Vineyards was a particularly good release, rated in the mid-80s by wine gurus. It has also produced some nice Chardonnays and a quaffable blended wine (Scrimshaw White) that is a good value.

RHODE ISLAND

Probably the best winery in the New England states, **Sakonnet** produces about twenty thousand cases per year, many of which are high-quality white wines made from *vinifera* and hybrid varieties. Their 1989 Chardonnay Southeastern New England Barrel Select is an especially flavorful wine. This winery is also doing an outstanding job with Vidal Blanc.

SOUTHERN REGION

In the southern United States you'll find a type of grape not seen in the other wine regions. The muscadine grape (*Vitis rotundifolia*) can be grown successfully wherever winter temperatures do not fall below 10°F. Muscadine grape varieties have been used to make wine in the South ever since people occupied the area. Locals have acquired a taste for it, but, being Yankees, we haven't. We don't find it especially offensive,[10] but newcomers to these wines are often put off by them.[11] Many southern vintners are now trying their hand with hybrids and *vinifera* varieties.

ARKANSAS

Wiederkehr Winery was developed by the Swiss immigrant Andreas Wiederkehr more than one hundred years ago; today it is now a large operation specializing more in *vinifera* than in native American varieties. You will find several blended wines here, along with Cabernet Sauvignon, Muscat, and Riesling. One of their best offerings, Altus Spumante, is reminiscent of Italian Asti Spumante. Its aromas and flavors resemble tropical fruits, and although sweet, it leaves a pleasant finish.

FLORIDA

Last year we visited **Lakeridge Winery and Vineyards** in Clermont. They are under the same ownership as **Lafayette**, which is located near Tallahassee. Since many southerners like their wines sweet, you'll find just such a finish on many of these wines. We were pleasantly surprised with the Stover Special Reserve, a pleasant, off-dry white wine that smelled and tasted a lot like Seyval Blanc. An off-dry wine made from Suwannee grapes also pleased our palates. They also offer two sweet but elegant Mèthode champenoise sparkling wines. Overall, you'll find a nice array of reasonably priced wines here.

GEORGIA

Chestnut Mountain Winery, located on the red soils of north Georgia, is putting all its eggs in the *vinifera* basket. The first results are

---

[10] One more politically correct statement from yours truly. Hope it helps to avoid another Civil War.

[11] Luigi says they "suck," but politesse has never been his strong suit.

encouraging. They feel they can produce wines similar to those found in the Piedmont of Italy, and have planted some Nebbiolo with that goal in mind. Their early releases of Cabernet Sauvignon and Merlot have been well received.

Chateau Elan is the largest Georgia winery and features a huge tourist complex. Its most popular wine to date is Summer Wine made from muscadine grapes and peach juice; it makes a good low-alcohol aperitif or dessert wine. The *vinifera* wines produced to date have been light-bodied and tailored for drinking within a few years of release.

MISSOURI

Perhaps the most well-known winery in Missouri is **Mount Pleasant**, which boasts a twenty-five-year history. Using mostly hybrid and *vinifera* grapes, its owners produce a varied array of average to good wines that seem a bit pricey. Their Port and Ice wines are quite good, but are priced at $20. Recent Chardonnays and Vidal Blancs were of average quality. With all the tourists pouring into the Branson area, it seems this region would be ripe for winery development. "Shit-kickin'" music nicely accompanies a lot of wines and food! (See Chapter 13)

MISSISSIPPI

Wineries seem to be as scarce as hen's teeth in this state. We did find **Claiborne Winery**, a small producer making several hundred cases a year. So far, the best wines produced there are Sauvignon Blancs.

Suggested Reading

Ensrud, B. *American Vineyards.* New York: Stewart, Tabori, & Chang, 1988. 244 pp.

Adams, L. D. *The Wines of America.* 4th ed. New York: McGraw-Hill, 1990. 528 pp.

Chapter 11

A Brief Look at Imported Wine

As confessed in Chapter 9, we sometimes stray from domestic wine to learn what is going on in other parts of the world. As you gain experience with wine you undoubtedly will want to sample a few exotics yourself. If you have an opportunity to travel to Europe or another wine-producing continent, sample the regional wines, which you will find at incredibly low prices. You may also find that the wine selection on site is completely different than the usual array of exports. In fact, eighty percent of the wine produced in France is *vin ordinaire*, the wine the French drink every day.

Exceptional buys in imported wines are now available in the United States as well, with consistent values coming from Australia and Chile and an occasional steal[1] from Spain and Portugal. Currently, the four largest exporters to the U.S. are France, Italy, Chile, and Germany. For the most part, the French, German, and Italian imports are fairly expensive. Many of these are of excellent quality, however, and could be considered for special occasions. Many wine connoisseurs regard the red wines of Bordeaux as the ultimate, which is why they are willing to pay hundreds of dollars for certain bottles. Remember that European wines are more likely to be named for a region rather than bear a varietal name. Many are carefully blended, which enhances rather than detracts from their quality.

This chapter will introduce you to the major wine-producing areas that export wines to the United States and a few specific products that

---

[1] Only figuratively speaking. Pay for the wine, Buster!

are definitely worth a try. This is only a brief overview. Entire books have been written about many of these regions (see Suggested Reading).

ARGENTINA

This South American country is one of the world's largest wine producers, although most of that production is consumed within its borders. The major grape-growing area, Mendoza, is an expansive plateau adjacent to the Andes Mountains. Most Argentines prefer heavy-bodied red wines (the ones we often refer to as robust)[2] that complement their hearty beef entrées. Recent years have seen a vast improvement in the quality of Argentine wine.[3] You will find a few of their reds (Cabernet, Malbec, Merlot, Pinot Noir, Syrah, or blends) in larger wine shops. You can find some nice Cabernets priced under $7. Good names to look for are **Navarro Correas**, **Bianchi Particular**, **San Felipe**, and **Trapiche**. **Navarro Correas** also makes an extremely nice Syrah that sells for less than $10. Other good buys are listed in Chapter 14.

AUSTRALIA

The Australian wine industry is best described as rapidly expanding and dynamic. There are now more than five hundred wineries spread over the continent's southern portion, which comprises several important wine-producing regions. Some of the better-known of these are Barossa Valley, Coonawarra, Hunter Valley, Southern Vales, and Swan Valley. Many of Australia's wine-producing regions are located in hot, arid areas, but some of the best wines come from cooler regions such as Barossa Valley (north of Adelaide), Hunter Valley (north of Sydney), and Coonawarra (southeast of Adelaide).

When we think of Australia, we think mainly of two varietals, Chardonnay and Shiraz (Syrah), along with a cast of reasonably priced blended wines. The Shiraz produced here are consistently among the best red wines in the world, and the neatest thing about them is the

---

[2] Luigi just calls them "Big Muthas"
[3] And believe us, it was needed.

145

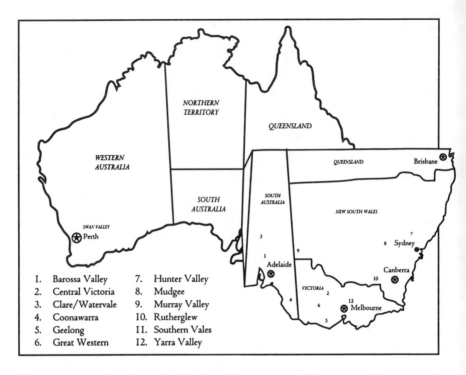

Most wine regions in Australia are located in the southeastern portion of the country, with the exception of the Swan Valley near Perth. Expanded depiction of the southeast shows the major wine-production areas.

price—you can find several for under $10 a bottle. Australia produces a number of Cabernet Sauvignons, but most have not greatly impressed us. Instead, we prefer the Cabernet/Shiraz blends, which are excellent values. Other varietals widely grown here are Sauvignon Blanc, Sémillon (often blended with Chardonnay), and Johannisberg Riesling (often sold as Rhine Riesling). Some very nice versions of all these are produced from year to year. So tie your kangaroo down, Sport, and let's look at some of the best Australian wine producers.

Australian Cabernet Sauvignons vary from lean- to full-bodied and can provide disappointments as well as pleasant surprises. Some of the better ones are **Black Opal, Cedar Creek** Bin 99, **Brown Brothers'** Family Reserve, **Hardy's** Bird Series, **Koala Ridge, Peter Lehmann, Lindeman's** Bin 45, **Mildara** Coonawarra, **Rosemount** Diamond,

Seppelt, and Wolf Blass.

Cabernet is frequently blended with Shiraz in Australia, and the blends that are predominantly Shiraz are among our favorites. Among the best of these are **Penfold's** Koonunga Hill and **Rosemount's** Diamond Reserve Red. Also worthy of mention are **Wirra Wirra** Church Block and releases from **Balgownie, Jacob's Creek, Mitchelton, Seppelt, Wolf Blass,** and **Yalumba.**

This brings us to Shiraz, the Persian name for Syrah, which is also labeled Hermitage in Australia. Australian Shiraz varies from smooth, medium- and full-bodied wines that are suitable for drinking young to darker, full-bodied, and somewhat tannic wines that require several years of bottle aging to smooth them out. Many American restaurants are now offering selections of Shiraz, and some of the nicer ones are **Peter Lehmann, Mitchelton, Montrose, Rosemount, Ryecroft,** and **Taltarni.** The latter is especially rich and full-bodied—and truly robust.

Australian Chardonnays can be as nice as any in the world. Many are loaded with fruit, spice, and butter blended in excellent balance. The good news is, many are still available in the $6 to $10 range. We've found many excellent vintages, including **Brown Brothers'** E. B., **Lindeman's** Bin 65, **Rothbury Estate** Brokenback, **Seppelt** Reserve Bins, and **Yeringberg** Lilydale, as well as selections from **Barrier Reef, Black Opal, Cedar Creek, Château Reynella, Hardy, Koala Ridge, Oxford Landing, Saltram,** and **Yalumba.**

Although Chardonnay dominates the white wine exports from down under, other pleasant white wines do find their way to the American market. We've enjoyed some good Sauvignon Blanc, including **Brown Brothers** E. B. and releases from **Roo's Leap, Oxford Landing,** and **Rothbury Estate.** Some of the best Rieslings are **Jacob's Creek, Pewsy Vale,** and **Wynn's** Coonawarra. Excellent Sémillon is also being produced here; it's either marketed as a varietal or blended with Chardonnay. A few of the best are **Lindemans, Penfold's** Koonunga Hill, **Rosemount** (Sémillon/Chardonnay), **Rothbury Estate,** and **Woodstock** McLaren Vale.

Australia also exports some proprietary blends that are of excellent quality and very reasonably priced. One of our favorites is **Tyrell's** Long Flat Red, which can usually be found for $5 to $6. **Rosemount** Diamond Reserve Red and White and **Hardy's** Premium Classic Dry Red and Dry White are also excellent values.

CANADA

Canada seldom gets mentioned in the wine books, but heck, dey produce some pretty good wine, eh?[4] We recently conducted a brief tour of the Niagara Peninsula of Ontario Province, where most Canadian wine is produced. We learned that the **Brights Wine Company** had actually pioneered the cultivation of *vinifera* grapes in the East, just ahead of vintners in New York. Current developments in the Ontario wine industry closely resemble those in the Great Lakes states. Certain *vinifera* varieties are doing quite nicely on selected sites near Lake Ontario and Lake Erie, and hybrids fill an important market niche. The quality of Ontario wine has made marked improvements in the past ten years, and several Ontario wineries have received international acclaim in world competition. The Canadians have instituted a program to improve product standards nationwide; their VQA (Vintners' Quality Alliance) Medallion is only placed on wines of the highest quality.

If you're bringing the new bride (or even the old one) to Niagara Falls, take a break from sightseeing and honeymooning[5] to enjoy some of the eighteen wineries nearby. The well-marked Niagara Winery Route starts near Niagara Falls and winds westward through the fruit-growing area to Winona. You can pick up a map at one of the Ontario Tourist Information Centers. Wineries definitely worth a visit are **Inniskillin**, whose best wines to date have been whites, mostly *vinifera;* **Brights**, a long-established company whose quality wines sometimes find their way into the United States; **Hillebrand Estates**, which offers

---

[4] Eh? is an expression widely used in Canada which many of us south of the border think is pretty cute. Actually it sounds a lot more intelligent than *our* widely used expression: Huh?

[5] Not to be confused with "mooning" your honey, which does not require a trip to Niagara Falls.

many pleasant whites including Chardonnay, Riesling, and Gewürztraminer; and **Stoney Ridge**, where you will find some outstanding Merlot and Cabernet Franc. Somewhat further inland is the "bench" area where **Vineland, Cave Spring Cellars**, and **Henry of Pelham** are located. Two other designated wine regions are located on the north shore of Lake Erie and on Pelee Island. You will definitely want to sample Canada's excellent *vinifera* and hybrid varieties on any visit there, since at this point few Canadian wines are exported to the United States.

CHILE

Reasonable quality and great prices have vaulted Chile into third place in U. S. imports, after France and Italy. Chilean Merlots and Sauvignon Blancs are especially competitive with those from the western United States, and their Cabernet Sauvignons and Chardonnays aren't far behind. Chile is blessed with sunny, dry weather, ample irrigation water, no *phylloxera* as yet, few other pests, and cheap land and labor. The Aconcagua Valley north of Santiago is the northernmost region, while the Maipo River and Maule River valleys to the south make up the major production regions. You may see regional or district names such as Curico, Rapel, or Lontue, on bottle labels. We'll use winery names to describe Chilean offerings, since at this point they'll probably will provide you better guidance than the regional ones.

Cabernet Sauvignon from Chile is bottled in two classes, regular and Reservas. Reservas, the best lots of wine, are aged longer and have more body and flavor; non-Reservas (regular) tend to be thin but quaffable. Reservas are still reasonably priced, with many in the $6 to $10 range. Some excellent choices are **Caliterra, Cousiño Macul** (Antiguas Reserva), **Errazuriz** Panquehue, **Los Vascos** (Reserva), **Santa Rita** Medalla Real, and **Santa Carolina** (Reserva).

Chilean Chardonnays don't seem to have nearly as much character as those from Australia, but we hope they'll improve in the future. One of the best we've tasted is **Caliterra**, which usually can be found in the $7

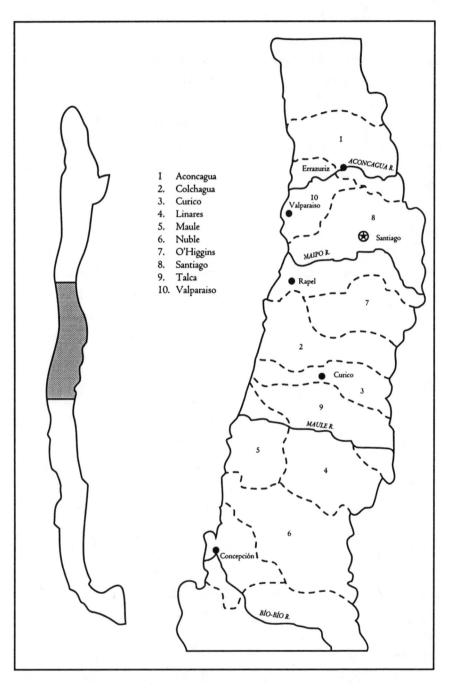

1   Aconcagua
2.   Colchagua
3.   Curico
4.   Linares
5.   Maule
6.   Nuble
7.   O'Higgins
8.   Santiago
9.   Talca
10. Valparaiso

Some major wine-producing regions of central Chile, several of which are located in the major river valleys.

range. Others worthy of a try are **Cousiño Macul, Miguel Torres,** and **Santa Rita** Reserva.

Chilean Merlots are quite nice for the price, although we would not rate their complexity with that of the gems now produced in Washington State. Better ones include **Concha y Toro, Errazuriz,** and **Santa Rita.** Numerous others quaffs and bargains compare to many domestic offerings.

We think Sauvignon Blanc is the finest wine now being produced in Chile. A glance at our best wine value listings in Chapter 14 will reveal many offerings. We consider the cream of the crop to be **Los Vascos** Reserva, **Caliterra, Errazuriz** Panquehue, and **Miguel Torres.**

FRANCE

France has gained a reputation as the premier wine-producing nation, and some of the world's highest priced and most sought after selections are produced here. France's many regions produce an enormous array of varieties and, fortunately for us, not all of them are expensive. France has strict regulations governing quality; the vast majority of its exported wines are in the *Appellation Controlee (AC)* category, which is the highest. Wines with this designation are guaranteed to be of specified origin, variety, and alcohol content, and must be produced by approved viticultural and enological techniques. Between *AC* and *vin de Table* (also known as the cheap stuff) are two other designations whose selections may be perfectly acceptable. They are *Vins Délimités de Qualité Supérieur (VDQS)*, which includes wines with sound regional characteristics, and *Vins de Pays (VDP)*, which are more recently introduced wines from specified regions. Look for some excellent values in the latter category. Incidentally, some *vin de Table* is perfect for everyday drinking and can be purchased for less than $2 a bottle in France. All fine French wines bear the name of a region and district; the exception to this is wine produced in Alsace (northeastern France), which more often carry varietal names.

When reading about French wines you frequently may see the term

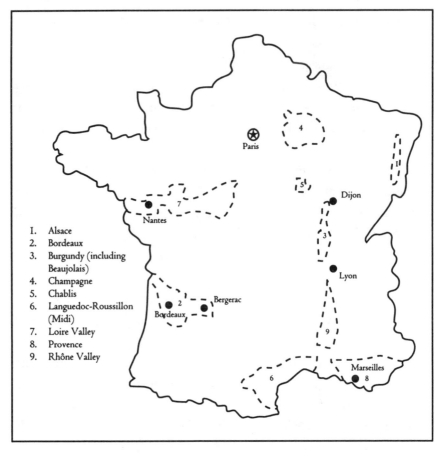

1. Alsace
2. Bordeaux
3. Burgundy (including Beaujolais)
4. Champagne
5. Chablis
6. Languedoc-Roussillon (Midi)
7. Loire Valley
8. Provence
9. Rhône Valley

Some of the major wine-producing regions of France. Many are close to France's scenic rivers or coasts.

cru (growth). *Grand cru* (first growth) refers to the vineyards or regions that are most highly ranked for quality. This usually turns out to be true, although there are a few exceptions. Some important wine-producing regions of France include Alsace, Bordeaux, Bourgogne or Burgundy (of which Beaujolais is a famous district), Chablis, Champagne, Languedoc-Rousillon, Loire Valley, Provence, and the Rhône Valley (Côtes du Rhône).

Alsace

Some of the premier white wines in the world are produced in Alsace;

most are vinted in a dry style. The major wines produced here are Gewürztraminer, Pinot Blanc, Pinot Gris, Riesling, Sylvaner, and Muscat. Although we usually don't expect white wines to age well, some of these dry versions can last five to ten years if properly stored. Many American winemakers are now trying to duplicate the Alsatian style, particularly with Gewürztraminer, Pinot Gris, and Riesling, and several are achieving good results.

Although it's becoming more difficult to find good Alsatian wine for less than $10 per bottle, a few shippers consistently export good values in the $7 to $10 range. Because these wines tend to be in less demand than the popular Burgundy and Bordeaux, you may find marked-down versions in your wine shop. Particularly good values in Gewürztraminer are **Lucien Albrecht, J. L. Mader, Trimbach,** and **Zind-Humbrecht.**

Pinot Blancs, which are perhaps the best values from this region, are crisp, dry, but fruity wines. Many are available in the $5 to $8 range and some of the better ones include **Leon Beyer, Dopff & Irion, Josmeyer Mise du Printemps, Pierre Sparr,** and **Zind-Humbrecht.**

Alsatian Rieslings with three to five years of bottle aging can be a delight.[6] At this point they fully develop their flowery bouquet and maintain their fruity character. Consistently good ones that are generally available for less than $10 are **Adam, Dopff "Au Moulin", G. Lorentz, Trimbach,** and **Zind-Humbrecht** Herrenweg Turckheim.

For good Sylvaner, try **Adam, Domaine Weinbach,** or **Trimbach.**

Bordeaux

The wines from this famous region in southwestern France can be either red or white. The premier districts for the reds are considered to be Graves, Haut-Médoc, Médoc, Pomerol, and St. Emilion. Adjacent to these areas are districts such as Fronsac, Côtes de Bourg, and Côtes de Castillon, which now produce some fine wines, many of which are excellent values in U.S. wine shops. The red Bordeaux are most often

---

[6] Afternoon or otherwise.

blends of Merlot, Cabernet Sauvignon, and Cabernet Franc, although other varieties may be used in certain districts. These wines are renowned for intense fruit and harsh tannins when young, with the capability of mellowing into complex and elegant wines after considerable bottle aging. As in most places, there are superb, good, and poor vintages from Bordeaux. The best vintages in recent history are generally considered to be 1990, 1989, 1988, 1986, 1985, 1983, and 1982.

Some good Bordeaux are available in the $8 to $12 range, although great ones will cost much more. Look for labels listing these châteaux for some exceptional values in Bordeaux[7]: **Beaumont** (Haut-Médoc), **de Belcier** (Côtes de Castillon), **Chantegrive** (Graves), **La Dauphine** (Fronsac), **Cap de Mourlin** (St. Emilion), **La Garde** (Graves), **Larose-Trintaudon** (Haut-Médoc), **Pitray** (Côtes de Castillon), **La Tour de By** (Médoc), and **La Vielle Cure** (Fronsac). There are also some proprietary brands that deserve your attention. Among these are **Château Bonnet, Mouton Cadet, Michel Lynch** Rouge, and **Château Timberlay**.

White Bordeaux is made from Sauvignon Blanc or Sauvignon Blanc blended with Sémillon. Although the best are produced in Graves, we don't consider these wines that much better than those now produced in Australia, or for that matter, the state of Washington. Many are overpriced, and for that reason alone we simply do not buy them. Those who do buy them recommend **Château Bonnet, Domaine Challon, Fondation 1725, Michel Lynch, Saint-Jovian,** and **Château de Sours** as good values.

Some of the world's best dessert wines, especially Sauternes and Barsac, also come from this region. These are discussed in more detail in Chapter 8.

Burgundy (Bourgogne)

This large region in eastern France is perhaps the second most famous wine producing area in the world. It extends from Chablis in the north to the Rhone Valley in the south, and is famous for Beaujolais (named for a district in Burgundy that specializes in lighter-bodied,

---

[7] Eaux, I'm a peauxet and didn't even kneaux it.

fruity reds from Gamay grapes), red Burgundy (produced from Pinot Noir grapes), and white Burgundy (mostly Chardonnay). The white wines range from the expensive Meursaults and Montrachets of the Côte d'Or to more reasonably priced Aligoté (a varietal), Bourgogne Blanc, Mâcon-Villages, and Saint-Véran. While the Meursaults and Montrachets are out of the range of most of our pocketbooks, almost everything else from this region can be found at reasonable prices.

Beaujolais wines have become extremely popular and are shipped all over the world. These light red, fruity, quaffing wines come in several quality levels. Simple Beaujolais are the lightest; many are very pleasing if drunk within a year of release. Beaujolais *nouveau* is the first Beaujolais to be released, traditionally on the third Thursday of November.[8] To realize its full raspberry bouquet and fruitiness, it should be drunk within four or five months of release.

Beaujolais-Villages are somewhat fuller in body than Beaujolais. The grapes originate in an area northwest of Villefranche containing about thirty villages. Many of the Villages selections are excellent *nouveau* candidates. They can be kept a bit longer than regular Beaujolais, but not much more than a year. The third and highest quality category of Beaujolais is called *crus*. These wines bear the names of ten specific locations such as Brouilly, Fleurie, and Morgon. In general, they have more body and fruit and a richer texture than the other categories of Beaujolais. They also cost two to three times as much, and can be held three years or more. Many Beaujolais and Beaujolais-Villages can be found in the $5 to $8 range, and even some of the *crus* sell for less than $10. Some good choices in each category are:

Beaujolais: **Georges Duboeuf, Louis Jadot, Louis Latour, Louis Tête**

Beaujolais *Nouveau*: **Jean Bédin, Georges Duboeuf, Prosper Maufoux, Antonin Rodet**

Beaujolais-Villages: **Paul Beaudet, Joseph Drouhin, Georges**

---

[8] This gives you a week before Thanksgiving to check it out.

Duboeuf, Louis Jadot, Maurice Descombes
Beaujolais-*crus*: Jean Bédin, Joseph Drouhin, Georges Duboeuf,
Jacky Janodet, Trenel

Some of the red wines made from Pinot Noir grapes are marketed as Bourgogne Rouge. They vary considerably in quality and price. Some good ones to look for are **Pierre Bourée, Joseph Drouhin, Jayer-Gilles, J. Monnier,** and **Domaine Tallmard.**

Some white Burgundy is elegant, and if you avoid those from the Côte d'Or you can find many values. White Burgundy is produced mostly from Chardonnay, and to a lesser extent from the Aligoté variety. In the latter category look for **Boillot, Louis Jadot, Louis Latour, Prosper Maufoux,** and **P. Morey.** Those labeled Bourgogne Blanc may originate anywhere in the region but will always be Chardonnay. Some of the better ones are **Charton & Trebuchet, Joseph Drouhin, P. Javillier, Louis Latour, J. Moreau** Chardonnay, and **J. Pascal.** White Burgundy from a region near the town of Mâcon is known as Mâcon-Villages or Mâcon Blanc. It is a crisp, fruity Chardonnay that is seldom aged in oak. Some good producers include **Domaine Fichet, Domaine des Roches, Joseph Drouin, Georges Duboeuf, Louis Jadot, Prosper Maufoux,** and **Domaine Tallmard.** Saint-Véran is another excellent appellation for White Burgundy that is aged in oak for short periods. Some of the best to find their way to the United States are **Paul Beaudet, Domaine Laroche, T. Guerin, Georges Duboeuf, Louis Jadot, Prosper Maufoux,** and **J. J. Vincent.**

Chablis

This small area includes the hillsides clustered around the town of Chablis, which is about 175 kilometers southeast of Paris. The white wines produced in this area express a magnificent flinty dryness, a green-tinged, yellow-gold color, and a delicate, perfumelike aroma. Unfortunately, the best (*Grand Crus*) are priced out of our reach. Occasionally you will find a *Premier Cru* (second rank) in the $12 to $15 range. Good ones are marketed by the grower's cooperative **La Chablisienne** under a variety of labels.

Champagne

This is the northernmost wine region of France, where many of the world's best sparkling wines are produced. The areas around Epernay and Reims are particularly famous for traditional Méthode champenoise Champagnes, many of which are very highly priced. For more details on sparkling wines, go directly to Chapter 7.[9]

Languedoc-Rousillon ("The Midi")

This region in south central France, sometimes called the Midi, lies just north of Spain and extends eastward to the western Mediterranean coast. The wines formerly produced here had a reputation for poor quality, but times have changed. A majority of the Midi vineyards have been replanted to more popular varieties and some excellent wines, most of which are reds, are now coming from this area. Considerable amounts of Cabernet Sauvignon, Merlot, and Syrah are being produced, some in a heavier Bordeaux style and some in a ready-to-drink-now style.[10] Some of the better reds imported from this area are produced by **Daniel Bessière**, **Château Grinou**, **Château de Jau**, **Domaine Les Jouglas**, **Château Montus Madiran**, **Rèserve St. Martin**, and **St. Chinian**.

An area east of Bordeaux known as Cahors produces some very nice red blends, mostly from Malbec, Tannat, Merlot, and Cabernet Sauvignon grapes. These are now coming to the United States, where a few can be found for less than $10. Look for **Château de Chambert**, **Domaine de Bovila**, **Moulin de la Grezette**, **Château Pech de Jammes**, or **La Tour de Vayrols**.

A region called Corbières has recently experienced extensive planting, and produces some very pleasant red, Rosé, and white wines. The

---

[9] Do not pass Go. Do not collect $200!

[10] For the impatient, that ready-to-drink-now stuff is a favorite.

reds and Rosés are being produced primarily from Carignane, Grenache, Mourvèdre, and Syrah grapes, while the whites are various blends of Bourboulenc, Chardonnay, Grenache Blanc, Sauvignon Blanc and Ugni Blanc. Since this area is growing rapidly, expect more labels to enter the marketplace each year. Good-value wines from this area are produced by **Château Beauregard, Clos Villemajou, Domaine Fontsainte** Reserve la Demoiselle, **Château Saint Auriol,** and **Château La Voulte Gasparets.**

Loire Valley

Along approximately six hundred miles of the Loire River as it flows from central France to the Atlantic Ocean are picturesque vineyards producing mostly white wines. Some of France's most famous wines (including Muscadet, Sancerre, Pouilly Fumé, and Vouvray) are named for the appellations or subregions here. Some of these are highly priced, and not all find their way to your corner wine shop. Since there are many appellations and a vast number of wines produced in this valley, we'll list only a few and recommend one or two good producers of each type.

Anjou: known particularly for crisp Rosés. Two good values are **Domaine de la Motte** and **Sauvion et Fils.**

Bourgueil: flavorful red wines made from Cabernet Franc. Excellent values are available from **Audebert, Domaine du Grand Clos,** and **Marcel Martin.**

Chinon: much like Bourgueil, but these red wines from Cabernet Franc tend to be more flavorful and pricey. Look for **Couly-Dutheil** and **Marcel Martin** for around $10.

Ménétou-Salon: high-quality whites, Rosés, and reds, but not many imported to the United States. Look for **Domaine Chatenoy** and **Le Brun St. Ceols.**

Muscadet: excellent, reasonably priced, crisp white wines that go great with seafood. Try **Barré Frères, Marcel Martin,** and **Sauvion et Fils.**

Pouilly-Fumé: excellent whites from Sauvignon Blanc, most of which will be out of our price range.

Quincy: poor man's Pouilly Fumé. Not as complex, but crisp and tasty. Look for **Sauvion et Fils.**

Sancerre: another excellent white made from Sauvignon Blanc. Rarely found for under $10, but watch for sales on **Château de Sancerre, Langlois,** and **Daniel Millet.**

Savennières: a unique and complex wine made from Chenin Blanc. One of the finest wines from the Loire; mostly expensive. You may find **Clos du Papillon** or **Roche aux Moines** on sale for around $10.

Vouvray: also made from Chenin Blanc. These wines vary in sweetness; the sweeter ones are labeled *demi-sec.* Sometimes you can find **Marc Brédif, Château de Montfort, Kermit Lynch,** and **Prince Poniatowski** for around $10.

Provence

This is another large area in southern France extending from the hills of Provence to the Midi. As in the Midi itself, expansion in Provence has been rapid and quality is on the rise. The bulk of France's everyday wine comes from these two areas. Some of the reds now produced here have distinctive qualities and are exported to the United States. A few whites here are also worth a try. Some excellent producers from this area are **Domaine La Moutête, Domaine La Rosière, Mas de Gourgonnier,** and **Mas de la Rouvière.**

Rhône Valley

This long, narrow region extends along the Rhône River from south of Lyons to Avignon. Some of the most famous French red wines come from this region; Côtes du Rhône is the appellation most often seen in the United States. Our brief summary lists the appellations and a few suggested producers from each. Again, we are primarily suggesting wines that can be found for $10 or less.

Côtes du Rhône: this appellation covers a variety of reds from the lighter-bodied blends (southern Rhône) to more intense ones made from Syrah grapes (northern Rhône). Of the latter, Hermitage, Côte Rotie, and Châteauneuf-du-Pape are famously delicious and pricey. Many others are excellent buys. Look for **Domaine Ste. Anne, E. Guigal, Les Gouberts, Jaboulet,** and **Kermit Lynch.**

Côtes du Ventoux: these tend to be lighter versions of Côtes du Rhône and although some possess good fruit, others may be too weak. Look for bargains from **Jaboulet, La Vieille Ferme,** and **Vidal-Fleury.**

Crozes-Hermitage: made from Syrah grapes from the area around a hill called Hermitage. These vary a lot in quality, but some can be exceptional for around $10. Look for **Domaine de Thalabert (Jaboulet), Michel Courtial, Moillard,** and Vidal-Fleury.

Gigondas: an area in the southern Rhône known for intense and tannic reds that age well. Some good ones are from **Grand Montmirail, Prosper Maufoux, Jaboulet,** and **Château du Trignon.**

Vacqueyras: vineyards near this town in the southern Rhône are allowed to use the appellation Côtes du Rhône-Villages for their intense, tannic reds. Ones you might be able to find in the $10 range are **Domaine de Couroulou, Dussen,** and **Jaboulet.**

GERMANY

Some people (mostly Chardonnay fans) turn up their noses at German wines because many of them tend to be on the sweet side. The fact of the matter is German wines, particularly Rieslings, are likable wines for both novice and expert. Many are now produced in a drier style that accompanies everyday meals nicely. Many of the sweeter ones drink nicely alone as aperitifs or desserts, or they can accompany a variety of desserts.

German wine sales in the United States may also be limited by the complex and intimidating German words that appear on their labels.[11] Fear not. We've already shown you a German wine label in Chapter 2, and we'll expound some more about these words in this chapter and in the Glossary.

---

[11] It is usually the umlauts that scare people. They are almost as frightening as mugwumps and hugmollies.

Good-quality German wines usually have a village and vineyard name on the label. The village names will always end in *er* (e.g., *Bernkasteler* or *Oppenheimer*). Another term you may encounter is *Bereich*, which refers to a subregion or a group of villages. These wines can vary quite a bit in quality. We seldom see the poorest grade German wine (*Tafelwein*) in the United States. Average grade wines in Germany are labeled *Qualitätswein* (*QbA*), while higher-quality wines are labeled *Prädikat* or *Qualitätswein mit Prädikat* (*QmP*). The *QmP* are ranked in order of increasing sweetness as *Kabinett, Spätlese, Auslese, Beerenauslese* (*BA*) *and Trockenbeerenauslese* (*TBA*). The latter three are probably unexcelled in their expressions of honey and flowers; they are usually considered some of the best dessert wines in the world..

German wines that are on the drier side are labeled *Trocken* (dry) or *Halbtrocken* (half-dry). Riesling is considered Germany's premier wine grape, and if a label does not say Riesling the wine probably was made from Müller-Thurgau, Kerner, Pinot Blanc, Pinot Gris, or Sylvaner grapes. You need to be cautious when buying wines labeled *Liebfraumilch*, *Piesporter Michelsberg, Piesporter Treppchen*, or *Zeller Schwarze Katz* because the quality of these will vary with the producer and the vintage. According to Barbara Ensrud (see Suggested Reading), German wines that bear the names of the following shippers or importers can be depended upon for consistent quality: **Deinhard, H. Sichel Söhne, Scholl & Hillebrand**, and **Terry Theise Estate Selection**.

Germany's eleven wine regions are located mostly along the Rhine River or its tributaries; not all of them export to the U.S. Let's put on our little pointed helmets and travel quickly through the most important ones.(As Artie Johnson used to say, "Interrrestink . . . but stupit!")[12] Other good value German wines are listed under the Riesling section in Chapter 14.

Baden

This southern German region borders Switzerland and the French Alsace. It is known for a few white wines, particularly those from the

---

[12] And Sergeant Schultz replied, "I know nutink!"

Bodensee, Kaiserstuhl-Tuniberg, and Ortenau districts, and for a few red wines produced from Spätburgunder grapes.

Franken (Franconia)

This region is located near Wurzburg along the Main River Valley. Wines produced here are primarily from Müller-Thurgau and Sylvaner grapes and are sold in a traditional flagon-type bottle called a Bocksbeutel.

Mittelrhein

This encompasses the area along the middle Rhine from Bonn south to Bingen. Some pleasant white wines are produced throughout the area, but you'll probably not see many on the U. S. market.

Mosel-Saar-Ruwer

The Mosel River is a major tributary of the Rhine; the Saar and Ruwer are tributaries of the Mosel. This area is almost exclusively devoted to its renowned Riesling. The good wines from this area are described as flowery and spicy. Wine labels from this area will include the names of famous wine villages such as Bernkasteler, Brauneberger, Piesporter, Urziger, Wehlener, and Zeltingner. Some of the best values can be found from these producers (and villages): **Sichel, Wegeler-Deinhard,** and **Weins-Prüm** (Bernkasteler); **F. Haag** and **Richter** (Brauneberger); **Deinhard, Milz Kabinett,** and **Moselland** (Piesporter); **Mönchhof, Christoffel,** and **Merkelbach** (Urziger); **Deinhard, Kerpen,** and **J. J. Prüm** (Wehlener); and **Friedrich Wilhelm,** and **Selbach-Oster** (Zeltinger).

Nahe

Nahe is another tributary of the Rhine, located south of the Mosel. Wines are produced here from Riesling, Ruländer, and Sylvaner grapes. Some excellent wines from this area (and its villages) are **Kronenberg** (Bad Kreuznacher) and **Staatsweingut** and **J. Schneider** (Niederhauser).

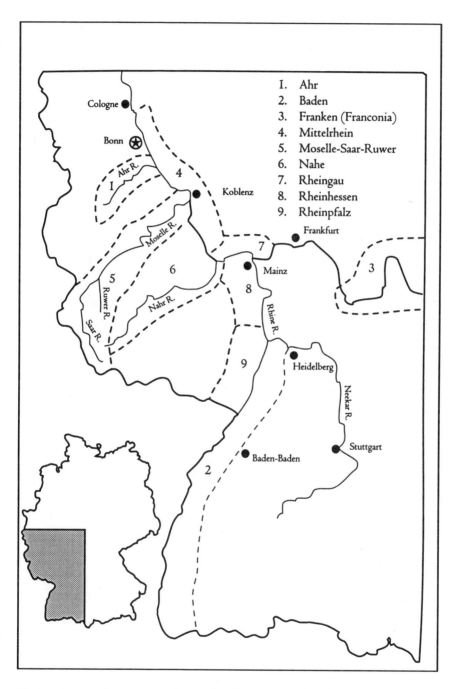

The major wine-producing areas of Germany line that country's scenic rivers.

Rheingau

This wine-producing region between Hochheim and Rüdesheim on the north side of the Rhine is widely considered to be Germany's finest. Wineries here produce every type of white wine, from high-quality *QbAs* to luscious (and expensive) dessert varieties. A few good producers (and villages) from this region are: **Staatsweingut**, and **von Simmern** (Eltviller); **Deinhard, Ress**, and **Schönborn** (Hochheimer); **von Metternich** (Johannisberger); and **Schloss Groensteyn**, and **Scholl & Hillebrand** (Rüdesheimer).

Rheinhessen

This region lies on the south side of the Rhine, facing Rheingau. Again, Riesling predominates, though considerable amounts of Sylvaner and Müller-Thurgau are also produced here. Many Liebfraumilchs (blended wines) are produced in this area; some are quite good, while others may disappoint you. The region's best wines are comparable to those made across the river. A few good ones (and villages) to look for are **Deinhard, R. Senfter**, and **Strub** (Niersteiner); and **Guldenmorgen** (Oppenheimer).

Rheinpfalz

The largest German wine region, this area is located on the west side of the Rhine south of the Rheinhessen. There are some real treats to be had from this area both in the *QbA* and *QmP* categories. Look for consistent quality from the following producers (and villages): **Basserman-Jordan, Bürklin-Wolf**, and **von Buhl** (Deidesheimer and Ruppertsberger); the above three plus **Deinhard** (Forster); and **Bürklin-Wolf** (Wachenheimer)

ITALY

Italy produces and drinks more wine per capita (about thirty gallons per person annually) than any other country in the world.[13] (Good

---

[13] It's been said that God created wine to keep Italians from taking over the world.

heavens, they're almost at the authors' level!) Since wines are produced from one end of the country to the other, there are numerous wine regions (about twenty at last count). Italian wines may bear a regional name or a varietal name, either of which may confuse the novice. As in many other countries, quality was once a problem, so in the 1960s Italy enacted legislation called *Denominazione di Origine Controllata* (*DOC*) to specify rules for labeling the best wines. More recently they established a *Denominazione di Origine Controllata e Guarantita* (*DOCG*) that includes only the "highest horsepower" wines. (We wish they would similarly control their automobile drivers. Every one of those SOBs thinks he needs to be first in line. Except for that—and the waiter in Sorrento who dropped a plate of pasta on my co-author's head!— Italians are a fun-loving group.)

Perhaps the most famous Italian red wines are Barolo, Barbaresco, Brunello, and Chianti Riserva. Unfortunately, their prices rose with their quality, and it is difficult to find many of these wines in the United States for under $10. Some of the best Italian whites are Pinot Bianco and Pinot Grigio, which also have escalated in price. As with our brief overviews of other countries, we'll point out the most important regions of Italy and a list few good wines from each one. We can't guarantee you'll be able to find all of these for $10 or less.

Alto Adige, Trentino, and Friuli-Venezia-Giulia

These northernmost wine regions primarily produce varietals, including Cabernet Franc, Merlot, Pinot Noir, Pinot Bianco, Pinot Grigio, and Gewürztraminer. Some of the best white wines from the region are Pinot Grigios, produced by **Bortoluzzi, Danieli, La Cadalora Valagarini,** or **San Valentino,** and Pinot Biancos, from **Enofriulia, La Cadalora, Maso Poli,** and **Ruffino Libaio.** You might also search out a white wine called Tocai, which is produced in Friuli. This is a unique wine with scents of wildflowers and almonds along with lots of fruit. Excellent ones are produced by **Marina Daniele, Jermann,** or **Doro Princic.** These wines are not well known in the United States. If you

1. Friuli-Venezia Giulia
2. Piedmont
3. Trentino-Alto Adige
4. Tuscany
5. Sicily
6. Veneto

A. Abruzzi
B. Apulia
C. Basilicata
D. Calabria
E. Campania
F. Emilia-Romagna
G. Latium
H. Liguria
i. Lombardy
J. Marches
K. Molise
L. Umbria
M. Valle D'Aosta

Italy's numerous wine regions. Those numbered 1 to 6 are briefly discussed in the text. Those identified A to M produce considerable wine, but export little to the United States. The Isle of Sardinia is hidden somewhere under the figure legend.

wish to try a robust, dark red wine from this area you might look for a Refosco (from the grape of that name) by **Durandi** or **Fantinel**, or a Teroldego Rotaliano by **Gaierhof, Maso Donati**, or **Zeni**. These are best as Riservas and some will age five years or more.

Veneto

This large region just south of Alto Adige includes the beautiful cities of Venice and Verona. You probably have seen Amarone, Soave, and Valpolicella wines at your grocery store. These are areas within the Veneto region. Some of the best white wines from this region are Bianco di Custoza, (a blend often better than Soave) from **Lamberti, Santa Sofia**, or **Tommasi**; and Soave Classico and Classico Superiore (consistently better than Soave) from **Anselmi, Bolla Castellaro, Masi**, or **Zenato**; and Breganze di Breganze, a proprietary blend from **Fausto Maculan**. Some of the best reds to look for are Campo Fiorin, a medium-bodied red from **Masi** in the Valpolicella region, and Valpolicella Classico Superiore from **Bertani, Bolla, Masi, Santa Sofia**, and **Tedeschi**. Try to avoid the lower grade Valpolicellas.

Piedmont

This northwestern region bordering the French Alps is famous for its red wines. Some of the more important wines produced here are Barolo, Barbaresco, Barbera, and Asti Spumante, many of which bear the names of towns in the region (e.g., Asti, Alba, Turin). One white wine produced here also deserves special mention: Gavi, which is produced from the Cortese di Gavi grape. It is delicate and full of fruit when drunk young. Some of the best producers of Gavi are **Bolla, Marchesi di Barolo, Massone**, and **Villa Banfi**.

Of the luscious red wines produced in the Piedmont, Barbera d'Alba and Barbera d'Asti are perhaps the best values now. D'Alba is the heaviest-bodied of the Barberas, and it literally fills your mouth—kind of making you want to chew the wine. Barbera d'Asti is a bit lighter in body, but often very good. Good producers to look for are **Castello di**

Nieve, Clerico, Aldo Conterno, Franco Fiorina, or **Mascarello.**

Two wines that have been likened to the Beaujolais of France are Dolcetto d'Alba and Dolcetto di Dogliani. They have lots of berry flavors and are meant to be drunk young. Look for **Elio Altare, Fennocchio, Paolo Cordero,** or **Valfieri.** Another red, Freisa, has become more popular in a newer, drier (*Secco*) style. Again, it is berrylike and a bit less expensive than the big reds. Look for **Aldo Conterno, Prunotto, Valentino,** and **Vietti.**

Another red deserving mention is Gattinara, which is made from the Nebbiolo grape. It is a lighter-bodied version of a Barolo, but the best ones can handle ten years of bottle age. Some of the better producers are **Fiore, L & G Nervi, Umberto,** and **Vallana.** You might also look for varietal Nebbiolo like Nebbiolo d'Alba from **Aldo Conterno** and **Luigi Einaudi,** which sometimes can be found in the $10 to $12 range. Unfortunately, the biggest reds (Barolos and Barbarescos) are all priced well above our pocketbook's capacity. If you've just won the lottery, how about a 1990 **Gaja** Barbaresco Sori Tildin for $139? It rated a perfect 100 from the *Wine Spectator.* **Gaja** had many other 1988-1990 vintage selections rated in the high 90s. If you'd rather drop your bankroll on Barolo, look for **Pio Cesare's** or **Prunotto's** 1988 and 1989 offerings, some of which can be had in the $30 range and some of which are yet to be released. Enough about expensive wine; it's depressing.

Tuscany

Tuscany is a large and important wine region located in west-central Italy, roughly between Florence and Viterbo. We visited several wineries here years ago, and remember buying good Chianti Classicos with a two dollar bill.[14] Those days have passed, but fortunately several of these wines are still within reach of middle-class Americans.[15]

Many Tuscan white wines are produced from Trebbiano or blends of

---

[14] The equivalent of two billion lira—but not an expensive wine!
[15] Those of us who pay most of the taxes.

that grape and other varieties such as Pinot Bianco, Chardonnay, Malvasia, or Sauvignon Blanc. Some of the better whites from this region are: Bianco di Toscana (look for **Antinori, Badia a Coltibuono, Poggio Garbato,** and **Vinattieri**), which shows a good balance of fruitiness and acidity; Pomino Bianco from the Chianti district, also a blended dry white with good character (produced by **Frescobaldi**); and Vernaccia di San Gimignano, which displays a touch of almond in its taste (good producers are **Riccardo Falchini, Teruzzi e Puthod,** and **Angelo del Tufo**).

Many different Tuscan reds are available for $10 or less. Perhaps the most famous reds from this area are the Chianti, which are simply blended red wines (containing predominantly Sangiovese grapes) from the Chianti district. Their quality has greatly improved in recent years, and prices of the best (Riservas) now often exceed our $10 barrier. Chianti is a light- to medium-bodied wine that will keep from two to four years, with the heavier-bodied Riservas cellaring eight years or more. Some of the more reliable producers of good-value Chianti are **Antinori, Berardenga-Fesina, Badia a Coltibuono, Luiano** (Riserva), **San Felice, Villa Banfi, Villa Cerna,** and **Villa Cilnia.** A small winery, **Selvapiana,** had the highest-rated Chianti (eighth) in *Wine Spectator's* 1992 top one hundred wines. This 1990 Chianti Rufina sells for $13. The 1990 vintage was particularly good for all Chianti. A **Renzo Masi** Chianti Rufina Fattoria di Basciano 1990 sells for $8.50, while a **Rodano** Chianti Classico 1990 can be found for $10. Both of these are highly recommended.

Other Tuscan reds you'll find very pleasing are: Monte Antico, a sturdy and well-balanced blend of Sangiovese and Canaiolo grapes (look for **Castello di monte Antico** and **La Pievanella**); and Rosso di Montalcino, another sturdy red, made from the Brunello grape (look for **Avignonesi, Banfi Centine, Col d'Orcia, Lisini, il Poggiolo,** and **San Filippo**).

Umbria

This important wine-producing area is located just to the south and east of Tuscany. One of the famous white wines from this region is

Orvieto, a fruity, fresh wine that needs to be drunk young. The *Secco* versions are best. Look for **Antinori Campogrande, Ruffino,** and **Palazzone.** In the reds, look for Montefalco Rosso, a blend produced by **Adanti,** or Rubesco, another sturdy red produced by **Lungarotti.**

Sicily

So we don't annoy any of our Mafia—oops, we mean *Sicilian* friends, we thought it appropriate to make mention of a Sicilian wine that often can be very good. It is a red called Corvo Rosso, and an excellent producer is **Duca di Salparuta.**

PORTUGAL AND SPAIN

We've decided to discuss the wines of these countries together because they have a lot in common besides lying side by side on the map. Both countries export red wines primarily, and both offer some exceptional values to those who appreciate big reds. The Portuguese dessert wines (Ports) are discussed separately in Chapter 8.

The best values in full-bodied, tannic, robust red wine currently come from Portugal, with many still priced in the $5 to $8 range. Some of these gems will cellar for ten years or more. Portuguese wines may bear regional names (e.g., Alentejo, Bairrada, Dao, and Ribatejo), proprietary names (e.g., Anfora, Conde de Santar, Quint da Camarate Clarete, and Serradayres) or varietal names (e.g., Periquita). The name Garrafeira indicates the best of the lot or proprietor's reserve. A few of the best Portuguese wines that you might find in a well-stocked wine shop (by category) are **Joao Pires** (Anfora); **Caves Sao Joao, Sogrape Terra Franca,** and **Sousellas Reserva** (Bairrada); **Caves Alianca, Conde de Santar** and **Caves Velhas** (Garrafeira); **Fonseca Terras Altas** (Dao); **José Maria da Fonseca** (Periquita); **Carvalho,** or **Ribeiro & Ferreira** (Serradayres), and **Caves Velhas Romeira** and **Romeira** Garrafeira (Ribatejo).

Spanish wines may also bear regional, proprietary, or varietal designations. A current wine map of Spain shows forty-one different Denominations of Origin. Obviously, we will not cover them all here.

The important wine regions of Spain and Portugal.

The best-known wine regions are Catalonia, which includes the Penedés; La Mancha, which produces most of Spain's quaffing wine; Rioja, known for its robust reds; and Ribera del Duero and Toro, also becoming known for hearty reds. A lot of the red wine in Spain is made from Tempranillo and Garnacha grapes. Rioja wines that are released young are called *Crianza*, while those with several years of bottling are called *Reservas* or *Gran Reservas* (best of the lot).

Some of the best Spanish red wine values are **J. Diaz** Colmenar Madrid, **Taja Jumilla** Tinto, and **Raimat** Cabernet Sauvignon; **Balbas or Penalba** (Ribera del Duero); **Martinez-Bujanda, Marques de Arienzo, Marqués de Cáceres,** and **Bodegas Palacio** Glorioso (Rioja); and **Fariña** Gran Colegiata, **Luis Mateos** Vega de Toro, and **Torres** Sangre de Toro Reserva (Toro).

Chapter 11

MISCELLANEOUS

Many other countries around the world produce wine, and every now and then their products appear in your favorite wine shop or grocery store. We'll offer a few brief comments on some that we've experienced:

Austria

You will not find many Austrian wines, but if you do see ones from **Siegendorf** or **Fritz Saloman** they will be of excellent quality.

Bulgaria

The only ones we've found to be fairly decent as well as excellent values are **Trakia** Cabernet Sauvignon and Chardonnay.

Greece

Some of the best Greek wines are produced by **Boutari** and **Carras**. If you're into dessert wines and want to try something different, try Commanderia or Samos. Both are sweet and delicious.

New Zealand

This is perhaps the best of the emerging cool-region production areas. You will continue to see New Zealand's impact on Sauvignon Blanc, Chardonnay, and Riesling markets. Look for **Cooks, Montana (Penfolds), Morton Estate**, and **Villa Maria**. Watch out for these folks, they may take over the wine world!

Rumania

The **Premiat** Cabernet Sauvignon and Merlot are acceptable at $3 to $4 per bottle when it's near the end of the month and you're short on cash.

South Africa

This country is now producing some very good wines which were seldom seen in U.S. wine shops because of sanctions. Look for **Backsberg** or **Nederburg** Chardonnay, **Kanonkop** or **Rustenberg** Cabernets and Bordeaux style blends.

Switzerland

Almost all Swiss wines are expensive, and many are very good. Again, they are seldom seen in U.S. wine shops. Look for **Domaine du Mont d'Or** and **Orsat, Caves SA.**

Suggested Reading

Ambrosi, H., and K. B. Stewart. *Traveller's Wine Guide: Germany*. New York: Sterling Publications, 1990. 144 pp.

Begg, D. *Traveller's Wine Guide: Spain*. New York: Sterling Publications, 1989. 144 pp.

Busselle, M. *The Wine Lover's Guide to the Rhône and South-East France*. London: Pavilion, 1990. 96 pp.

Duijker, H. *The Traveller's Guide to the Wine Regions of France*. London: Mitchell Bearzley, 1989. 176 pp.

Ensrud, B. *Best Wine Buys for $10 or Less*. New York: Villard Books, 1992. 170 pp.

Halliday, J. *Australian Wine Guide*. North Ryde NSW , Australia: Angus and Robertsons Publishers, 1986. 325 pp.

Millon, M., and K. Millon. *The Wine Roads of Spain*. London: Harper Collins Publishers, 1993. 497 pp.

Millon, M., and K. Millon. *The Wine Roads of Italy*. London: Harper Collins Publishers, 1991. 416 pp.

Read, J. *Chilean Wines*. London: Sotheby's Publications, 1988. 175 pp.

Chapter 12
Wine and Your Health

R ecent developments in this area deserve your undivided attention.[1] Some people say we shouldn't touch this topic with a
ten-foot pole because we're not medical doctors. Well believe us,
lots of "experts" out there with no knowledge of health issues have been
spreading false information and/or telling outright lies for years. The fact
that one of us (Al, the senior author) spent twenty-five years as a research
scientist trying to sort out scientific facts from falsehoods hopefully gives
us some credibility. If you don't trust our health suggestions, pick up all the
references cited at the end of this chapter and read them thoroughly.

Sandi and I have become particularly interested in lifestyle changes
that might prolong my life, since all the male members of my family for
the past three generations have died of heart problems before the age of
fifty. Statistics like that really capture your attention! Recently, health-
related literature has placed more emphasis on the prevention of serious
ailments such as heart disease and cancer. What impact, if any, does wine
consumption have on the incidence of these diseases? Rather than try to
answer this question ourselves, we'll present you with statements from
the medical community that address wine and health.

The Mediterranean Lifestyle and Health

This subject has received a great deal of attention in the past three
years. Why do southern Europeans outlive us Yanks by an average of two

---

[1] Well, only if you're interested in living a longer and healthier life.

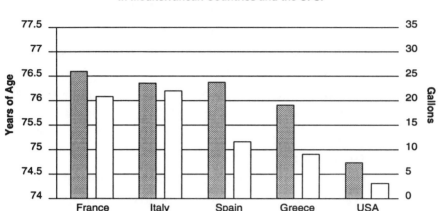

**Life Expectancy and Per Capita Wine Consumption
In Mediterranean Countries and the U. S.**

Life expectancy and per capita wine consumption in several Mediterranean countries, as compared to ours in the United States. Courtesy of the Wine Institute's Research and Education Department.

to two and a half years? Why do the French suffer forty percent fewer heart attacks than we do, in spite of the fact that they smoke more, eat much more fat, and exercise less? This situation, called "The French Paradox," got worldwide attention when it was covered by CBS's *60 Minutes* in 1991. In 1992, the book *The French Paradox and Beyond* (see Suggested Reading) clearly summarized the possible benefits of wine and the Mediterranean lifestyle.

According to Dr. R. Curtis Ellison, M.D., chief of Preventive Medicine and Epidemiology and professor at Boston University School of Medicine, the French differ from us in their intake of food and beverages in the following ways:

* They regularly consume moderate quantities of alcohol, particularly red wine, with their meals.
* They eat more fresh fruits and vegetables.
* They take longer to eat their meals and snack less.
* They eat less red meat.
* They eat more cheese and less whole milk.
* They use more olive oil and less lard or butter.

175

These dietary habits are maintained in other Mediterranean countries, whose citizens also experience lower heart disease rates than ours. Interestingly, the two countries with the lowest heart disease rates, France and Italy, also are the two countries with the highest per capita wine consumption (averaging 2.5 glasses per day). Before you run out and gulp down a flood of red wine, consider what medical authorities have to say about a variety of other wine-related health issues.

Alcohol Consumption and Health

After summarizing all the studies, Dr. Ellison maintains that moderate drinkers of alcohol have significantly lower death rates (usually twenty to forty percent lower) from all causes than abstainers or heavy drinkers. In 1989, Mary Ann Armstrong and Dr. Arthur L. Klatsky conducted a study that examined the relationship between alcohol intake and hospitalization. By studying case histories of 82,430 people, they found that those who drank more than one but less than three drinks per day spent the least time in the hospital.

A recent study published in the *American Journal of Public Health* indicates that moderate drinkers have more resistance to the common cold. The subjects from the various drinking groups were all inoculated with a virus known to cause colds, and those who drank in moderation caught sixty-five to eighty-five percent fewer colds than abstainers. Smoking wiped out any benefit from moderate drinking, however.

Dr. Helen Rodgers and associates recently published the results of their study in the journal *Stroke*. Their findings indicate that those who abstain from alcohol roughly double their risk of stroke. Stroke is similar to coronary thrombosis, except that in stroke the artery blockage occurs in the brain instead of the heart. These researchers suggest that moderate drinkers' reduced risk of stroke may be attributed to similar mechanisms that appear to protect against coronary heart disease.

In addition, according to research presented at the 1993 Annual Meeting of the Society for Behavioral Medicine in San Francisco, moderate drinkers are better able to cope with stress. Robert Lipton,

Ph.D., of the Berkeley Alcohol Research Group, found that moderate consumers of alcohol were less likely to become depressed when under stress than abstainers or alcohol abusers. This study indicates that moderate alcohol consumption can improve emotional health as well as physical health.

What is moderate drinking? Luigi told me that in his college days he only had one drink per day, but it was a quart of Absolut Vodka. Everyone has his/her idea of moderate drinking, but the medical community has pretty much agreed it consists of about twenty-five grams of alcohol per day, which translates into two to two and a half glasses of wine per day, depending on the alcohol content.

Wine consumption does differ appreciably from that of other forms

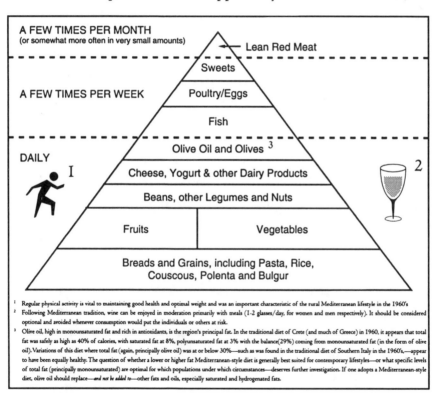

A FEW TIMES PER MONTH
(or somewhat more often in very small amounts) — Lean Red Meat

Sweets

A FEW TIMES PER WEEK — Poultry/Eggs

Fish

DAILY — Olive Oil and Olives [3]

Cheese, Yogurt & other Dairy Products

Beans, other Legumes and Nuts

Fruits — Vegetables

Breads and Grains, including Pasta, Rice, Couscous, Polenta and Bulgur

[1] Regular physical activity is vital to maintaining good health and optimal weight and was an important characteristic of the rural Mediterranean lifestyle in the 1960's

[2] Following Mediterranean tradition, wine can be enjoyed in moderation primarily with meals (1-2 glasses/day, for women and men respectively). It should be considered optional and avoided whenever consumption would put the individuals or others at risk.

[3] Olive oil, high in monounsaturated fat and rich in antioxidants, is the region's principal fat. In the traditional diet of Crete (and much of Greece) in 1960, it appears that total fat was safely as high as 40% of calories, with saturated fat at 8%, polyunsaturated fat at 3% with the balance(29%) coming from monounsaturated fat (in the form of olive oil). Variations of this diet where total fat (again, principally olive oil) was at or below 30%—such as was found in the traditional diet of Southern Italy in the 1960's,—appear to have been equally healthy. The question of whether a lower or higher fat Mediterranean-style diet is generally best suited for contemporary lifestyles—or what specific levels of total fat (principally monounsaturated) are optimal for which populations under which circumstances—deserves further investigation. If one adopts a Mediterranean-style diet, olive oil should replace—*and not be added to*—other fats and oils, especially saturated and hydrogenated fats.

Pyramid depicting a traditional Mediterranean diet and lifestyle. First presented by Walter Willett, M.D., at the 1993 International Conference on the Diets of the Mediterranean. Courtesy of the Oldways Preservation and Exchange Trust and the Harvard School of Public Health.

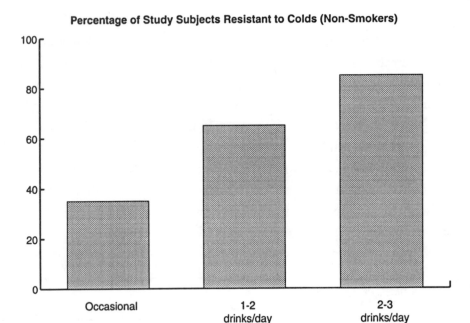

Percentage of Study Subjects Resistant to Colds (Non-Smokers)

Increased resistance to the common cold displayed by moderate consumers of alcohol. Data from Cohan, et al., American Journal of Public Health, 83 (9):1277. Courtesy of the Wine Institute's Research and Education Department.

of alcohol. About seventy-five percent of wine drinking takes place in a home setting; of that, eighty-three percent occurs at mealtime, most often as part of a family gathering. For the most part, wine consumers are moderate and responsible drinkers.

The problem with alcohol is its potential abuse. It is estimated that seven to ten percent of the United States population abuses alcohol. Alcohol abusers create serious health problems for themselves and, all too frequently, pose a serious threat to the rest of us. These people should not drink, and society should insist on (and assist with) a solution to their problem. It would be better to spend taxpayer money on this effort than on a campaign to prevent moderate consumption. Unfortunately, fanatical groups in this country would rather issue total bans than seriously attempt to resolve the real issues.

One of the greatest challenges we all face is alcohol education. We certainly do not want our children to become abusers or alcohol-related accident statistics. Many experts believe that American parents fail to teach their children about the moderate and responsible use of alcohol. Too often, the entire subject becomes taboo. (By the way, sex education faces the same problem.) Again, the fanatics in our society confuse *teaching* kids about good behavior with *advocating* bad behavior. They fight our schools' attempts to teach young people the basic facts about alcohol (or sex) and foolishly suppose that a few cute slogans like "Just say no!" will suffice.

Interestingly, alcohol education isn't much of a problem in Italy, France, or the other Mediterranean countries. In Europe, children are routinely exposed to moderate wine drinking at mealtimes and accept it as normal behavior. They might even be allowed the occasional taste or a watered-down drink, so they know what the stuff is *before* they reach those rebellious years. In a 1990 editorial Dr. Ellison wrote, "Many who have studied the etiology of alcoholism believe that the complete prohibition of exposure to alcoholic beverages until 'adulthood' is not an appropriate way of preventing alcohol abuse". On this same subject, Dr. Margaret Deansley (affiliated with the Stanford Medical School and a practicing physician) said, "We expect to raise these people to the age of twenty-one, open the door, and say, 'Now drink; it will be fine, dear.' And of course we know now how badly that has failed." Deansley advocates making education about responsible drinking an important part of parental teaching, and if necessary, part of the school curriculum.

The potential benefits of moderate alcohol consumption are obscured by extremists' attempts to equate alcohol abuse with moderate alcohol intake. They consistently use this tactic to influence government policy concerning the regulation of alcohol. Dr. John P. Callan, an Illinois psychiatrist who treats chemical dependency patients, wrote something we agree with in the winter 1992 issue of *Priorities*:

These NeoProhibitionist "drys" are not only generating intemperate propaganda against overindulgence, but also against the publication of healthful effects of moderate drinking. Alcohol

179

has been shown, in reputable scientific studies, to be beneficial to good health. The one-sided attacks should not go unanswered. Legitimate voices should speak out lest unscientific opinion prevail and Prohibition be re-enacted.

Wine Consumption and Heart Disease

The only type of heart problem related to high alcohol consumption is cardiomyopathy, (the actual injury of heart tissue). This is a rare disease. Coronary artery disease, the big killer (about 500,000 deaths annually), involves the plugging of the arteries by platelets; when severe, this can cause coronary thrombosis. What effect does moderate alcohol consumption, and more specifically wine consumption, have on coronary heart disease? Here's what medical doctors say about this subject:

• Dr. Serge Renaud, head of the Lyon Center of INSERM [the French equivalent of our National Institutes of Health (NIH)] says, "It's well documented that a moderate intake of alcohol prevents coronary heart disease by as much as fifty percent."

• Studies published by Klurfield and Kritchevsky in the *Journal of Experimental and Molecular Pathology* (1990) indicate that rabbits administered red or white wine had sixty percent (red) and thirty-three percent (white) less arteriosclerosis than the control group. Those fed ethanol or whiskey had twenty-five percent and seventeen percent less respectively; those fed beer were similar to the control group.

• Studies headed by Dr. Eric Rimm (Harvard University School of Public Health) and published in *Lancet* (August 1991) found that male physicians who drank, on average, one drink (or slightly less) per day had twenty-one percent fewer instances of coronary artery disease than abstainers. Those that consumed slightly more than one drink per day reduced their risk by thirty-two percent, and those who consumed up to three drinks per day reduced their risk by twenty-seven percent. While coronary artery disease was also reduced by even higher levels of consumption, heavier drinking may increase the risk of other diseases.

• Dr. Arthur Klatsky of Kaiser Permanente Medical Center in Oakland, California, addressed a criticism regarding the control groups used in some older studies. He published a paper in the *American Journal of Cardiology* (October 1986) that corrects for these factors and still supports the view that alcohol protects against coronary artery disease.

• Dr. A. S. St. Leger of the British Medical Research Council's Epidemiology Unit looked at ischemic heart disease deaths in eighteen developed countries to determine what factors were associated with the deaths. His paper appears in a 1979 issue of *Lancet*. He found strong positive correlation between smoking, total fat intake, total calorie intake and ischemic heart disease. The most surprising finding was a

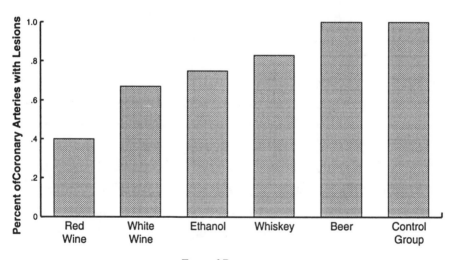

Incidence of Arteriosclerosis in Test Rabbits

Incidence of coronary lesions in test rabbits fed various alcohol-containing beverages. Data from Klurfeld, et al., Journal of Experimental and Molecular Pathology, *and adapted from Perdue, et al.,* The French Paradox and Beyond.

strong negative correlation between alcohol consumption and heart attack deaths. In other words, those who used alcohol had the least heart problems. In his study group, this was attributed primarily to wine consumption.

• Dr. Arthur Klatsky, Dr. Gary D. Friedman, and Mary Ann Armstrong published a paper in the November 15, 1990 issue of the *American Journal of Cardiology*. It says moderate consumers of wine, compared to abstainers, have a fifty percent lower risk of dying of heart attack and a twenty percent lower risk of dying of all causes.

• A research team led by Dr. M. Seigneur reported in the *Journal of Applied Cardiology* (May 1990) that consumption of red Bordeaux wine— but not white wine or ethanol—induced platelet hypoaggregation as well as an increase in HDL ("good") cholesterol levels. These platelets and HDL levels have cardioprotective properties in humans.

• Dr. J. Michael Gaziano (Brigham and Women's Hospital, Boston, MA) reported in the *New England Journal of Medicine* (1993) that moderate wine consumption increases HDL cholesterol levels.

• Dr. Robert Langer reported in the March 1992 issue of *Circulation* that "the explanation for the residual fifty percent benefit attributable to alcohol is unknown but may include interference with thrombosis."

• Dr. Y. H. Kimura and associates have shown that a chemical called resveratrol induced platelet hypoaggregation in rat cells. Dr. H. Arichi and associates also found that this chemical reduced lipid (fat) deposition in rats' livers. (Several published scientific findings from 1982-1985.)

• In 1991, Drs. Evan Siemann and Leroy Creasy extracted resveratrol from several types of red and white wines. They found this chemical in higher quantities in red Bordeaux and Zinfandel than in white wines, though some Chardonnay did contain fairly high amounts. (Published in the February 1992 issue of the *American Journal of Enology and Viticulture*.)

• Drs. E. Frankel, A. Waterhouse, and J. Kinsella (University of California-Davis) recently found that antioxidants (quercetin, catechin, and resveratrol) from red wine were effective inhibitors of LDL ("bad") cholesterol oxidation. Oxidized LDL is believed to cause clogged arteries. The wine components were even more effective than vitamin E in stopping LDL oxidation.

• David Fitzpatrick, Ph.D., a researcher at the University of South Florida at Tampa, has found that substances found in grape skins relaxes blood vessels. This would presumably improve blood flow to the heart. The study is published in the *American Journal of Physiology* (1993).

To quickly summarize these findings: Moderate consumption of alcohol appears to reduce the risk of heart disease, and wine appears to be more effective than other alcohol sources in this regard. In addition, several antioxidants have been isolated from wine that can (1) prevent blood clot formation in arteries, (2) increase the good HDL cholesterol level in the bloodstream, and (3) decrease the bad LDL cholesterol level in the bloodstream.

Every year, about 500,000 people die from heart attacks caused by coronary artery disease. It appears that this number could be reduced significantly by moderate consumption of wine, particularly red wines containing the beneficial antioxidant chemicals. Many doctors perceive the truth of these findings, and now practice moderate wine consumption themselves—which tells us they believe in wine's benefits.[2]

Wine Consumption and Cancer

Undoubtedly, you have heard conflicting reports about the relationship between alcohol consumption and cancer. Much of the con-

---

[2] To find out what they are cellaring and drinking, see the *Wine Spectator*, March 14, 1994, pp. 46-47.

troversy stems from a 1987 report by the International Agency for Research on Cancer (IARC), a branch of the World Health Organization (WHO), which said, "The consumption of alcoholic beverages is causally related to the occurrence of cancers of the oral cavity, pharynx, larynx, esophagus and liver which tend to be rare." They indicated no increased risk for any other types of cancers. Many doctors do not agree with their conclusions.

• Dr. Emanuel Rubin, professor and chairman of the Department of Pathology and Cell Biology at Jefferson Medical College and adjunct professor at the University of Pennsylvania Medical school says, "A review of the evidence relied upon by the IARC working group reveals that the putative causal relationship between alcohol and cancer is based upon inconsistent and limited epidemiological evidence, that animal studies fail to support a causal link, and that no satisfactory explanation for a possible causal relationship has been elucidated. The animal studies have failed to support a conclusion that alcohol is carcinogenic at any level."

• Dr. Parviz Pour, professor at the University of Nebraska's Epply Institute for Research in Cancer, says, "I have concluded that alcohol cannot be considered a carcinogen or co-carcinogen of the esophagus nor can it be regarded as a promoter of esophageal carcinogenesis."

• Dr. Michael Anderson, Senior Research Fellow, Cancer Research Campaign (Britain), says, "Many of the IARC studies were poorly designed or reported."

• Paul Levy, Sc.D., professor and director of the Epidemiology and Biometry Programs at the University of Illinois School of Public Health, says, "The IARC's conclusions were based on flawed methodology."

• Marvin Goldman, Ph.D., professor of Toxicology at the University of California-Davis, says, "The overwhelming and consistent trend in the laboratory experiments is that alcohol is not a carcinogen."

• John Doull, M.D., Ph.D., professor and director of the Center of Environmental and Occupational Health at the University of Kansas Medical Center, says, "Experimental studies do not provide a basis for the conclusion other than there is, at this time, no demonstration of the carcinogenicity of alcohol."

Another cancer issue which hits the press from time to time is a possible link between alcohol consumption and breast cancer. Dr. Keith Marton of the California Pacific Medical Center and University of California-San Francisco Medical School initially reviewed twenty-three major studies on this topic and more recently reviewed several more. Twelve of the studies indicated there was some positive correlation between breast cancer and moderate alcohol consumption. The majority of the more recent studies indicate little or no risk at a consumption level of two or fewer drinks per day. No clear conclusion can be drawn from these studies; in the worst case scenario, wine consumption increases a woman's chance of dying from breast cancer by about four percent.

Quercetin, a chemical found in wine, onions, garlic, and several other vegetables, has been shown to block the human oncogene H-RAS (cancer gene) that converts normal cells into cancerous ones. Dr. Terance Leighton, professor of Biochemistry at the University of California-Berkeley said, "Quercetin is a powerful anti-cancer compound."

Researchers at Cornell University discovered a positive effect of wine which they had not expected. In experiments designed to assess the effects of the chemical ethyl carbamate on cancer in mice, they administered the chemical to the mice in water, in plain alcohol, and in red or white wine. Mice that received ethyl carbamate in water or alcohol had higher levels of cancer than the controls. Mice receiving the chemical in white wine had lower levels of cancer than the controls, and mice that received it in red wine had the lowest cancer levels in the experiment. Other preliminary studies also indicate that both red and white wine may reduce the incidence of cancer in test animals. It is known

185

that wine contains one strong anticancer chemical that is released into its active form during the fermentation process.

We've personally not seen data which specifically separates effects of wine and those of other forms of alcohol on humans. Most medical people feel the current evidence shows no increase in cancer from moderate wine consumption, though few would question the need for more studies.

Wine Consumption and Fetal Alcohol Syndrome

Fetal Alcohol Syndrome (FAS) can develop whenever a fetus is exposed to abusive amounts of alcohol *in utero*. The key here is *abusive amounts*. The symptoms are varied and tragic, one of the worst being mental retardation. Still, the rate of occurrence of FAS has been exaggerated and distorted by anti-alcohol groups so that many women have concluded that it is unsafe to drink any amount of alcohol during the entire term of pregnancy.

This topic has been summarized recently in a straightforward manner by Dr. Wells Shoemaker, a pediatrician. The facts of this matter, according to Dr. Shoemaker, are as follows: "There have been no cases of 'full blown' FAS in children whose mothers consumed moderate amounts of alcohol. The problem does occur with ingestion histories that range from two to three six-packs of beer or the better part of a fifth of distilled spirits a day. There have been no cases reported in which wine was the source of ethanol." Interestingly, pediatricians in Mediterranean countries do not see an increase in the number of FAS children, even though wine consumption there is many times higher than in the United States, and pregnant women routinely take wine with their meals.

Fetal Alcohol Effect (FEA) is a term to describe the behavioral problems of alcohol-injured children who do not have the physical appearance of FAS. Numerous studies have investigated the possible effects of moderate alcohol intake on FEA. Dr. Keith Marton reviewed these studies and found no indication that moderate consumption had a harmful effect on birth weights. Similar conclusions were drawn about possible effects on the children's intelligence. In the September 1991 issue of the *British Journal of Addiction*, Dr. Genevieve Knupfer wrote, "An examination of the research literature on the results of drinking during pregnancy does not provide any evidence that light drinking is harmful to the fetus." Scottish research physicians Forrest and Florey published a paper in the *British Medical Journal* (July 1991) that verified the alcohol consumption of 846 pregnant women and followed 592 of their newborns through eighteen months of age. They found no increase in alcohol injury indicators until consumption reached twelve drinks per week and concluded, "Pregnant women probably need not abstain from alcohol altogether as no detectable adverse relation was found between the child's mental and physical development and the mother's weekly consumption at levels less than one hundred grams absolute alcohol." To allow an adequate safety margin, they recommended that pregnant women not drink more than one drink per day.

Dr. Shoemaker points out that the greatest risk from a fetal toxin is in the first trimester of pregnancy. He feels there is no danger to the fetus from the occasional glass of wine at mealtime, but also urges potential mothers with drinking problems to get professional help immediately.

The anti-alcohol group spearheaded the effort that resulted in "danger to pregnant women" warnings on all alcoholic beverages. Folks in the wine industry are angry about this warning that fails to distinguish between alcohol use and alcohol abuse. In light of recent evidence that moderate wine drinking may actually have other health benefits, this reaction is understandable.

Alcohol Consumption and Cirrhosis of the Liver

In cirrhosis of the liver, healthy cells are replaced by fibrous scar tissue that cannot perform the necessary chemical functions. When too much scar tissue forms, the liver fails and death is the result. In the United States, the death rate from cirrhosis is about 17 per 100,000 (compared to 464 per 100,000 for cardiovascular disease). France, which has almost twice the per capita consumption of alcohol as the United States, has a death rate from cirrhosis of 31 per 100,000 (and 310 per 100,000 for cardiovascular disease). Naturally, anti-alcohol forces jumped on these statistics, claiming that all alcohol consumption causes cirrhosis.

Let's take a closer look at France. It turns out that the areas of France having the highest wine consumption (and lower consumption of beer and spirits) also have the lowest cirrhosis rates (7 to 14 per 100,000). Areas where beer and spirits are heavily consumed (especially Alsace and Lorraine) have the highest cirrhosis rates (50 to 100 per 100,000).

Most doctors agree that alcohol abuse—but not moderate use—contributes to the development of cirrhosis. It appears that alcohol abuse plus other factors that often go along with it can be involved. Dr. David Zakim, Distinguished Professor of Medicine at Cornell University Medical School, says, "Neither malnutrition nor ethanol ingestion causes serious liver disease, yet abuse of ethanol plus malnutrition produces liver disease in some patients." Once again, the problem of excessive alcohol use becomes apparent. Certainly it must be avoided.

It is natural to focus on the liver when discussing the effects of alcohol because this organ has an important role in the degradation of alcohol. The liver contains the enzyme alcohol dehydrogenase, as does the lining of the stomach. This enzyme becomes saturated (reaches its maximum efficiency) when the blood alcohol level reaches .046. This means if you continue to consume alcohol beyond this point, you will outstrip your liver's metabolic capacity, and your blood alcohol level will continue to increase.

Many doctors feel that wine consumption provides a more favorable situation; when wine is consumed with meals, as it frequently is, its alcohol enters the blood stream gradually. Furthermore, even when spirits are diluted and beer is spiked to approximate the alcohol content of wine, the alcohol in wine is still absorbed more slowly. In any event, there is certainly no evidence to suggest that moderate wine consumption will lead to cirrhosis or other health problems. Just the opposite is true: a great deal of evidence suggests that wine may provide important health benefits.

Wine Consumption and Aging

As we all grow older, we hope to be like a nice bottle of red wine that ages gracefully. Does this mean we will have to abstain from alcohol? The average life span is now pushing seventy-two years for men and seventy-nine years for women. We live longer these days, but does that mean we live better? A study conducted by Dr. Jack M. Guralnik of the U.S. National Institute on Aging and George A. Kaplan of the California Department of Health Services that ran in the June 1989 *American Journal of Public Health* offers good and bad news. We won't bore you with many of the details, but the one finding that may interest you concludes that individuals who drank alcohol moderately were 3.1 times more likely to age successfully than abstainers and 2.5 times more likely to age more successfully than heavy drinkers. (It's no surprise that cigarette smokers were 6.1 times more likely to be dead or low-functional.)

You might also be interested to know over half of the hospitals in the top sixty-five metropolitan areas of the United States are now offering wine service to patients (with doctor approval, of course).

Wine, Sulfites, and Health

Many foods naturally contain low concentrations of sulfites, and sulfite-containing chemicals may sometimes be added to foods as preservatives. The chemical most commonly added is bisulfite, which converts to sulfur dioxide upon contact with the acids in food. Almost all commercially produced wines have added bisulfite, because vintners do not want to risk spoilage.

Sulfites do not pose any problem for the vast majority of people. A small percentage of the population suffer allergic reactions to them, however. These people may also be asthmatics; about five percent of the sulfite-sensitive group are. People who have this sensitivity must follow their doctor's advice regarding consumption of foods or wines containing sulfites. Producers of these products are required to issue a warning on their label to protect those who have this problem.

Lead, Wine, and Health

The issue of lead in wine hit the newspapers back in 1991. Like so many other spectacular stories, it had its little fling and then everyone seemed to return to reality. Along the way, the Food and Drug Administration (FDA) decided to establish a limit of 150 parts per billion (ppb) for lead residues in wine. To our knowledge, all domestic and imported wines sampled were well below this standard. How does lead get in wine? Very small quantities appear there naturally, and some additional amounts may get in because the capsules used on the necks of wine bottles previously were manufactured from a lead foil material. This practice has now been discontinued. A few years back there was additional clamor about lead from expensive lead crystal glassware. Supposedly, if you let wine sit in this glassware for several days you can pick up a few more parts per billion.

Here's what Dr. Curtis Klaasen, professor of Pharmacology and Toxicology at the Kansas Medical School (and an expert on heavy metals poisoning), said: "Lead levels in wine are irrelevant from a health standpoint." Dr. John Osterloh from the University of California-San Francisco Medical School said, "If you drink enough wine for lead to be a problem, you've got one hell of an alcohol abuse problem."

Wine and Chubbiness

This is one topic where I[3] don't have to rely on medical doctors. As songwriter and vocalist Paul Simon sings, "How come I'm so soft in the middle now, when the rest of my life is so hard?" What we're getting to here is wine and calories. After age forty, it becomes a con-

---

[3] Alias Bubba.

stant battle of diet and exercise to keep some semblance of slimness. The bad news, folks, is that wine contains a fair amount of calories. The caloric content varies with the sugar and alcohol content of the wine. Alcohol packs a lot of calories per gram, about a third more than carbohydrates and protein, and only a quarter less than fat. Two four-ounce glasses of wine provide about two hundred calories. There are some "light" versions of wines on the market that have seven to eight percent alcohol and a lower sugar content.[4] But if you want to continue enjoying the health benefits from moderate wine consumption and don't want to "blimp out," you'd do well to start modifying your food intake (especially fats) and increasing your exercise regimen.

The Bottom Line

After reviewing the allegations against wine, frankly, the worst we can say about it is it does contain a lot of calories. As far as the other allegations are concerned, we find no validity in any of them. We believe moderate consumption of wine is good for us; being the health conscious people we are, we wouldn't drink it otherwise.[5] On the other hand, we're aware of the tragedy that goes with alcohol abuse and strongly support efforts to reduce this problem in our society. We believe the secret to good health and longevity is to eat healthy diets including lots of fresh fruits and vegetables, cut down on saturated fats, get regular exercise, participate in frequent sexual activity, and drink moderate amounts of good wine in the presence of fun-loving people.[6]

Suggested Reading

Coats, D. "Moderate Drinking and Coronary Heart Disease Mortality: Evidence from NHANES I and the NHANES." *American Journal of Public Health* 83 (1993): 888-90.

---

[4] Luigi says they lack "gusto."

[5] Ha!

[6] Not necessarily in the order presented.

Cohen, S., et al. "Smoking, Alcohol Consumption, and Susceptibility of the Common Cold." *American Journal of Public Health* 83 (1993): 1277-82.

Fitzpatrick, D. "Endothelium-Dependent Vaso-relaxing Activity of Wine and Other Grape Products." *American Journal of Physiology* 265 (1993): 774-8.

Frankel, E., et al. "Inhibition of Human LDL Oxidation by Resveratrol." *The Lancet* 341 (1993): 1103-4.

Frankel, E., et al. "Inhibition of Oxidation of Human Low-Density Lipoprotein by Phenolic Substances in Red Wine." *The Lancet* 341 (1993): 454-7.

Friedman, G. D., and A. L. Klatsky. "Is Alcohol Good for Your Health?" *The New England Journal of Medicine* 329(1993): 1883-5.

Gaziano, J. M., et al. "Moderate Alcohol Intake, Increased Levels of High-Density Lipoprotein and Its Subfractions, and Decreased Risk of Mycardial Infarction." *The New England Journal of Medicine* 329(1993): 1829-34.

Klatsky, A. "Correlates of Alcohol Beverage Preference: Traits of Persons Who Choose Wine, Liquor or Beer." *British Journal Addiction* 85 (1990): 1279-89

Klatsky, A., and M. Armstrong. "Alcoholic Beverage Choice and Risk of Coronary Artery Disease Mortality. Do Red Wine Drinkers Fare Best?" *American Journal of Cardiology* 71 (1993):467-9.

Matthews, T. "Wine: Prescription for Good Health." *Wine Spectator* (March 1994): 37-44.

Peele, S. "The Conflict Between Public Health Goals and the Temperance Mentality." *American Journal of Public Health* 83 (1993):805-10.

Perdue, L., et al. *The French Paradox and Beyond.* Sonoma, Calif.: Renaissance Publishing, 1992. 273 pp.

Renaud, S., and M. De Lorgeril. "Wine, Alcohol, Platelets and the French Paradox for Coronary Heart Disease." *The Lancet* 339 (1992): 1523-6.

Rodgers, H., et al. "Alcohol and Stroke. A Case-Control Study of Drinking Habits Past and Present." *Stroke* 24 (1993): 1473-7.

Rosenberg, L., et al. "Alcohol Consumption and Risk of Breast Cancer: A Review of the Epidemiologic Evidence." *Epidemiologic Reviews* 16 (1993): 133-44.

Siemann, E., and L. Creasy. "Concentration of the Phytoalexin Resveratrol in Wine." *American Journal of Enology and Viticulture* 43 (1992): 49-52.

St. Leger, A. "Factors Associated with Cardiac Mortality in Developed Countries with Particular Reference to the Consumption of Wine." *The Lancet* 1 (1993): 1017-20.

Chapter 13
Wine and Food—and Music

This chapter came close to straining our marriage! The chubby half (Bubba) kept saying, "I need you to write this part be cause you know a lot more about food and cooking than I do." I didn't care to do it because I've never really envisioned any clear-cut rules about what food to serve with what wine. But Bubba persisted, "You know how confused people get when they go to a restaurant and try to match the proper wine with their food." He convinced me when he complained, "Do you remember how ticked off the Boldts were at our dinner party when we played Eric Clapton's *Unplugged* and it clashed with that great bottle of **Ravenswood** Zinfandel?" It became clear that we needed to make the ultimate marriage of food, wine, and music, or risk jeopardizing all the friendships we've nurtured over the years.

All the great wine and gourmet publications have missed one of the obvious reasons food and wine might or might not meld: the synergistic influence of music that creates a holistic experience far exceeding the sum of its parts. Imagine how horrid it would be to put together a wholly antagonistic combination of wine, food and music. Truly a hostess's nightmare, and as Luigi says, "Sounds like the makings of a pretty shitty evening, too."

Because individual tastes differ, it is impossible to make infallible statements[1] about wine and food matches. Wine neophytes seem to be particularly afraid of making the Big Mistake: bringing or serving the

---

[1] Only the Pope is good at that stuff.

wrong wine to dinner parties. Whenever people discover we are knowledgeable about wine, their most frequent questions inevitably relate to what wine is best to serve with what food. They assume there is a "politically correct"[2] aspect to it. Although we go so far as to suggest music to drink by, there's no real "right" or "wrong" when matching food, wine, and song.

We can give you some tips, though. Many people have expounded about wine and food matches. Joe Heitz (**Heitz Cellars**) said it best, "It's drinking what you like with what you like to eat." Frankly, we are less concerned about perfect matches than we are clashes. Experience tells us foods with spiced sauces (e.g., hot Mexican dishes) can completely overpower a wine, and that some salad dressings with high acids (e.g., vinegar) can crush a wine's delicate flavors. The taste components of food can drastically change your impression of a wine. If you want to check this out for yourself, experiment with a bottle of dry or off-dry white wine. Take a sip of the wine by itself, then follow with a saltine cracker and another sip. In turn, try a slice of apple, then a sip; a few peanuts, then a sip; a bite of dill pickle, then a sip; a tostada chip dipped in some hot salsa, then a sip, and so forth. This simple experiment will demonstrate how foods influence wine. A wine that may have been pleasant by itself or with the neutral cracker progressively changes from perhaps slightly better with the apple to decidedly worse with the overpowering peanuts, pickle, and salsa. Conversely, a big, tannic red wine might completely blow away a lovely fettucini nestled in cream sauce, but form a perfect marriage with its cousin, a meaty, mushroom-tomato[3]-onion-garlic-laden linguini. The important point to remember is this is a two way street; food can annihilate the wine, or the wine can annihilate the food. And even worse, we argue, clashing music can annihilate both.

One of the better habits Europeans practice and which many Ameri-

---

[2] A philosophy implying it's worse to verbally insult someone than to murder one's parents or whack off a spouse's pee-pee. Whatever happened to the good old days when verbal abuse was okay?

[3] Notice the spelling, Dan.

cans neglect is making dinner a social event that might last several hours. A European's evening meal involves several courses of food and a few different wine selections. Most importantly, it includes good, relaxed conversation, and often depends on the proper music playing quietly in the background. Such dinners help to build strong relationships. We Americans tend to eat and run, taking little time to savor anything but covering lots of territory in pursuit of more money or fame. If the members of our society spent more time sitting at the table together, savoring a good bottle of wine or two, and thoroughly chewing their food (as well as the "fat"), we think there would be fewer conflicts! Hell, if we'd spend a little time listening to what kids have to say at dinner, they might even quit taking guns to school.

The same quality time can be relished with good old friends or interesting new ones. Some of our most enjoyable entertainment consists of sitting at the table with special friends and several bottles of delicious wine, discussing every major world event—or just running off at the mouth about trivial subjects.

Do We Match Wine with Food or Vice Versa?

If you're a beginning or intermediate wine drinker you'll probably decide on the food first, then try to select a wine to complement it. As you gain more experience with wine, you may find that wine becomes the focus. You may want to share certain special bottles with fun-loving friends, so the decision-making involves what food to serve with these special wines. Sometimes when we go to a restaurant, we are purposely looking for a wine we may have read about, and we build our food order around that particular wine. We consider ourselves decadent (but always deserving) when we spend more on our wine than on our food.[4]

More often, you'll probably want to find good wine matches for a particular entrée, either at home or at a restaurant. And here we raise the specter of an ugly problem. It is virtually impossible to perfectly match

[4] Easier done than said.

one bottle of wine with every component of a meal. For example, the wine may nicely complement the steak, but not the vegetable dish, salad, or dessert. If there are just two of you, and you are only interested in one glass or one bottle, it's probably better to drink the wine when the main course is served. If you're not having some other cocktail before dinner, you might want to try a nice aperitif wine (by the glass) that will carry you through the soup or salad course. And if you're really eager to experiment, order all your wine by the glass: one as an aperitif, one for the main course, and finally, one for the dessert.

But how does the music component fit in? Well, the problem of music and wine matching is perfectly analogous to that of food and wine matching. When you put on an album (compact disc or cassette for anyone born in the modern era), a variety of songs will play. Do not expect each song to perfectly match the wine, any more than each course of a meal will. And for God's sake don't try to do what Luigi did. You guessed it! He attempted to drink a different wine for each song on a CD and passed out before it finished playing!

There are a few simple rules to remember about matching music and wine. For the most part, instrumental music sounds better with white or blush wines, while vocals have the depth required to accompany a big red wine. Sweet wines suggest sweet music, robust wines require raucous music, and naturally, delicate wines dictate delicate music. Tempo seems to be more important than the category of music (pop, classical, country, etc.).

Traditional Rules and Myths

One of the oldest axioms we've heard regarding wine and food is "white with fish or poultry and red with red meat." You can't go terribly wrong with this approach; the problem is, if you adhere to this rule you are going to miss some great matches. For example, one of the finest wines to enjoy with grilled salmon or swordfish is Pinot Noir, a red wine. With a big Thanksgiving turkey and all the fixin's its damn hard to beat a nice robust Zinfandel, another red wine. So much for the white with fish and poultry rule! Although the latter part of the rule, "red with red meats," is a pretty good policy, the choice of red will depend on whether your meat is simply grilled or smothered in a sauce. Red meats which tend to be high in protein and fat are a good match with tannic red wines, because they soften the tannin, allowing the best characters of both food and wine to be expressed. In general, strongly flavored foods need a robust wine with enough power to stand up to them.

Acidity and sweetness should always be considered when matching food and wine. In this case you want to match rather than contrast. If you're serving a salad with an acidic dressing (containing vinegar, lemon juice, etc.) your wine will need to be fairly high in acid so it is not overpowered by the dressing. Many of the white wines fall in this category. Similarly, if your entrée contains a sweet sauce, don't serve a bone dry wine. Rather, look to something in the *demi-sec* category. And if its dessert time, your wine choice should probably carry even more residual sugar.

It's really tough to find a wine that is not overpowered by strongly spiced foods, particularly those flavored with chilies or other hot peppers. The only wine we've found that stands up moderately well to hotly spiced oriental dishes is Gewürztraminer. Perhaps that is because it has a spicy character itself. Many Mexican dishes have overpowered the wines we've tried with them.[5] Other than a few strong mustards, pickles, and relishes, these are the only foods that have given us difficulty with wine matches.

Pasta dishes present an interesting array of wine opportunities because they can be served in a myriad of sauces. The simple dishes containing only a little butter and garlic might nicely accompany a dry Riesling or Chenin Blanc. Pasta dishes with a flavorful, creamy sauce and seafood might make a perfect marriage with a buttery Chardonnay (the glycerol content of the Chardonnay will probably tie the knot). On the other hand, pastas with sturdy meat sauces require robust red wines like Barbera, Chianti Classico, or Syrah.

---

[5] Even Luigi prefers a Margarita or a Corona beer and lime with south-of-the-border fare.

What about some of the myths? We've heard that no wine will go well with salty foods. Wrong! Try a nice sparkling Brut Champagne, even with an anchovy. Some say no wine goes with eggs. It depends on how they are prepared, but serve a little fruit along side, open a bottle of fresh, fruity white wine (Chenin Blanc or Riesling) or even a Champagne, and you'll be doing all right. No wine goes well with citrus fruit—another myth. Find a wine with some citrus overtones, such as Seyval Blanc or Vignoles made in a dry style. No problem!

What about chocolate? Some claim no wine goes well with it. Wrong again! We've had wedges of fudge accompanied by a nice, fruity, but high-alcohol late-harvest Zinfandel—a beautiful match. Even a sip of Whidbey's isn't too shabby with chocolate desserts,[6] especially if they also contain a little fruit.

Others have claimed no wine goes well with artichokes or asparagus. Hey, watch out—you're messin' with two of our favorite vegetables here! The naysayers probably put heavy sauce on these veggies to disguise their taste. Go light instead. Artichokes with a little lemon butter and a nice fresh Sauvignon Blanc? Perfecto! One time in a motel room in Ukiah, California, we steamed freshly picked asparagus in our electric coffee pot, added a little Molly McButter seasoning and found the spears went nicely with a **Parducci** Gewürztraminer and a **Kenwood** Chenin Blanc. A perfect match, and we didn't even have music! Seriously, folks, be skeptical about most of these myths.

Since this is a beginning wine book and only one chapter is devoted to this subject, don't expect a detailed list of gourmet recipes here. You can find good recipes in a variety of other places including food and wine magazines and cookbooks. In the interest of brevity we've compiled a table of good food, wine, and music combinations. This will get you started; later on, you can let your imagination run wild. We did as we wrote this chapter! In addition to our own preferences, we've drawn upon a few ideas presented by The Wine Institute as well as

---

[6] Come to think of it, **Whidbey's Ltd.** makes a chocolate confection containing a bit of Whidbey's liqueur inside.

Barbara Ensrud and Hugh Johnson in some of their recent books. Our personal favorites in each category are marked with an asterisk (*). The second table is a chart that categorizes wine types and offers a few suitable food matches for each style of wine.

GOOD COMBINATIONS OF FOOD, WINE & MUSIC

FOOD	WINE	MUSIC
NONE	*White:* Aurore, Cayuga, Chablis, Chenin Blanc, Fumé Blanc, Gewürztraminer*, Müller-Thurgau, Pinot Bianco, Riesling (Kabinett, halbtrocken), Sémillon, or Seyval, Vidal and Vignoles* (in *demi-sec* style)	Mark O'Connor - *The New Nashville Cats,* Golden Strings - *Greatest Hits I,* Bonnie Raitt - *Nick of Time*,* The Seekers - *The Very Best of The Seekers,* Jackie Wilson - *Higher and Higher*
	Blush: Pinot Noir Blanc, Rosé of Cabernet*, White Grenache, White Zinfandel	Fiedler/Boston Pops -*Concert in the Park,* Buckwheat Zydeco - *Menagerie**
	Light-Bodied Reds: Beaujolais-Villages, Gamay Beaujolais, Pinot Noir*	Huey Lewis and the News - *Sports,* Alan Jackson - *Here in the Real World**
LIGHT FARE (hors d'oeuvres, first courses, lunches)		
Artichokes (without vinegar)	Grey Riesling, Sauvignon Blanc*	K.T. Oslin - *K. T. Oslin,** Patty Loveless - *Up Against My Heart*
Asparagus	Gewürztraminer (dry)*, Saint Véran, Sauvignon Blanc	Emmy Lou Harris - *At the Ryman*,* Billy Joel - *Glass Houses*
Caesar Salad	Sauvignon Blanc, Sparkling wines, Vignoles (dry)*	Kenny G - *Breathless*,* Fiedler/Boston Pops - *The Pops Goes West*

Cheese (mild to medium)	Chenin Blanc, Gamay Beaujolais, Gattinara, Merlot, Riesling, Sémillon, Seyval*, Vidal Blanc, Zinfandel	Jimmy Buffet - *Feeding Frenzy*, Bach - *Violin Concerto No. 1*, Roy Orbison - *Hits You Remember**
Cheese (hearty)	Barbaresco, Cabernet Sauvignon, Merlot*, Pinot Noir, Sauternes, Syrah, Zinfandel	Billy Joel - *River of Dreams*, Sawyer Brown - *Outskirts of Town*, Creedence Clearwater Revival - *Gold**
Chicken Salad	Aurore, Chenin Blanc (dry), Gewürztraminer, Riesling*, Sémillon, Vouvray	Whitney Houston - *Whitney*, David Sanborn - *Up Front*, Lyle Lovett - *Lyle Lovett and His Large Band**
Clam Chowder (and other Bisque)	Chardonnay, Pinot Gris*, Riesling (*Spätlese*), fino Sherry	Neil Young - *Old Ways*, Guy Clark - *Boats to Build**, Lorrie Morgan - *Watch Me*
Fruit (fresh)	Aurore, Blush, Cayuga, Chenin Blanc, Riesling, Sémillon, Seyval Blanc, Vidal Blanc* (all in *demi-sec* style)	Vince Gill - *Pocket Full of Gold*, Paul Simon - *Rhythm of the Saints* *, George Gershwin - *The Best of George Gershwin*
Guacamole	Chardonnay, Sangria*	Freddy Fender - *The F.F. Collection*, Jimmy Buffet - *Changes in Attitude**
Meats (cold cuts, spiced)	Barbera*, Cabernet Sauvignon, Chianti Classico, Zinfandel	Guy Clark - *Old Friends*, Garth Brooks - *In Pieces**
Melon	Grey Riesling*, Madeira, Muscat, Port, Sherry	Natalie Cole - *Take a Look**, Delbert McClinton - *Delbert McClinton*, Cher - *Love Hurts*
Pasta Salads	Beaujolais, Chianti, Pinot Grigio*, Sauvignon Blanc	Luciano Pavarotti - *Greatest Hits**, Billie Holiday - *The Silver Collection*, Lionel Hampton - *Just Jazz*
Pâté (liver)	Gamay Beaujolais, Gewütztraminer, Pomerol, Seyval Blanc*, Vouvray	Engelbert Humperdink - *Greatest Hits*, Tchaikovsky - *The Best of Tchaikovsky : 1840-1893**

Pizza	Barbera, Chianti, Rioja, Syrah, Zinfandel*	Sha Na Na - *Anthology I*, Bruce Springsteen - *Born in the USA**, John Anderson - *Solid Ground*
Quiche	Côtes du Rhône, Fleurie, Riesling (dry)*, Sémillon, Sparkling Wine	Elton John - *Rare Masters**, Beethoven - *Symphonies No. 6 and 8*
Salmon (smoked)	Blush (dry), Chardonnay, Pinot Gris, Pinot Noir*, Sauvignon Blanc	Abba - *Gold (Greatest Hits)**, Smokey Robinson - Motown *25th*
Shrimp Cocktail	Chenin Blanc, Pinot Blanc, Sauvignon Blanc*, Sparkling Wine	Paula Abdul - *Spellbound*, Mariah Carey - *Music Box*, Neil Diamond - *Up on the Roof**
Soup (excluding Bisque)	Beaujolais, Chenin Blanc, Fumé Blanc, Dry White Blends*	Restless Heart - *Fast Movin' Train*, Juice Newton - *Greatest Hits**, John Denver - *Greatest Hits*
Spinach Salad	Blush, Gamay Beaujolais, Sparkling Wine, Zinfandel (light-bodied)*	Debbie Gibson - *Body and Mind*, James Taylor - *Live**
Trout (smoked)	Chardonnay, Pinot Blanc, Pinot Gris*, Sauvignon Blanc	Traveling Wilburys - *Vol. I**, Jim Croce - *His Greatest Hits*
Tuna Salad	Chenin Blanc (dry), Blush (dry), Marsanne*, Pinot Gris, White Blends	K.T. Oslin - *Love in a Small Town**, Johnny Cash - *Original Golden Hits, Vol.II*

ENTRÉES - FISH

Abalone	Blush (dry), Pinot Gris, Riesling (dry)*	Wynton Marsalis - *Hot House Flowers*, Strauss - *The Best of Johann Strauss 1825-1899**
Bass (freshwater) (grilled or fried)	Chablis, Chardonnay, Pinot Blanco, Seyval Blanc (dry)*, Soave	Hal Ketchum - *Past the Point of Rescue**, Simon and Garfunkel - *Concert in the Park*

Bass (striped) (baked or poached)	Burgundy (white)*, Chardonnay	Eric Clapton - *Unplugged*, Vangelis - *Chariots of Fire*
Bluefish	Beaujolais-Villages*, Chablis, Sauvignon Blanc	Fiedler/Boston Pops - *Familiar Music for Family Fun*, Michael Martin Murphy - *River of Time*
Clams (fried)	Chardonnay, Gamay Beaujolais, Pinot Noir*, Sauvignon Blanc, Sparkling Wine	Bob Seger - *Against the Wind*, Earth, Wind, and Fire - *Millenium*, Van Halen - *Fair Warning*
Clams (steamed)	Chardonnay, Pinot Blanc, Pinot Gris*, Sauvignon Blanc, Vignoles (dry)	Sting - *Ten Summoners Tales*, Frank Sinatra - *Duets*, Don Henley - *End of Innocence*
Cod - see Bass (freshwater)		
Crab (cold)	Chenin Blanc, Fumé Blanc, Pouilly Fumé*, Seyval Blanc, Vidal Blanc	Michael Bolton - *Time, Love, and Tenderness*, Julio Iglesias - *1100 Bel Air Place*
Crab (steamed or in a sauce)	Chardonnay, Vignoles (dry), Viognier*	Barbra Streisand - *Back to Broadway*, The Judds - *River of Time*
Fish and Chips	Bordeaux (white), Chablis, Riesling (dry), Sauvignon Blanc, Seyval Blanc*, Vidal Blanc	Marty Brown - *Wild Kentucky Skies*, Randy Travis - *Heroes and Friends*, UB 40 - *Promises/Lies*
Haddock - see Bass (striped)		
Halibut (grilled)	Chardonnay, Riesling (*Spätlese, Auslese*), Sémillon-Chardonnay Blends, Vignoles*	Michael Bolton - *The One Thing*, The Isley Brothers - *Tracks of Life*, Vern Gosdin - *Greatest Hits*
Lobster (with drawn butter)	Burgundy (white), Chardonnay*, Sparkling Wine, Vignoles (dry)	Leon Redbone - *On the Track*, Alan Jackson - *Don't Rock the Jukebox*, Neil Diamond - *Up on the Roof*
Mahi Mahi (Dolphin) - see Bluefish		

Chapter 13

Mussels	Chardonnay, Pinot Blanc*, Pinot Grigio, Sauvignon Blanc, Sparkling Wine	Bryan Adams - *So Far So Good*, Moody Blues - *A Night at Red Rocks**
Oysters (on the half-shell)	Chardonnay, Fumé Blanc, Sparkling Wine, Vignoles*	Buddy Holly & The Crickets - *Golden Greats**, Fiedler/Boston Pops - *The Pops Goes West*

Oysters (fried) - see Clams (fried)

Red Snapper - see Bass (striped)

Salmon (broiled or grilled)	Beaujolais-Villages, Chardonnay, Pinot Noir*, Sauvignon Blanc, Sparkling Wine	Earl Thomas Conley - *The Heart of It All*, The Righteous Brothers - *Greatest Hits**
Scallops (sauteed or in sauce)	Chablis, Chardonnay*, Chenin Blanc, Montrachet, Sauvignon Blanc, Vignoles, Viognier	Marty Brown - *High and Dry*, Mozart - *The Life, Times & Music Series 1756-1791**

Scallops (fried) - see Clams (fried)

Shrimp (in garlic butter)	Chardonnay*, Sauvignon Blanc, Sparkling Wine, Vignoles	Bobby McFerrin - *Simple Pleasures*, Bach - *Brandenburg Concerto No. 2**
Shrimp (breaded & fried)	Blended Whites*, Chablis, Pinot Blanc, Sauvignon Blanc	Roger Whittaker - *Love Will Be Our Home*, Mark Chestnut - *Too Cold at Home**

Swordfish (grilled) - see Salmon (broiled or grilled)

Trout (grilled or fried)	Chenin Blanc, Riesling*, Pinot Blanc, Pinot Gris, Seyval Blanc	Aaron Tippin - *Read Between the Lines*, Common Thread - *Songs of the Eagles**

Tuna (grilled) - see Salmon (broiled or grilled)

ENTRÉES - POULTRY

Chicken (barbecued)	Blush, Gamay Beaujolais, Gewürztraminer, Riesling*, Zinfandel (light-bodied)	Ray Charles - *Anthology*, Tina Turner - *Simply the Best*, Jim Stafford -*Jim Stafford*
Chicken (in cream sauce)	Burgundy (white), Chardonnay, Côtes du Rhône, Vignoles Viognier*	Little Richard - *20 Greatest Hits*, Aaron Neville - *Orchid in the Storm*
Chicken (herbed, roasted)	Côtes du Rhône, Chardonnay, Marsanne, Merlot, Sauvignon Blanc, Vidal Blanc*	Jerry Reed - *The Bird*, The Everly Brothers - *20 Greatest Hits*, Randy Travis - *Old 8 x 10*
Chicken (vegetable stir fry)	Chenin Blanc, Gewürztraminer*, Riesling, Tocai	Martin Del Ray - *Get Rhythm*, Billy Joel - *Glass Houses*
Duck	Burgundy (red), Gewürztraminer (dry), Pinot Noir*, Riesling (*Spätlese*)	Hall & Oates - *Greatest Hits Rock'n Soul Part I,* London Philharmonic - *Tchaikovsky Spectaculars*
Gamebirds (grouse, pheasants, quail)	Burgundy (red), Cabernet Sauvignon, Hermitage, Pinot Noir*, Petite Sirah	Merle Haggard - *Kern River*, Doug Kershaw - *Alive and Pickin*

Goose - see Duck

Turkey (roasted, with gravy & dressing)	Blush (dry), Gamay Beaujolais, Pinot Noir, Sparkling Wine, Zinfandel*	Leon Redbone - *Champagne Charlie*, Nitty Gritty Dirt Band - *Will the Circle Be Unbroken II*

ENTRÉES - PINK AND RED MEATS

Beef (roast)	Barbaresco, Barolo, Bordeaux, Cabernet Sauvignon (and blends), Merlot, Rioja Riserva, Syrah*	Clint Black - *The Hard Way*, Neil Young - *Harvest Moon*

Beef (steak: broiled or grilled)	Barbera, Barbaresco, Cabernet Sauvignon (and blends), Chancellor, Lemberger, Merlot, Syrah, Zinfandel*	Garth Brooks - *No Fences*, Lyle Lovett - *Joshua Judges Ruth**, Marty Stuart - *Tempted*
Beef (stew)	Barbera, Bordeaux, Petite Sirah*, Syrah, Zinfandel	Highway 101 - *Highway 101*, Travis Tritt - *Country Club**
Beef (vegetable stir fry)	Blush, Gamay Beaujolais*, Zinfandel (light-bodied)	Billy Joel - *Glass Houses**, Neil Diamond - *Hot August Night*
Chili (spicy)	Barbera, Cabernet Sauvignon, Chianti, Petite Sirah*, Zinfandel	Doug Kershaw - *Alive and Pickin'*, Marty Stuart - *Tempted**
Ham (honey baked)	Blush, Gamay Beaujolais, Beaujolais-Villages*, Gewürztraminer, Riesling, Vidal Blanc (*demi-sec*)	Randy Travis - *Heroes and Friends*, Asleep at the Wheel - *Western Standard Time*, Ricky Van Shelton - *Ricky Van Shelton III**
Hamburgers	Beaujolais-Villages, Cabernet Sauvignon (and blends), Lemberger*, Merlot, Pinot Noir, Zinfandel	Traveling Wilburys - *Vol. I**, Pam Tillis - *Homeward Looking Angel*
Hot Dogs	Beaujolais, Blush*, Red or White Blends (including Thunderbird and Mad Dog 20/20)	M.C. Hammer - *Please Don't Hurt 'Em* (or any rap music)
Lamb (chops)	Cabernet Sauvignon* (and blends), Merlot, Pinot Noir, Zinfandel	Johnny Cash - *Gold Hits II*, The Righteous Brothers - *Greatest Hits**
Lamb (roast)	Bordeaux*, Cabernet Sauvignon, Merlot, Rioja Riserva	Harry Chapin - *Greatest Stories - Live**, Clint Black - *The Hard Way*

Liver (and various other innards)	Beaujolais, Pinot Noir, Merlot*, Zinfandel	Bryan Adams - *So Far So Good,* Gladys Knight & The Pips - *Gladys Knight & The Pips**
Meatloaf	Barbera*, Lemberger, Merlot, Pinot Noir, Red Blends, Zinfandel	Patsy Cline - *12 Greatest Hits,* Meatloaf - *Bat Out of Hell, II**
Pork (barbecued ribs)	Gamay Beaujolais, Red Blends, Syrah*, Zinfandel (light-bodied)	Keith Whitley - *I Wonder Do You Think of Me,* Aretha Franklin - *What You See Is What You Sweat**
Pork (herbed, roasted)	Beaujolais, Chardonnay, Pinot Noir*, Riesling, Sparkling Wine, Zinfandel	Strauss - *The Best of Johann Strauss 1825-1899,* Eartha Kitt - *The Fabulous Eartha Kitt**
Pork (sweet and sour)	Blush, Chenin Blanc, Gewürztraminer*, Riesling, Sparkling Wine	Ray Charles - *Anthology*,* Johnny Clegg & Savuka - *Cruel Crazy Beautiful World,*
Rabbit	Chianti, Lemberger Merlot, Zinfandel (light-bodied)*	James Taylor - *Live*,* Eddie Rabbit - *Jersey Boy*
Sausage (Italian)	Barbera, Chianti Classico*, Petite Syrah, Rubesco, Zinfandel (big)	Frank Sinatra - *Duets,* Tony Bennett - *Tony Bennett**
Veal (chops or Marsala)	Bordeaux, Cabernet Sauvignon*, Chancellor, Chianti Classico, Pinot Noir, Zinfandel	Randy Travis - *Wind in the Wire,* Vince Gill - *When I Call Your Name**
Venison (antelope, deer, elk)	Barolo, Bordeaux, Cabernet Sauvignon, Petite Sirah*	Tina Turner - *Simply the Best*,* Van Halen - *Fair Warning,* Creedence Clearwater Revival - *More Creedence Gold*

Chapter 13

ENTRÉES - MISCELLANEOUS

Chinese food (richly sauced)	Gewürztraminer, Petite Sirah, Tocai, Tokay d' Alsace, Zinfandel*	Adrian Legg - *Wine, Women & Waltz**, Joshua Kadison - *Painted Desert Serenade*
Chinese food (spicy)	Gewürztraminer*, Rosé (off-dry)	Bob Dylan - *30th Annual Concert Celebration**, The Temptations - *Greatest Hits*
Eggplant (stuffed or parmesan)	Barbera*, Chianti, Syrah	Luciano Pavarotti - *Greatest Hits**, Barbra Streisand - *Back to Broadway*
Japanese food	Light dry whites like Chenin Blanc* or Mâcon, Sake	Harry Chapin - *Greatest Stories - Live*, Tina Turner - *Simply the Best**
Mexican food (mild)	Beaujolais, Rioja Blanco, Sangria*	Gloria Estefan - *Into the Light*, Julio Iglesias - *1100 Bel Air Place**
Pasta (with cream sauce)	Chardonnay*, Gamay Beaujolais, Orvieto, Pinot Blanc, Sauvignon Blanc, Sparkling Wine	Wynton Marsalis - *Hot House Flowers*, Moody Blues - *A Night at Red Rocks**
Pasta (with pesto sauce)	Barbera, Pinot Grigio*, Sauvignon Blanc, Blended dry Whites	Michael Bolton - *Timeless (The Classics)**, Bob Seger - *Against the Wind*
Pasta (with tomato and meat sauce)	Barbera, Cabernet Sauvignon and blends, Lemberger, Merlot, Petite Sirah*, Zinfandel	Martina McBride - *The Way That I Am**, John Mellencamp - *Human Wheel*
Peppers (sweet, stuffed)	Chianti Classico, Lemberger, Petite Sirah, Syrah*, Zinfandel	Juice Newton - *Greatest Hits*, Buddy Holly & The Crickets - *20 Golden Greats**
Thai food (Lightly spiced)	Beaujolais-*Nouveau*, Chenin Blanc, Gewürztraminer*, Pinot Bianco, Riesling	Traveling Wilburys - *Vol. I*, Vince Gill - *When I Call Your Name**

208

| Vegetarian dishes | Chablis, Chenin Blanc*, Seyval Blanc, Vidal Blanc, Blushes or light reds with bean dishes | Emmy Lou Harris - *Cowgirl's Prayer*, Righteous Brothers - *Greatest Hits* |

DESSERTS

None	A glass of almost any sweet wine makes a fine dessert by itself.	Leon Redbone - *Sugar*, Paul Simon - *Rhythm of the Saints*
Apples (with cheese)	Vignoles (late harvest)*, Vintage Port	Jimi Hendrix - *Kiss the Sky*, Kenny G - *Breathless**
Apple pie or strudel	Riesling (*Auslese** or *Beerenauslese*)	Neil Young - *Old Ways*, James Taylor - *Live*
Berries (fresh)	Muscat, Riesling (*demi-sec*)*, Vidal or Vignoles (late harvest), Berry Wine	Emmy Lou Harris - *At the Ryman**, Vince Gill - *When I Call Your Name*
Cake (excluding chocolate)	Bual or Malmsey Madeira, Oloroso or Cream Sherry, Sweet Muscat*, Zinfandel (late harvest)	Michael Martin Murphy - *River of Time** Strauss - *The Best of Johann Strauss 1825-1899*, Hank Williams, Jr. - *Born to Boogie*
Cake (chocolate)	Bual Madeira, Port, Zinfandel (late harvest)*	Fiedler/Boston Pops - *Concert in the Park*, Lyle Lovett - *Pontiac**
Cheesecake	Vignoles* (late harvest), Vouvray (sweet)	Abba - *Gold (Greatest Hits)**, Aaron Neville - *Orchid in the Storm*

Custard (vanilla) - see Cake (excluding chocolate)

| Fruit (fresh) | Gewürztraminer, Muscat, Riesling, Vidal Blanc*, Vignoles | Billie Holiday - *The Silver Collection**, Simon and Garfunkel - *Concert in the Park* |

Chapter 13

Fruit (dried)	Madeira*, Port, Sherry, Zinfandel (late harvest), Fruit Wines	George Gershwin - *The Best of George Gershwin*, Kathy Mattea - *Willow in the Wind*
Fruit (cooked)	*Beerenauslese*, Muscat*	Natalie Cole - *Take a Look*, David Sanborn - *Upfront*
Fruit (with cream)	Sauternes, *Trockenbeerenauslese*	Mariah Carey - *Music Box*, Elton John - *Rare Masters*
Ice Cream	Sweet Fruit Wines, Whidbey's Liquer*	Cher - *Love Hurts*, Marty Stuart - *Tempted*
Melon (with blue cheese)	Grey Riesling*, Vidal Blanc	Frank Sinatra - *Duets* Holly Dunn - *Milestones*

Mousse (chocolate) - see Cake (chocolate)

Nuts	Bual Madeira, Oloroso Sherry, Vintage or Tawny Port*	Berlin Philharmonic - *Beethoven Symphonies Nos. 6 and 8*, Bach - *Brandenburg Concerto No. 2*
Pears (with blue cheese)	*Auslese*, Sauternes, Vignoles (late harvest)*	Debbie Gibson - *Body and Mind*, Smokey Robinson - *Motown 25th*

Pudding (chocolate) - see Cake (chocolate)

Strawberry Shortcake	Fruit Wines, Vouvray (sweet)*	Elvis - *The King of Rock 'n Roll*, Johnny Cash - *Golden Hits II*, Bonnie Raitt - *Nick of Time*

THE "QUICKIE" TABLE OF WINE STYLES AND FOOD MATCHES

WHITE WINE STYLE	FOOD MATCHES
Dry, Light-Bodied: Aurore, Chardonnay, Côtes du Rhône Blanc, Frascati, Mâcon-Villages, Muscadet, Orvieto, Pinot Bianco, Riesling (*Kabinett*), Rioja Blanco, Seyval Blanc, Soave, Trebbiano, Vidal Blanc, Vouvray (sec)	Mild cheeses, Mild fish dishes, Lighter poultry dishes, Lighter pasta dishes, Vegetarian dishes
Dry, Medium-Bodied: Aligoté, Fumé Blanc, Gavi, Graves, Marsanne, Pinot Blanc, Pinot Grigio, Pinot Gris, Pouilly-Fuissé, Pouilly-Fumé, Riesling (Alsace), Saint-Véran, Sancerre, Seyval Blanc, Tokay d' Alsace	Fish and shellfish without heavy sauces, Lighter meat dishes, Pâté, Medium pasta dishes
Dry, Full-Bodied, and Complex: Chablis (French), Chardonnay, Gewürztraminer (Alsace), Hermitage Blanc, Meursault, Montrachet, Vignoles, Viognier	Fish, poultry, shellfish, or veal in rich sauces, Sausages
Demi-Sec: Aurore, Chablis (California), Chenin Blanc, French Columbard, Gewürztraminer, Grey Riesling, Riesling, Seyval Blanc, Vidal Blanc, Vouvray, and an array of Blended Wines	Alone as an aperitif, Fruit, Mild cheeses, Oriental dishes, Poultry and other light meats
Sweet: Asti Spumante, Barsac, Eiswein, Gewürztraminer (late harvest), Moscato, Muscat Canelli, Riesling (*Spätlese, Auslese, Beerenauslese, Trockenbeerenauslese*), Sauternes, Vignoles (late harvest), Vin Santo, Vouvray (doux)	By themselves or with fruit, nuts, fruit pies, or other desserts

211

Chapter 13

BLUSH OR ROSÉ WINE STYLE	FOOD MATCHES
Dry: Bandol Rosé, Castel del Monte, Côtes de Provence Rosé, Dechaunac Rosé, Foch Rosé, Rosé of Pinot Noir, Sancerre Rosé, Tavel	Almost all foods except red meat dishes that are heavily seasoned
Lightly Sweet: Cabernet d'Anjoi, Rosé of Cabernet, Foch Rosé, White Grenache, White Zinfandel	Many lunches and hors d'oeuvres including lighter cheeses, cold meats, pasta salads, baked ham, etc.

RED WINE STYLE

Light, Fruity: Bardolino, Beaujolais, Brouilly, Chambourcin, Chinon, Côtes de Beaune-Villages, Côtes du Rhône, Dolcetto D'Albia, Foch, Gamay, Gamay Beaujolais, Lambrusco, Napa Gamay, Pinot Noir, Saint-Amour, Sancerre Rouge, Valpolicella	Lighter cheeses, Pasta, Lighter meat dishes, Pizza, Some fish dishes
Full-Bodied, Rich: Barbera, Barbaresco, Bordeaux, Cabernet Sauvignon, Chancellor, Lemberger, Merlot, Pommard, Syrah (Shiraz), Taurasi, Volnat, Zinfandel	Wild fowl, Medium cheeses, Beef roast and steaks, Lamb, Pork, Meatloaf
Full-Bodied, Robust: Amarone, Barolo, Brunello di Montalcino, Charbono, Châteauneuf-du-Pape, Côte Rotie, Gigondas, Hermitage, Mourvèdre, Petite Sirah, Syrah (Shiraz), Zinfandel	Strong cheeses, Meat stews, Beef steaks, Venison steaks
Sweet, Dessert: Berry & Fruit Wines Commanderia, Madeira, Marsala, Muscat, Port, Sherry, Zinfandel (late harvest)	Dried fruits, Cake, Cheesecake, Just by themselves

The suggested wine and food matches are only general guidelines for you to follow; try experimenting with other combinations. By the way, if you haven't figured it out by now, we were really just kidding about the music, although atmosphere is always important!

Does Your Restaurant Have a Wine List?

As we travel throughout the United States, we are amazed by the number of restaurants paying little attention to wine service. Many offer only a limited selection of house wines (red, white, or pink) on the lower end of the quality scale. When in a new area, we always hope to find a restaurant that provides at least a basic, even minimal, wine list from which we can choose a match for our evening meal. The list does not have to include hundreds or thousands of wine selections like the famous big city restaurants. Rather, we wine lovers would be satisfied with a list of about twenty wines of medium to good quality. We'd be particularly excited to see a few of the local wines listed, because we're always eager to learn about new wines.

Restaurants buy wholesale, and we patrons pay restaurant prices that are roughly two times retail. Since it is not uncommon for restaurants to make sixty to seventy percent profit on wine sales, these sales obviously can have a favorable impact on the restaurant's "bottom line."

Here are some guidelines for putting together a restaurant wine list. After a few month's trial, selections that people routinely request can be added and those that just don't seem to sell can be eliminated. Specific selections can be made from the lists in Chapter 14. Try to provide wines in the $12 to $20 range.

Suggested Reading

Ensrud, B. *Wine With Food.* New York: Fireside/Simon & Schuster, 1991. 256 pp.

Johnson, H. *Pocket Encyclopedia of Wine.* New York: Fireside/Simon & Schuster, 1993. 208 pp.

A BASIC RESTAURANT WINE LIST

WHITE WINES (10)		ORIGIN
Dry (5)	Chardonnay (2)	One California or Australia, One local.
	Sauvignon Blanc (1) (Fumé Blanc)	California, Chile, or local.
	Imported Dry (1)	Vouvray, Pinot Grigio, Pinot Blanc, Orvieto, etc.
	Blended Dry (1)	Local.
Off-Dry (4)	Sparkling Wine (1)	Imported or domestic.
	Gewürztraminer (1)	California or local.
	Johannisberg Riesling (1)	Local.
	Any one of these (1)	Chenin Blanc, German *Kabinett*, or a local blended white.
Semi-Sweet (1)	Any one of these (1)	German blend, German *Spätlese*, or a local favorite.

ROSÉ WINES (2)		
	White Zinfandel (1)	California.
	Rosé or blush (1)	Local.

RED WINES (10)		
Light-bodied (2)	Beaujolais or Beaujolais-Villages (1)	France or local.
	Pinot Noir (1)	Local.
Medium-bodied (4)	Chianti Classico (1)	Italy.
	Syrah or Shiraz (1)	California or Australia.
	Merlot (1)	California, Chile, or Pacific Northwest.
	Varietal or blend (1)	Local.
Robust (4)	Bordeaux (1)	France.
	Cabernet Sauvignon (1)	California or local.
	Zinfandel (1)	California.
	Varietal or blend (1)	Local.

Chapter 14
Best Wine Values and Best Wine Shops

L isting every good wine buy and all the best places to buy wine is a formidable task; as Luigi says, "It's also a damn hard thing to do." As much as we've traveled and read, there are undoubtedly many wine values we're not aware of. And surely there are some neat wine shops we haven't had the opportunity to visit. In preparing this chapter we've drawn upon our own tasting experiences and two other sources with which we frequently agree, namely, the *Wine Spectator* and a recent book by Barbara Ensrud (see Suggested Reading). We've also tried to provide a good mix of domestic and imported wines.

There is one catch to our best wine values listing. Since considerable time may elapse between the writing and actual publication of this book, and since many of these wines may have received good publicity through other publications, some of the wines may be sold out before you learn about them. As Pete, another of our good friends, said, "Time passed and night fell and the good cheap wine was all gone." Do not despair! Many of the wineries on this list consistently produce good values. Remember, we are not talking about the greatest wines here, just very good wines at reasonable prices. Another tip worthy of mention: you might stand a better chance of finding these best-value wines on the dusty shelves of small wine shops off the beaten track than at wineries or wine shops connoisseurs visit weekly. Wineries often sell out of particular items within a month of receiving Best Buy ratings in national magazines. If you have a good wine dealer nearby, he/she can probably order case lots of these items shortly after the ratings come out. After that, many of these wines will be hard to come by. The fact of the matter is, magazines like the *Wine Spectator* and *The Wine Advocate* are very effective wine sellers.

What criteria have we chosen for the selection of our best wine values? First, the wines must be priced at $10 or less per 750 ml bottle. It is difficult to find high-quality dessert and sparkling wines for under $10, so we have altered the price guideline for these and offer our suggestions in Chapters 7 and 8. Second, the wines we have chosen must have either impressed us or have been strongly recommended by trusted sources. In no way do we mean to suggest that this is a complete list of bargain wines. We hope that you will be fortunate enough to find many others on your own.

What makes a great wine shop? Again, our list isn't all-inclusive, and we must rely on our own experience and reports from our scouts. We prefer stores with large selections of domestic and imported wines and lots of sale items. Some sale items may actually be "loss leaders" that bring no profit for the store but attract shoppers who may buy other items, too. Another important characteristic of a good wine shop is a knowledgeable, unintimidating staff who can and will provide good service. They should always be willing to order selections that may not be in stock. We were once in a Melbourne, Florida, wine shop with our friend Paul, searching for a recent vintage Zinfandel we were specifically interested in. We didn't mind that they didn't stock it, but we stormed out after the smartass clerk told us, "all red wine gets much better with age." We've been trying to decide if the guy was just ignorant or if he often used that line to get rid of old Beaujolais that should have been drunk two years ago.

Some states allow in-store tastings, and they are a great way to familiarize yourself with particular wines. Some of the best wine shops offer these events periodically. Some shops also provide newsletters or sell magazines, books, and other educational materials about wine. Other shops may have developed arrangements to directly import certain bargain wines, providing customers with a steady flow of good quality everyday drinking selections.

Is it more economical to buy directly from the winery? Sometimes, but usually not. Wineries occasionally offer sales such as mixed-case specials, but often you will find their premium wines more reasonably priced at discount wine shops. Wineries offer discounts of ten to twenty-five percent on case quantities, but so do many wine shops. Don't be afraid to ask for case discounts, wherever you are. In our view, wineries primarily offer the opportunity to gain overall knowledge and sample items not widely distributed; they aren't the best places to find bargains.

You do have to be a bit careful about wines that are marked down as sale specials. Granted, some of these may be exceptional buys, especially if they haven't moved at the regular price and the retailer is making an honest attempt to move them before they lose their quality. On the other hand, beware of old (and undoubtedly tired) versions of wines that should normally be drunk young (e.g., Chenin Blanc, Gewürztraminer, Beaujolais, Rosé). As a general rule, we'd be suspicious of anything offered for less than $3 per 750 ml. The few exceptions are some wines from eastern Europe, which may be okay, and some jug wines in larger-volume containers.

Our best value wines are listed by variety or category, then by price range, then alphabetically by winery. Some popular varietals like Cabernet Sauvignon and Chardonnay are produced by hundreds of wineries, so we've narrowed the selection to a reasonable number and marked our own personal favorites within a group with an asterisk (*). Because individual tastes vary, these will not necessarily be your favorites. And remember, there are a lot of great wines out there for slightly more than $10 per bottle, and sometimes they go on sale!

BEST WINE VALUES - VARIETALS

BARBERA - $8 to $9
Dessilani Barbera 1990 (Italy) $8
Michele Chiarlo Barbera d'Asti 1990 (Italy) $9
*Monteviña Barbera 1991 (CA) $9
Prunotto Barbera d'Alba Fiulot 1992 (Italy) $8

CABERNET FRANC - $7 to $10
Konocti Cabernet Franc 1989 (CA) $9.50
Madroña Eldorado 1989 (CA) $9.50
*Parducci Cabernet Franc 1989 (CA) $7.75
Sebastiani Sonoma County 1989 (CA) $10
Shooting Star Clear Lake 1991 (CA) $9

CABERNET SAUVIGNON - $3.50 to $6.50
Alameda Maipo Valley 1988 (Chile) $5.50
*Bandiera Napa Valley 1989 and 1990 (CA) $6.50
*Bel Arbors 1990 Founder's Selection (CA) $6.50
Bodegas San Telmo Mendoza Cuesta del Madera 1987 (Argentina) $4.50
Caliterra Maipo 1989 (Chile) $6
Carmen Maipo Valley Alto Jahuel 1990 (Chile) $6
Cedar Creek S. E. Australia Bin 99 1990 $6
Cook's California Captain's Reserve 1988 $5.50
Côtes De Sonoma Sonoma County 1990 (CA) $6.50
Glen Ellen California Proprietor's Reserve 1989 $6.50
La Playa Maipo Valley 1988 (Chile) $5
Los Catadores Lontue Seleccion Especial 1986 (Chile) $5
Maison Du Lac Maipo Valley 1989 (Chile) $5
Monterey Vineyard Monterey County Classic 1989 and 1990 (CA) $6
*Napa Ridge Cabernet Sauvignon California 1989 $5.50

Oak Bluffs   Colchagua 1990 (Chile) $6
Portal Del Alto   Maipo Valley 1987 (Chile) $3.50
*Round Hill   Cabernet Sauvignon California 1989 $6
San Jose De Santiago   Colchagua Valley 1990 (Chile) $5
Santa Rita   Maipo Valley 120 1988 (Chile) $6
Sebastiani   Country Cabernet Sauvignon NV (CA) $7/1.5L
Stony Hollow   San Fernando 1988 (CA) $6
Valle De San Fernando   San Fernando Gran Reserva 1986 and
   1988 (Chile) $5
Villa Montes   Curico Villa Montes 1989 (Chile) $6

CABERNET SAUVIGNON - $7 to $10
Arrowwood   Domaine Du Grand Archer Sonoma County 1991
   (CA) $8.25
Black Opal   Cabernet Merlot S.E. Australia 1990 $9
Bon Marche   Sonoma County 1991 (CA) $7
Canyon Road (Geyser Peak)   California 1991 $7
Castoro   Paso Robles 1989 (CA) $9.50
Chestnut Hill   California Coastal Cuvée 1990 $8
Columbia Crest   Columbia Valley 1988 (WA) $9
Corbett Canyon   Alexander Valley Reserve 1989 and 1990 (CA)
   $8.50 and $9
Creston   Paso Robles 1989 (CA) $10
Errazuriz   Aconcagua Valley Don Maximiano Estate Reserva 1991
   (Chile) $9
Estancia   Alexander Valley 1990 and 1991 (CA) $9
Fetzer   California Valley Oaks 1990 $8
Finca Flichman   Mendoza Proprietors Private Reserve 1988
   (Argentina) $7
Glass Mountain Quarry (Markham)   California 1990 $9
*Hardy's   S. Australia Bird Series 1988 $8
*Hedges   Cabernet-Merlot 1990, 1991, and 1992 (WA) $9 to
   $9.50

J. Lohr   California Cypress 1990 $7.75
Jekel   Arroyo Seco 1990 (CA) $10
Koala Ridge   Barossa Valley 1988 and 1990 (Australia) $10 and $9
Laurel Glen   Sonoma County and Napa Valley Terra Rosa 1989 and 1990 (CA) $9
Lava Cap   El Dorado 1989 (CA) $10
Liberty School   California Vintner Select Series Three 1990 $7.50
Los Vascos   Colchagua 1990 and 1991 (Chile) $7 and $9
Miguel Torres   Curico District 1989 and 1990 (Chile) $7
Montes   Curico 1988 (Chile) $8
Phillippe-Lorraine   Napa Valley 1989 (CA) $10
Raimat   Costers del Segre 1989 (Spain) $8
Santa Rita   Maipo Valley Reserva 1990 (Chile) $9
Santa Rita   Maipo Valley Cabernet Sauvignon 120 1989 (Chile) $7
*St. Francis   Sonoma County 1989, 1990 and 1991 (CA) $10
Ste. Chappelle   Washington 1988 (ID) $10
Stevenot   Calaveras County Reserve 1990 (CA) $10
Stevenot   California 1991 $8
Sunnycliff   Coonawarra 1990 (Australia) $7
Tyrell's   S. E. Australia Old Winery 1986 $9
Villa Mt. Eden   California Cellar Select 1988 $8
*Wildhurst   Clear Lake 1990 (CA) $10
Wolf Blass   S. Australia Yellow Label 1988 and 1990 $10
Yalumba   Cabernet-Shiraz S.E. Austalia Oxford Landing 1989 $7

CHARDONNAY - $5.50 to $8
Bandiera   Napa Valley 1991 (CA) $6.50
Barrier Reef   S. E. Australia 1992 $7
Barton & Guester   Macon St. Louis 1991 (France) $8
Bel Arbors   Founder's Selection 1992 (CA) $6.75
Caliterra   Curico 1991 and 1992 (Chile) $6
Canyon Road   California 1992 $7

*Columbia   Columbia Valley Woodburne Cuvée 1991 (WA) $8

Columbia Crest   Columbia Valley 1991 and 1992 (WA) $8

Côtes De Sonoma   Sonoma County 1992 (CA) $7.50

Estancia   Monterey County 1992 (CA) $8

Fetzer   California Sundial 1992 $8

Fortaut   Vin de Pays d'Oc 1992 (France) $7

Georges DuBoeuf   Vin de Pays d'Oc 1992 (France) $6.50

Glen Ellen   California Proprietors Reserve 1990 and 1991 $6.50

Hardy's   S. Australia Nottage Hill 1991 $8

Hardy's   E. Australia Bird Series 1991 $7.50

Labouré-Roi   Bourgogne Blanc Chardonnay 1991 (France) $7.50

La Crosse   Napa Valley 1991 (CA) $6

*Lindemans   S. E. Australia Bin 65 1991, 1992, and 1993 $7

Marion   Sonoma County 1991 (CA) $7

Monterey Vineyard   Classic Chardonnay Monterey County 1992
   (CA) $6

*Napa Ridge   Central Coast 1992 and 1993 (CA) $5.50 and $7

Normans   S. Australia Chandlers Hill 1991 $7

Orlando   S. E. Australia Jacob's Creek 1991 $7

Oxford Landing   S.E. Australia 1992 $7

QC Fly   California 1991 $8

Raymond   California Selection 1991 $8

Saltram   S. E. Australia Classic 1991 $7

Santa Rita   Maipo Valley 120 1991 (Chile) $7

Seppelt   S. E. Australia Reserve Bin 1991 $8

Seghesio   Sonoma County 1992 (CA) $9

Wente Brothers   Central Coast Estate Grown 1991 (CA) $8

Wyndham Estate   S. E. Australia Oak Cask 1992 $8

Yalumba   S. E. Australia Oxford Landing 1991 $7

CHARDONNAY - $8.50 to $10

Belvedere   Alexander Valley 1991 (CA) $8.50

Brutocao   Mendocino 1991 (CA) $10

Black Opal S. E. Australia 1991 $9

Cambria Katharine's Vineyard 1990 and 1992 (CA) $10

Castoro San Luis Obispo County 1991 (CA) $10

Chateau de Baun Russian River Valley 1992 (CA) $10

Chateau Potelle Napa Valley 1991 (CA) $9.50

Château St. Jean Sonoma County 1991 (CA) $10

***Covey Run** Yakima Valley 1991 (WA) $10

Estancia Monterey County 1991 (CA) $9

Estate William Baccala Sonoma County 1991 (CA) $9

Fetzer Barrel Select Mendocino County Organically Grown Grapes 1991 (CA) $9

J. Fritz Sonoma County 1991 (CA) $9.50

Geyser Peak Sonoma County 1991 (CA) $9

Hogue Cellars Columbia Valley 1992 (WA) $10

Latah Creek Washington 1991 $10

Lawrence J. Bargetto Central Coast Cypress 1991 (CA) $9

Meridian Santa Barbara County 1991 and 1992 (CA) $9.75 and $10

Roo's Leap Coonawarra Barrel Fermented 1991 (Australia) $10

Rosemount S. E. Australia 1991 $9.50

Rothbury Hunter Valley 1991 (Australia) $9.50

St. Andrew's Winery Napa Valley 1991 (CA) $10

***St. Francis** Sonoma County 1991 (CA) $10

***Taft Street** Sonoma County 1992 (CA) $8.50

Ventana Monterey Gold Stripe Collection 1991 (CA) $10

Vina Del Mar Lontue Reserve 1991 (Chile) $9

Waterbrook Columbia Valley 1992 (WA) $9

Wente Bros Central Coast Estate Grown 1992 (CA) $9

CHENIN BLANC - $4.75 to $7.50

Beringer Napa Valley 1992 (CA) $6.25

Chappellet Napa Valley Dry 1991 (CA) $7.50

Chateau Ste. Michelle Columbia Valley 1992 (WA) $4.75

*Covey Run   Yakima Valley 1992 (WA) \$5.25
Hogue   Columbia Valley Dry 1992 (WA) \$5.25
Hogue   Washington State 1992 \$5.25
*Kenwood   California 1991 \$6
*Parducci   Chenin Blanc 1992 (CA) \$6
Ste. Chappelle   Dry Chenin Blanc 1992 (ID) \$5.50
Sutter Home   California 1991 \$5.85

GEWÜRZTRAMINER - \$6.00 to \$9.00
   *Adler Fels   Sonoma County 1992 (CA) \$8
   Bouchaine   Russian River Valley Dry 1991 (CA) \$8.50
   Columbia Crest   Columbia Valley 1991 (WA) \$6.50
   DeLoach   Russian River Valley Early Harvest 1992 (CA) \$8.50
   Fetzer   California 1992 and 1993 \$6
   Firestone   Santa Ynez Valley 1991 (CA) \$8.50
   Firestone   California 1992 \$9
   Great Western   Finger Lakes 1992 (NY) \$6.50
   Hillebrand Estates   Niagara Peninsula 1992 (Canada) \$8
   Hoodsport   Washington 1992 \$8.50
   Hop Kiln   Russian River Valley M. Griffin Vineyards 1992 (CA)
      \$7.50
   Lawrence J. Bargetto   Monterey County 1992 (CA) \$8
   Louis M. Martini   Russian River Valley 1992 (CA) \$7.50
   *Madroña   El Dorado 1992 (CA) \$7
   Mill Creek   Dry Creek Valley 1992 (CA) \$7
   *Navarro   Gewürztraminer Anderson Valley Cuvée Traditional 1991
      and 1992 (CA) \$8.50 and \$9.50
   Parducci   Mendocino County 1991 (CA) \$6.50
   *Rochioli   Sonoma County 1991 (CA) \$8.50
   *St. Francis   Sonoma County 1991 (CA) \$7.50

MERLOT - \$4.50 to \$7
   Bel Arbors   California 1990 \$6.50

Canepa   Maipo Valley 1990 (Chile) $6
Dunnewood   California Barrel Select 1990 $6
*Glen Ellen   California Proprietors Reserve 1991 $6.50
La Playa   Maipo Valley 1990 (Chile) $6
Les Jamelles   Merlot Vin de Pays d'Oc 1991 (France) $7
Monterey Vineyard   Monterey County Classic 1989 (CA) $6
Paul Masson   California Vintners Selection 1989 $4.50/1.5 L
*Roundhill   California 1990 $7
San Pedro   Merlot Lontue 1989 (Chile) $7
Santa Rita   Maipo Valley 120 1989 (Chile) $6
Vina Del Mar   Merlot Lontue 1990 (Chile) $6
Walnut Crest   Merlot Rapel 1989 and 1990 (Chile) $4.50 and $5

MERLOT - $8 to $10
*Arbor Crest   Columbia Valley 1991 (WA) $10
Bogle   California 1991 $9
Bonverre (St. Supery)   California Famille Lot No. 8 NV $8
Cecchetti Sebastiani   Sonoma County 1989 (CA) $10
Chateau Julien   Monterey County 1989 (CA) $9
Chateau Souverain   Alexander Valley 1989 and 1990 (CA) $10
Chateau Souverain   Sonoma County 1990 (CA) $10
*Columbia Crest   Columbia Valley 1990 and 1991 (WA) $10
Concha y Toro   Rapel Marques de Casa Concha Peumo Vineyard
   1989 (Chile) $9.50
Crosswoods   North Fork of Long Island Ressler Vineyards 1987
   (NY) $10
Errazuriz   Maule Valley 1992 (Chile) $8
Hahn   Merlot Monterey 1990 and 1991 (CA) $10
Konocti   Lake County 1989 (CA) $10
J. Lohr   California Cypress 1989 and 1991 $8.50 and $9
Montes   Merlot Curico 1990 (Chile) $8
Ravenswood   North Coast Vintners Blend 1990 and 1991 (CA)
   $9.50 and $10

Santa Carolina Maipo Valley Santa Rosa Vineyard 1991 (Chile) $8
Sebastiani Sonoma County 1989 (CA) $9
Stevenot North Coast Reserve 1989 (CA) $10
***Stoney Ridge** North Coast Limited Release 1991 (CA) $10
Stratford Merlot California 1990 $9.75
Wildhurst Clear Lake 1991 (CA) $8

PETITE SIRAH - $6 to $10
Aberdeen-Angus Sirah Mendoza 1987 (Argentina) $6
***Bogle** Petite Sirah California 1991 (CA) $6.25
Foppiano Sonoma County 1990 (CA) $10
Mirassou Monterey County Family Selection 1990 (CA) $7.50
***Parducci** Petite Sirah 1989 and 1991 (CA) $6 and $7

PINOT BLANC - $7 to $10
Benziger Sonoma County 1991 (CA) $10
Mirassou Pinot Blanc Monterey 1989 and 1991 (CA) $7 and 7.50
***Trimbach** Pinot Blanc Alsace 1990 (France) $8.50

PINOT GRIS (GRIGIO) - $9 to $10
***Argyle** Oregon Dry Reserve 1991 $9.50
Domaine Paul Blanck Tokay Pinot Gris Alsace Graffechen 1991 (France) $9

PINOT NOIR $5.50-$10
Aries Los Carneros 1992 (CA) $10
Bon Marche Sonoma County 1991 (CA) $8
Bouchaine California Q.C. Fly 1991 $8
***Bridgeview** Willamette Valley 1990 and 1991 (OR) $6
Carneros Creek Fleur de Carneros 1991 (CA) $9
Chateau De Baun Sonoma County 1991 (CA) $10
Chateau De Leu Napa Valley 1991 (CA) $9.50

Creston   Paso Robles 1992 (CA) $9.75
Domaine De Clarck   Monterey County Villages (CA) 1992 $10
Fetzer   Barrel Select 1992 (CA) $7.50
Grateful Red   Willamette Valley NV (OR) $10
J. Pedroncelli   Dry Creek Valley 1991 (CA) $8.50
Jaffelin   Bourgogne 1989 (France) $10
*Knudsen-Erath   Dundee Villages NV (OR) $7
Labouré-Roi   Bourgogne Pinot Noir 1991 (France) $7.50
Lupe-Chalet   Bourgogne Pinot Noir Comte de Lupe 1989 (France) $7.50
Mark West   Russian River Valley 1991 (CA) $10
Napa Ridge   North Coast 1991 (CA) $6
Navarro   Anderson Valley Cuvée 90/91 (CA) $9
*Parducci   Mendocino County 1990 and 1992 (CA) $7
Pepperwood Grove   California Cask Lot 2 1992 $5.50
*Saintsbury   Carneros Garnet 1990 and 1992(CA) $10

RIESLING (JOHANNISBERG) - $6 to $7.50
Chateau Ste. Michelle   Johannisberg Riesling Columbia Valley 1992 (WA) $7
Chateau Ste. Michelle   Dry Riesling Columbia Valley 1992 (CA) $7
Deinhard   Riesling QbA 1992 (Germany) $7
*Fetzer   Johannisberg Riesling 1991 and 1992 (CA) $6.50
Latah Creek   Dry Riesling 1991 (WA) $6
Knudsen Erath   Dry Riesling 1990 and White Riesling 1991 (OR) $5
Sichel   Rheingau Bereich Johannisberg Riesling 1991 (Germany) $6.25
*Ste. Chappelle   Johannisberg Riesling Idaho 1992 $6
Woodbury   Dry Riesling New York 1990 $7

RIESLING (JOHANNISBERG) - $8 to $10

*Alexander Valley Vineyards Johannisberg Riesling Alexander Valley 1991 (CA) $8

Alfred Merkelbach Riesling Spätlese Mosel Urziger Wurzgarten 1992 (Germany) $10

Bonny Doon Riesling California Pacific Rim 1991 and 1992 $8

Carl Graff Kabinett Mosel Urziger Wurzgarten 1992 (Germany) $8

*Chateau Grand Traverse Dry Johannisberg Riesling Old Mission Peninsula 1992 (MI)$8.50

Claiborne & Churchill Dry Riesling Central Coast Alsatian Style 1991 (CA) $9.50

Christoffel Urziger Wurzgarten 1991 (Germany) $9

*Dr. Becker Dienheimer Falkenberg Riesling Kabinett 1992 (Germany) $8

Dr. Fischer Ockfener Bockstein Riesling Spätlese 1991 (Germany) $9

*Gainey Santa Ynez Valley 1991 (CA) $8

Hagafen Napa Valley 1991 (CA) $9

Hillebrand Estates Riesling Classic 1991 (Canada) $9.50

Hop Kiln Russian River Valley M. Griffin Vineyards 1992 and 1993 (CA) $8

H. Kerpen Wehlener Sonnenuhr Kabinett 1991 (Germany) $8

Joh. Jos. Christoffel Erben Riesling Spätlese Mosel Urziger Wurzgarten (Germany) $10

Josef Leitz Riesling Kabinett Rheingau Rudesheimer Bischofsberg 1992 (Germany) $9

Karlsmuhle Riesling QbA Saar-Ruwer Lorenzhofer 1992 (Germany) $10

Kendall-Jackson California Vintner's Reserve 1992 $9

Kurt Darting Riesling Spätlese Pfalz Ungsteiner Bettlehaus 1992 (Germany) $9

Meulenhof Erdener Treppchen 1991 (Germany) $8

Schloss Saarstein Riesling QbA Trocken Saar-Ruwer 1992 (Germany) $9

Ste. Chapelle Idaho Winery Hill Vineyard Special Harvest 1992 $9

Van Duzer Dry Riesling Oregon 1990 $8

Von Kesselstatt Graacher Josefshoffer Riesling Kabinett 1991 (Germany) $8.50

Willi Haag Brauneberger Juffer Riesling Kabinett 1991 (Germany) $9

Zeltinger Himmelreich Halbtrocken 1992 (Germany) $8

SAUVIGNON BLANC - $5 to $7

Arbor Crest Columbia Valley Bacchus Vineyard 1992 (WA) $7

Bogle Fumé Blanc Lake County 1992 (CA) $5.75

*Canepa Maipo Valley 1991 and 1992 (Chile) $5

Clos du Bois Alexander Valley Barrel Fermented 1992 (CA) $7

Columbia Crest Columbia Valley 1992 (WA) $7

Corbett Canyon Central Coast Coastal Classic 1992 (CA) $4.50

Cousiño-Macul Maipo 1992 (Chile) $6

Errazuriz Maule Valley Reserva 1991 (Chile) $7

Fetzer Dry Fumé Blanc California 1992 $7

*Geyser Peak Sonoma County 1991 (CA) $6.50

LaPlaya Maipo Valley 1992 (Chile) $5

Miguel Torres Curico District 1991 and 1992 (Chile) $7 and $6

Mirassou California 1991 $5.50

Oxford Landing S. E. Australia 1992 $7

R. H. Phillips California Night Harvest 1991 and 1992 $4/500ml

Robert Mondavi California Woodbridge 1991 $6

Robert Pecota Napa Valley 1992 (CA) $7

Sage Estate Maipo Valley 1992 (Chile) $6

Santa Monica Ranagua 1991 (Chile) $6

Santa Rita Maipo Valley 120 1991 (Chile) $6

Springbok Coastal Region (South Africa) 1992 $6

*Taft Street Sonoma County 1990 and 1991 (CA) $6.50 and $6

Vina Del Mar Fumé Blanc Lontue 1991 (Chile) $6

Wildhurst Clear Lake 1991 (CA) $7.00

SAUVIGNON BLANC - $7.50 to $10

Benziger Fumé Blanc Sonoma County 1992 (CA) $9.50

Bernardus Monterey County 1992 (CA) $8.50

Buena Vista Lake County 1991 and 1992 (CA) $7.50

*Brutocao Mendocino 1991 (CA) $8.50

Byron Santa Barbara County 1992 (CA) $9

Caymus Napa Valley Barrel Fermented 1992 (CA) $10

Chalk Hill Chalk Hill 1991 (CA) $10

Chateau Souverain Alexander Valley 1992 (CA) $7.50

Chateau St. Jean Fumé Blanc Sonoma County 1991 (CA) $8

Chateau Ste Michelle Columbia Valley 1992 (WA) $9

Coopers Creek Marlborough New Zealand 1992 $10

DeLoach Fumé Blanc Sonoma County 1991 (CA) $10

Fieldbrook Mendocino County Quillen Vineyard 1992 (CA) $9

Flora Springs Napa Valley Floréal 1992 (CA) $8

Gary Farrell Russian River Valley Rochioli Vineyard 1992 (CA) $10

Guenoc Guenoc Valley 1991 (CA) $9

Hanna Sonoma County 1992 (CA) $8

*Hogue Cellars Fumé Blanc Columbia Valley 1992 (WA) $8

House of Nobilo Marlborough New Zealand 1990 $10

*J. Fritz Dry Creek Valley 1991 (CA) $7.50

Markham Vineyards Napa Valley 1991 and 1992 (CA) $9

Navarro Mendocino Cuvée 128 1991 (CA) $10

*Preston Dry Creek Valley Cuvée de Fumé Barrel Fermented 1991 (CA) $9.50

Quail Ridge Napa Valley 1991 (CA) $8

*Robert Pepi Napa Valley Two-Heart Canopy 1992 (CA) $9

Rooiberg Sauvignon Blanc Robertson 1991 (S. Africa) $8

Roo's Leap Fumé Blanc Barossa Valley 1991 (Australia) $8

*Santa Rita Maipo Valley Reserva 1991 (Chile) $7.50

Stoneleigh Marlborough 1992 (New Zealand) $9

Stratford California Partner's Reserve 1991 $9.50

Waterbrook Columbia Valley 1991 and 1992 (WA) $9

SÉMILLON - $6 to $9
Arbor Crest Columbia Valley Dionysus Vineyard 1992 (WA) $6.25
Chateau St. Michelle Columbia Valley 1990 (WA) $7
*Columbia Columbia Valley 1992 (WA) $6
*Decoy (Duckhorn) Napa Valley 1990 (CA) $7.25
Hogue Columbia Valley 1990 and 1992 (WA) $7 and $8
*Preston Sémillon 1992 (CA) $9

SEYVAL BLANC - $6.50 to $7.50
Bully Hill Great Tree Seyval Blanc 1991 (NY) $6.50
*Fenn Valley Seyval Blanc 1993 (MI) $6.50
Rivendell Seyval Blanc New York Sarabande Sur Lie 1990 $7.50

SYRAH (SHIRAZ) - $7 to $10
Black Opal Shiraz S.E. Australia 1991 $10
D'Arenberg Shiraz McLaren Vale Old Vine 1989 (Australia) $8
Les Jamelles Vin de Pays d'Oc 1991 (France) $7
McGuigan Brothers Shiraz S. E. Australia Black 1992 $7
McLarens Shiraz S. E. Australia 1991 $8.50
Mitchelton Shiraz Victoria 1991 (Australia) $9
*Rosemount Shiraz S. E. Australia 1990, 1991, and 1992 $9.50
*Ryecroft Shiraz McLaren Vale Flame Tree 1992 (Australia) $8.50

VIDAL BLANC - $6 to $6.50
Boordy Maryland Semi-Dry 1990 (MD) $6
Bully Hill Special Reserve 1991 (NY) $6.50
*Lemon Creek Vidal Blanc-Dry NV (MI) $6

VIGNOLES (RAVAT) - $6.50 to $10
Bully Hill Ravat Blanc 1991 (NY) $6.50
Good Harbor Leelanau Peninsula 1989 (MI) $7.50
*L. Mawby Vignoles 1991 (MI) $10

ZINFANDEL - $5 to $7.50

Bel Arbors   California Founders Selection 1990 $6

Canterbury   Zinfandel California 1990 $5

Chateau Souverain   Dry Creek Valley 1990 (CA) $7.50

Chestnut Hill   San Luis Obispo 1989 (CA) $6

E. & J. Gallo   Northern Sonoma 1987 (CA) $5

*Karly   Amador County Pokerville 1990 (CA) $6

Monteviña   Amador County Brioso 1990 (CA) $7.50

Parducci   Mendocino County 1991 (CA) $6

Robert Mondavi   California Woodbridge 1990 $7

Rosenblum   California Vintners Cuvée IV and VI NV $7 and 7.50.

*Round Hill   Napa Valley 1989 and 1990 (CA) $6

Santa Barbara   Central Coast Beaujour 1991 (CA) $7.50

Sebastiani   Sonoma County 1989 (CA) $7

*Seghesio   Sonoma County 1989 and 1990 (CA) $7.50

Shenandoah   Amador County Classico Varietal Adventure Series 1990 (CA) $6

Stratford   California 1991 $7.75

Sutter Home   California 1991 $5

Vendage   Zinfandel California 1989 $6

Wildhurst   Clear Lake 1990 and 1991 (CA) $7

ZINFANDEL - $8 to $10

Belvedere   Dry Creek Valley 1989 (CA) $9

Beringer   Napa County 1989 (CA) $8.50

Beringer   Napa Valley 1990 (CA) $8.50

*Boeger   El Dorado Walker Vineyard 1990 and 1991 (CA) $10

Buehler   Napa Valley 1992 (CA) $8

Chateau Souverain   Dry Creek Valley 1991 (CA) $8.50

De Moor   Napa Valley 1991 (CA) $10

*Fetzer   California Barrel Select 1989 and 1991 $9

Fitch Mountain   Dry Creek Valley 1989 (CA) $10

Foppiano   Dry Creek Valley 1991 (CA) $10

Franciscan   Napa Valley Oakville Estate 1990 and 1991 (CA) $10
Frey   Mendocino 1990 (CA) $8
J. Fritz   Dry Creek Valley Eighty Year Old Vines 1989 (CA) $10
Guenoc   Zinfandel California 1989 and 1991 $9.50 and 9
*Karly   Amador County 1990 and 1992 (CA) $9.25 and $9.50
Konrad   Mendocino County 1989 and 1990 (CA) $10 and $9
Manzanita Ridge   Alexander Valley 1988 (CA) $8
Marietta   Sonoma County 1988 (CA) $8
Meeker   Dry Creek Valley Gold Leaf Cuvée 1990 (CA) $10
Nevada City   Sierra Foothills 1990 (CA) $8
Rabbit Ridge   Dry Creek Valley 1991 (CA) $10
*Ravenswood   North Coast Vintners Blend 1991 (CA) $7.75
Ridge   Sonoma County 1990 and 1991 (CA) $8.50 and $10
Rosenblum   Contra Costa County 1991 (CA) $9.50
Sobon Estate   Sierra Foothills 1989 (CA) $10
Story   Shenandoah Valley 1991 (CA) $10
Sutter Home   Amador County Reserve 1988 (CA) $10
Villa Mt. Eden   California Cellar Select 1989, 1990, and 1991 $8
White Oak   Sonoma County 1989 and 1991 (CA) $10

BEST WINE VALUES - BLENDED WINES

RED BLENDS - $3.50 to $7[1]
*Antinori   Santa Cristina 1991 (Italy) $7
Barton & Guestier   Côtes du Rhône (France) 1990 $7
Bichot   Côtes de Duras 1989 (France) $6
Bodegas Campo Viejo   Rioja Albor 1990 and 1991 (Spain) $6
Bodegas Jaume Serra Penedés   Tempranillo 1988 (Spain) $6
*Bodegas Martinez Bujanda   Rioja Valdemar Vino Tinto 1991
   (Spain) $7
Bodegas Montecillo   Vina Cumbrero Rioja 1987 (Spain) $6
Bodegas Pedro Rovira   Tarragona Cataloma Reserve 1987 (Spain) $6

---

[1] Several that are widely available in 1.5 liter magnums are also listed in Chapter 6.

Caves Alianca Bairrada Reserva 1990 (Portugal) $6

Château De Blomac Minervois Cuvée Tradition 1988 (France) $6

Château De Fontauche St. Chinian Cuvée Grand Veneur 1990 (France) $7

Chateau De Leu Brunolino North Coast 1991 (CA) $6

Château Guibon Entre-Deux-Mers 1990 (France) $5.50

Coldridge Shiraz-Cabernet Sauvignon S.E. Australia 1992 $6

Domaine De St. Luc Côteaux du Tricastin 1989 (France) $7

Domaine Des Pervenches Côtes du Rhône 1990 (France) $5.50

El Domino Jumilla 1990 (Spain) $7

Finca Flichman Mendoza 1989 (Argentina) $5.50

Gallo Hearty Burgundy NV (CA) $4

Georges Duboeuf Côtes-du-Rhône 1992 (France) $5

*Glen Ellen Proprietor's Reserve Red NV (CA) $3.75

Gran Corpas Tarragone 1988 (Spain) $5.50

Grant Smith LTD. Shiraz-Cabernet Riverina Valley Bin 95 Vintner's Reserve 1990 (Australia) 1990 $7

Hallcrest Clos de Jeannine 1990 (CA) $7

Hardy's Shiraz-Cabernet S.E. Australia Captain's Selection 1991 $6

L. De Valloint Côtes du Rhône St. Vincent 1990 (France) $7

Le Jaja de Jan Vin de Pays des Côtes Catalanes 1991 (France) $7

Les Producteurs DeMont Tauch Vin de Pays du Torgan Le Sanglier 1991 (France) $6

Lucien Deschaux Côtes du Rhône LeVieux Presbytere 1989 (France) $6

Maison L'Aiglon St. Chinian Grand Reserve 1990 (France) $6

Marques De Arienzo Rioja 1986 (Spain) $7

Millesime Fitou A.O.C. Rouge 1990 (France) $7

Montrose Poets Corner S. E. Australia 1991 $6

Parducci Vintage Red 1990 (CA) $3.75

*Parducci Bono-Sirah Mendocino 1990 (CA) $7

Pellegrini Family Côtes de Sonoma Deux Cepages 1991 (CA) $6

Pere Anselme Côtes du Ventoux 1991 (France) $7
R.H. Phillips California Night Harvest Cuvée Rouge $4/500ml
Straccali Chianti Vernaiolo 1991 (Italy) $6
Tobin James Château Le Cacheflo[2] Paso Robles NV (CA) $6
Torres Sangre de Toro Penedés 1989 (Spain) $7
*Tyrell's Long Flat Red S. E. Australia 1990 and 1991 $6.50
Urbion Ribera del Duero Tinto 1991 (Spain) $7
Verdillac Bordeaux Rouge 1990 (France) $7
Woodley Shiraz-Cabernet S. E. Australia Queen Adelaide 1988 $7
Zonin Montepulciano d'Abruzzo 1990 (Italy) $7

RED BLENDS - $7.50 to $10

Abbaye De Valmagne Côteaux du Langvedoc 1991 (France) $10
*Barnard Griffin Cabernet-Merlot Columbia Valley 1990 (WA) $10
Bodegas Martinez Bujanda Rioja Conde de Valdemar Crianza 1990
  (Spain) $9
Ca' Del Solo Big House Red California 1992 $8
Castello Banfi Rosso di Montalcino "Centine" 1990 (Italy) $8
Castello de Verrazzano Chianti Classico 1991 (Italy) $9.50
Catherine De St. Jurey Côteaux du Languedoc 1992 (France) $9
Château De Cabriac Corbières 1992 (France) $8.50
Château Des Vallonnieres Côtes du Rhône 1990 (France) $8.75
Château Hauterive Le Haut Corbières 1990 (France) $10
Château Larose-Trintaudon Bordeaux Haut-Médoc 1989 and 1990
  (France) $10
Château Trocard Bordeaux Superieur 1988 (France) $8.50
*Cline Côtes d' Oakley Contra Costa County 1990 and 1991
  (CA) $7.50
Cune Rioja Viña Real Crianza 1989 (Spain) $9
Domaine B. Serveau Bourgogne 1989 (France) $10
Domaine D'Aupilhac Vin de Pays du Mont Baudille Le Carignan
  1992 (France) $8
Dr. Cosimo Taurino Salice Salentino Riserva 1986 (Italy) $8

---

[2] Get it? Ha! Ha!

Fetzer Red Table Wine Mendocino County Organically Grown Grapes 1990 (CA) $9

Francesco Candido Salice Salentino Riserva 1988 (Italy) $8

Georges Duboeuf Beaujolais Moulin-à-Vent 1992 (France) $10

Georges Duboeuf Côtes du Rhône 1990 (France) $8

Georges Duboeuf Julienas Domaine de la Siegneurie de Julienas 1992 (France) $8.50

Georges Duboeuf Regnie 1991 (France) $8

Gilbert Alquier Faugères 1991 (France) $9

***Hedges Cellar** Cabernet-Merlot Washington State 1991 and 1992 $9.50

Hop Kiln Marty Griffin's Big Red Sonoma County 1991 (CA) $8

Jaume Serra Penedés Crianza 1989 (Spain) $7.50

Jean Claude Boisset Côtes du Rhône 1990 (France) 1990 $8.50

Jean Garandet Bourgogne Passetoutgrains 1990 (France) $10

J. Vidal-Fleury Vacguegras 1990 (France) $9

Lar De Barros Tierra de Barros Tinto Reserva 1989 (Spain) $8.50

La Vieille Ferme Côtes du Rhône Reserve 1990 (France) $8

Madroña Eldorado Estate Claret 1990 (CA) $8

Marqués De Cáceres Rioja 1989 and 1990 (Spain) $9

Martinez Bujanda Rioja Conde de Valde mar Crianza 1990 (Spain) $9

Masi Valpolicella Classico Superiore 1989 (Italy) $8

Meeker Dry Creek Valley Red Table Wine First Rack 1991 (CA) $8

Mongeard-Mugneret Bourgogne 1989 (France) $9.50

Ochoa Navarra 1988 (Spain) $8

Paul Jaboulet aine Côtes du Rhône Parallele 45 1990 (France) $9

Penfolds Shiraz-Cabernet Koonunga Hill S. Australia 1990 $9

***Preston** Faux Dry Creek Valley 1992 (CA) $9

Prosper Maufoux Côtes du Rhône 1990 (France) $8

Rocca Delle Macie Chianti Classico 1991 (Italy) $9

Rosemount Shiraz-Cabernet Sauvignon S. E. Australia 1992 $7.50

Torres Coronas Penedés 1989 and 1990 (Spain) $9 and $8

BLENDED WHITES - $3.50 to $6[3]

Firestone   Prosperity White Santa Ynez Valley NV (CA) $5

*Good Harbor   Trillium NV (MI) $6

*Hardy's   Sémillon-Chardonnay S. E. Australia Captains Selection 1991 $6

Harvard   Sémillon-Chardonnay S. E. Australia 1991 $6

Parducci   Vintage White 1991 (CA) $3.75

Seppelt   Sémillon-Chardonnay S. E. Australia Classic 1992 $6

Signorello   Il Taglio Napa Valley 1991 (CA) $5

Tyrell's   Long Flat White S. E. Australia 1992 $5.50

Vina Talca   Sauvignon-Sémillon Maule Valley 1990 (Chile) $5

Wine Cask   Melange Blanc Santa Barbara County NV (CA) $5

BLENDED WHITES - $6.50 to $10

*Barone Ricasoli   Orvieto Classico Secco 1990 (Italy) $8

Château Bonnet   Entre-Deux-Mers Blanc 1992 (France) $7

Château Coucheray   Pessac-Leognan 1990 (France) $8

*Columbia Crest   Sémillon-Chardonnay Columbia Valley 1990 (WA) $7.50

E. Guigal   Côtes du Rhône 1991 (France) $10

*Fenn Valley   Classic Reserve NV (MI) $6.50

Geyser Peak   Semchard California 1991 and 1992 $9 and 7.50

Laboure-Roi   Pouilly-Fuissé 1991 (France) $10

Liberty School (Caymus)   Three Valley Select 1991 (CA) $7.50

L. Mawby   P. G. W. Pun 1992 (MI) $6.50

*L. Mawby   Sandpiper 1992 (MI) $7.50

Marquis De Chasse   Bordeaux Blanc 1991 (France) $7

Masi   Soave Classico Superiore 1991 (Italy) $8

Moillard   Côtes du Rhône Les Violettes 1992 (France) $8

*Navarro   Edelzwicker Mendocino 1990 (CA) $6.50

Penfolds   Sémillon-Chardonnay S. Australia Koonunga Hill 1991 $7

Rabbit Ridge   Mystique Sonoma County 1991 (CA) $7

Tyrell's   Long Flat White S. E. Australia 1991 $7

Vichon   Cheurignon Napa Valley 1992 (CA) $9.75

---

3 Several that are widely available in 1.5 liter magnums are listed in Chapter 6.

BEST OF THE BEST FOR VALUE

After compiling lists of best value wines for several years, some wineries obviously emerge as superstars. We recognize this fact not only because they appear so frequently on our lists, but because they also appear frequently in our own cellar.[4] Two California superstar wineries are **Fetzer Vineyards** (marketed both as **Fetzer** and **Bel Arbors**) and **Parducci Wine Cellars**. Other California wineries appearing frequently on our Best Value lists are **Beringer, Chateau St. Jean, Glen Ellen, Napa Ridge, Navarro, Preston, Sebastiani, St. Francis,** and **Sutter Home.** Great value superstars from other U. S. areas are **Chateau Ste. Michelle** (WA), **Columbia Crest** (WA), **Fenn Valley** (MI), **Hogue Cellars** (WA), and **Ste. Chappelle** (ID).

Picking superstars among the imports is tougher because of the extensive number of wineries and countries involved. Among our favorites for value are **Hardy's, Lindemans,** and **Rosemount** (Australia); **Caliterra, Errazuriz,** and **Santa Rita** (Chile); **Georges Duboeuf** and **Prosper Maufoux** (France); and **Deinhard** (Germany).

Please remember that these comments relate strictly to value and not necessarily overall quality. There are many other wineries offering exceptional products which exceed the arbitrary $10 price tag we have imposed.

BEST WINE SHOPS

Obviously, we haven't been everywhere, so we are listing several shops we have visited plus others whose reputations we know. Several of these stores have mailing lists and will be happy to keep you updated on the availability of wines throughout the country. Not all of these shops are large. Some of the smaller ones are listed because they provide excellent service for special wine orders, and many provide discounts for the purchase of case lots. If you know of a good shop that should be listed, please drop us a note; if it fits our criteria, we'll include it in the next edition.

---

4 Being the tightwads that we are.

Arizona	Scottsdale	Newman's Liquor Barn
California	Berkeley	Kermit Lynch
	Costa Mesa	Hi-Time Cellar
	Los Angeles	Wally's,
		Trader Joe,
		Duke of Bourbon,
		Wine Warehouse
	Menlo Park	Beltramos
	Mill Valley	Mill Valley Market
	Redwood City	K & L Wines & Spirits
	Sacramento	Corti Brothers
	San Francisco	Cost Plus,
		Draper & Esquin,
		The Jug Shop,
		K & L Wines & Spirits,
		Liquor Mart,
		Pacific Wine Co.
	Santa Barbara	Wine Cask
	Santa Rosa	Bottle Barn
Colorado	Denver	Applejacks
District of Columbia	Washington	Calvert Woodley,
		MacArthur's,
		Mayflower,
		Pearson's
Florida	Fort Lauderdale	Crown Liquor
	Miami	Sunset Corners
Georgia	Atlanta	Skinflint's
Hawaii	Honolulu	Vintage Wine Cellar
Illinois	Chicago	Sam's Wine Warehouse,
		Knightsbridge
	Skokie	Schaefer's
Kentucky	Covington	Cork 'n Bottle

Louisiana	New Orleans	Martin Wine Cellar
Massachusetts	Boston	Brookline Liquor Mart,
		Cirace & Son
Michigan	Detroit	Merchant of Vino
	East Lansing	Goodrich's
	Grand Haven	D & W Foods
	Grand Rapids	G. B. Russo and Son
		D & W Foods
	Kalamazoo	D & W Foods
Minnesota	Minneapolis	Haskell's
Missouri	Kansas City	Berbiglia,
		Gomer's
	St. Louis	Wine Cellar
	Springfield	Brown Derby
Montana	Big Sky	Sky Spirits & Gifts
New Jersey	Ho-Ho-Kus	Wine & Spirit World
New York	Albany	Barbara's World
	Buffalo	Premier Center
	Hastings-on-Hudson	Rockwood & Perry
	Long Beach	Pop's
	Manhassett	Young's
	New York City	Astor Wines and Spirits,
		Crossroads,
		Garnet,
		K & D Morrell & Co.,
		Sherry-Lehmann,
		Heights Cellars (Brooklyn),
		Van Vleck (Brooklyn),
		Goldstar (Queens)
	Rochester	Century
	Scarsdale	Zachy's
Rhode Island	Providence	Town Wine & Spirits

Tennessee	Memphis	Buster's
Texas	Dallas	Marty's
	Houston	Richard's
Washington	Seattle	Larry's Markets, Thriftway

Suggested Reading

Ensrud, Barbara. *Best Wine Buys for $10 or Less*. New York: Villard Books, 1992. 170 pp.

Johnson, Hugh. *Pocket Encyclopedia of Wine*. New York: Fireside/Simon & Schuster, 1993. 208 pp.

Wine Spectator. Published biweekly by M. Shanken Communications, Inc., New York.

Glossary

Acetic: containing the smell or taste of vinegar.

Acidity: that portion of a wine's taste attributed to the acids, mostly lactic and succinic; a tartness or dryness counteracting the sweetness of sugar in a wine. Acids contribute to wine's overall balance. (See also **Fixed Acidity, Volatile Acidity, Total Acidity,** and **pH.**)

Alcohol: ethyl alcohol, or ethanol, is one of the chemicals produced by the fermentation process. It is usually present in wine at ten to fifteen percent by volume.

Amelioration: any addition (such as sulfur or sugar) to grape juice or wine for the purpose of improving its quality.

Aperitif: a wine taken as an appetizer.

Appellation: a wine-growing region, presumably one with sufficient climatic or soil characteristics to provide special attributes to the grapes and wine produced there.

Aroma: technically, that portion of a young wine's odor attributed to the grape variety making up the wine. Often the term is interchanged with **bouquet** or **nose.**

Astringency: the portion of a wine's taste that puckers your mouth and lingers on your taste buds. It is primarily attributed to tannins and acid, and often indicates that the wine will be long-lived.

"Attack": a term used to describe the first impression a wine makes in your mouth. A good wine should attack your mouth.

"Attractive": a polite (but pukey) term to describe an okay wine. (See **"Charming".**)

Auslese: medium-bodied dessert wines produced from selected bunches of overripe grapes. Originally produced and named in Germany.

Balance: when all the components of wine (i.e., acidity, sugar, alcohol, and tannin) are present in proper proportions, the wine is said to be balanced.

Beaujolais: a region in southern Burgundy, France, producing light red wines from Gamay grapes.

Beerenauslese: full-bodied dessert wines with considerable sweetness, made from *Botrytised* grapes. Originated in Germany.

Bereich: German word for district.

Berries: a term used to describe aromas or flavors in wine that resemble berries (e.g., blackberries, raspberries, currants).

Bianco: Italian word for white.

"Big": Robert Mondavi defined this best, saying, "A big wine fills your mouth." Usually a wine with a high glycerol content.

Blanc: French word for white.

Blanc de Blanc: a sparkling wine made entirely from white grape varieties.

Blanc de Noirs: white wine from red grapes.

Blanco: Spanish word for white.

Body: the consistency of a wine. Related somewhat to its viscosity and texture, but more importantly, to what extent it fills your mouth.

Bordeaux: wines produced in the Bordeaux region of France. Bordeaux wines are made from different grape varieties, depending on the district.

Botrytis: [also Noble Rot or *Edelfaule* (German)] the fungus *Botrytis cinerae* which sometimes infects grapes and gives them exceptional qualities for dessert wines.

Bouquet: technically, that portion of a wine's odor that is attributed to the fermentation and aging process. Often used interchangeably with **aroma** and **nose**.

Brandy: distilled wine. Many of the best are aged in oak barrels.

Brix: a term to express the sugar content (percent by weight) of grapes. Grapes with high sugar content have the potential to make wines with higher alcohol content.

Brut: (pronounced "brute") a dry champagne, one without noticeable sugar content.

Burgundy: wine produced in the Burgundy (now called Bourgogne) region of France. Many of the red Burgundys are Pinot Noirs, while most of the white Burgundys are Chardonnays. In California, Burgundy is a generic red wine.

"Buttery": a term used to describe wine aromas and flavors akin to butter. Usually found in Chardonnay or white Burgundy.

Carafe: a glass bottle for serving wine.

Chablis: a famous white burgundy made from Chardonnay grapes in the Chablis area of France. In California, blended white wines made in a dry to off-dry style.

Chaptalisation: addition of sugar to fermenting wine to increase alcohol content. Now closely controlled by law.

Charmat process: a process for making sparkling wine in which the fermentation takes place in large tanks instead of individual bottles. Named after the French enologist Eugene Charmat.

"Charming": one of those sickening terms we wish were never used to describe wine. Also applies to "lovely."

Château: in France, a wine estate.

Chianti: light red wines (often blended) produced in the Chianti region of Tuscany in central Italy.

Chianti Classico: the best Chianti from select districts that produce medium- to full-bodied red wines with good aging potential.

Claret: an English word for the red wines of Bordeaux. Now more loosely used to describe many red wines made in that style.

Clarification: any procedure to remove particulate matter from wines.

Clarity: how clear the wine is. Wines that have no particulate matter look very transparent in good light.

Classico: Italian term for the superior wine produced in a region.

"Clean": a term to describe wine that is "fresh" in appearance, aroma, and flavor.

Color: an important factor in judging a wine. Is it typical for that wine or too light, off-color, brownish, etc.?

Complex: a term to describe wine that possesses many different tastes and aromas. Complexity is essential to greatness.

Cooper: a craftsman who makes barrels or casks.

Cooperage: the type of barrel (French oak, American oak, etc.) used to age wine. Also used to indicate the length of time a wine spends in the barrel, i.e., cooperage time.

"Corky": wine that smells of cork (due to a faulty cork).

Côte: French term for a slope with vineyards.

"Crisp": a term to describe a fresh wine with pleasing acidity.

Cru: French term for growth. The word denotes a vineyard of high quality.

Cuvée: a blended wine.

Dao: Portugese wines from vineyards south of Dours.

Decant: to pour wine from its bottle to another container from which it will be served.

"Deep": usually denotes a complex wine that presents an array of flavors in sequence. Such wines "have depth."

Demi-sec: half dry.

"Delicate": a wine which is light in aroma, body and flavor.

Dolce: Italian word for sweet.

Doux: French word for sweet.

"Dry": a term to describe wine that leaves no impression of sweetness.

"Earthy": a term to describe wines that smell of soil. Considered appealing when not overpowering.

"Easy": a term for wines that are quaffs or pleasant drinks without complexity.

Einzellage: German term for a specific vineyard.

Eiswein: this German word literally translates as "ice-wine" and refers to the German technique of allowing the grapes to freeze prior to harvest and making wine from the frozen fruit.

"Elegant": a term reserved for wines that combine excellent color, aroma, taste, and overall impression.

"Empty": a term for wine that virtually lacks flavor.

Enologist: one who practices enology.

Enology: the science and art of winemaking.

Estate bottled: a term often found on wine labels indicating that the wine was made from grapes grown in the winery's own vineyard.

"Fat": see **"Big"**.

Fermentation: a process by which yeast converts sugar to alcohol and carbon dioxide.

Filtration: a procedure to clarify wine by passing it through very fine filters.

Fingers: see **Legs**.

Fining: a procedure to clarify wine by binding the particulates with materials such as bentonite clay, egg white, or gelatin and allowing them to settle. Also called collage.

Finish: the flavors and aromas that linger after a wine is swallowed. The longer these persist the better. This is a fancy term for aftertaste. "Long" or "length" are also used in this regard.

"Firm": a term to describe wine with flavors that strike the palate rather boldly because of the acidity or tannin content of the wine. This often indicates a youthful wine that will age well. It is a positive attribute.

First Growth: the highest-ranked châteaux of the Bordeaux region in France.

Fixed Acidity (F.A.): acidity from tartaric, malic, and citric acids in grapes as well as lactic and succinic acids produced by fermentation.

"Flat": a wine that lacks firmness or "grip."

"Flinty": a term to describe wine with a dry mineral character from the soil in which the grapes were grown.

Flor: a white blanket of yeast that develops on fine sherries.

"Floral" or "flowery": a term for wine that has the bouquet and taste of flowers.

Flute: an elongated wineglass used for sparkling wine. Also a tall wine bottle traditionally used for Alsatian and Rhine wines.

"Foxy": a term to describe the distinctive flavor of wines made from *Vitis labrusca* (American grapes such as Concord).

"Fresh": a term often used to describe white wines that possess good fruity acidity or tanginess.

"Fruit" or **"fruity"**: a term describing aromas or flavors of wine that resemble fruit or a mixture of fruits (e.g., apples, apricots, berries, figs, grapefruit).

"Full": a term for wines that fill the mouth with lots of flavors. Synonymous with full-bodied.

Generic: wines that carry the name of a wine-producing region or a proprietary name rather than a varietal name (e.g., Burgundy, Chablis, Rioja).

Glycerin (glycerol): a trihydroxy alcohol formed during fermentation of grape juice. It is believed to contribute a "fatness" or "buttery" character to wine.

"Grip": a term for firmness of flavor and composition.

Grosslage: German term for a group of neighboring vineyards.

Halbtrocken: a term often found on German wine labels that translates as "half dry." To most non-Germans, these wines taste dry.

"Harmonious": a term for a wine with all its components in perfect balance.

"Herbaceous": a term for wines with grassy aromas or flavors.

"Hollow": a term for wine that noticeably lacks flavor.

"Honest": a term for wine without noticeable flaws, but nonetheless not outstanding.

Horticulturist: a person who studies or practices the culture of fruit, vegetable, or ornamental plants. Not to be confused with a "blooming idiot."

Kabinett: a German term to describe naturally light wines. Many are Rieslings, off-dry wines with crisp acidity, a pleasant aroma, and about ten percent alcohol.

Lambrusco: a sweet, sparkling red wine produced in Italy.

Liebfraumilch: a German word roughly translating as "Holy Mother's milk." It originally referred to wines made in Worms, in the Rheinhessen region of Germany, and is now a trade name for blended wines from many areas of Germany.

"Lean": a term to describe wine that is lacking in texture and flavor, but which may be appropriate for a lighter style.

Lees: see Sediment.

Legs: rivulets that run down the side of a wineglass after the wine is swirled inside.(Also commonly referred to as fingers.)

"Light": a term for wines with relatively little alcohol or body. These might be just fine as quaffing wines.

Limousin oak: oak from the Limousin Forest in France. Traditionally used to age red wines.

Madeira: rich dessert wines produced on the Isle of Madeira.

Malolactic fermentation: fermentation in barrels or bottles converting malic acid to lactic acid with the release of carbon dioxide. It adds complexity (new flavors) to the wine.

Marsala: an important dessert wine of Italy that has a taste reminiscent of burnt sugar.

Mature: a wine that has fully developed and is ready to drink.

"Meaty": a term for wines with substance that you can almost chew. They cling to your gums.

Médoc: one of the great Bordeaux districts.

Meritage: American blends of Bordeaux grape varieties.

Méthode champenoise: the traditional method of making champagne in which still wine is fortified with sugar and yeast and refermented in the bottle. The sediment is disgorged and the wine remains in the same bottle.

Midi: a vast wine-producing area in southern France (also called Languedoc-Rousillon).

Must: a mixture of grape juice, skins and pulp that will undergo fermentation.

"Musty": a term for a wine with a stale aroma.

Nevers oak: a type of French oak used to age Bordeaux wines.

"Noble": a term for a great wine or one which is perfectly balanced.

Noble Rot: *Botrytis cinerea.*

Nose: a slang term used to describe the aroma and bouquet of wine.

Great smelling wines have a "big nose." Next thing you know we'll be calling them "Cyranos" or "Pinocchios."

"Nutty": a term for a wine having a nutlike aroma.

Oak or "Oaky": the wood from which most wine-aging barrels are made. "Oaky" describes the flavors and aromas of oak released by the wine.

Oxidation: chemical reactions in which the alcohol in wine is converted to acetaldehyde and acetic acid (vinegar), resulting in spoiled wine.

Pétillance: very tiny bubbles of carbon dioxide dispersed in wine which give it a lightly sparkling appearance (not a true sparkling wine).

pH: a measurement of the strength of acidity on a scale of 1 to 7 (1 being most acid and 7 being neutral).

Phylloxera: a root-feeding insect which severely damages or kills grapevines. This pest has wiped out entire vineyards in many areas of the world and is now attacking many vineyards in California.

"Plump": a term to describe wine that has enough "fat" to be pleasing.

Port: dessert wines, the authentic versions of which are produced in Portugal.

Pouilly-Fuissé: fine dry white wines from France's southern Burgundy, made from Chardonnary grapes.

Pouilly-Fumé: excellent dry white wines from France's Loire Valley, made from Sauvignon Blanc grapes.

Private Reserve: a wine that in the winery's opinion is of superior quality. These wines are bottled separately.

Proprietary: similar to generic wines (i.e., not varietals) except the names are coined by the winery and are not names of the growing region. (e.g., Trillium, Proprietors Red, Village White).

Qba: German abbreviation for quality wine of designated regions. The middle level of German wines.

Qmp: German abbreviation for quality wines with special attributes. These include the five top levels of German wine, *Kabinett, Spätlese, Auslese, Beerenauslese,* and *Trockenbeerenauslese.*

Quaff: a wine that drinks easy, with no great characteristics.

Reserve: the best lot of wine from a varietal, which the wine maker bottles separately.

Residual sugar: the amount of sugar remaining in a wine (usually expressed as a percentage).

"Rich": a term to describe a wine with opulence, exceptional sweetness, or depth.

Riddling: a technique of rotating Champagne bottles so the sediment settles in the neck.

Rioja: a wine-producing region in northern Spain.

"Robust": a term to describe a wine that "attacks" fairly vigorously and finishes nicely.

Rosé: a wine with a pink to salmon color that is usually produced by leaving red grape varieties on the skin for the first few hours of fermentation. Some are also produced by blending, but they are considered inferior. *Rosato* in Italian; *Rosdao* in Spanish.

Rosso: Italian word for red. *Tinto* in Spanish; *Rouge* in French.

"Rough": a term to describe a wine noticeably out-of-balance which gives no pleasure.

"Round": a well-balanced wine which may be "big" or "fat".

Saké: a Japanese wine made from fermented rice.

Sauternes: a dessert wine that is usually made from Sauvignon Blanc and Sémillon grapes. Named for the district, Sauternes, in Bordeaux, France.

Schloss: the German version of a French château.

Secco: Italian word for dry. *Seco* in Spanish; *Sec* in French.

Sediment: solid matter in wine which may require that the wine be decanted. Also called Lees.

"Sharp": a term to describe wine that bites the tongue because of high acid or tannin.

Sherry: Dessert or aperitif wines, the authentic versions of which are produced in southern Spain.

"Short": a term to describe a wine that lacks finish.

Sommelier: a restaurant employee who is in charge of the wine service.

Spätlese: medium-bodied German white wines, usually with a floral and fruity nose and rich fruit flavors. They vary from slightly sweet to dry.

"Spicy": a term to describe wine that has the aroma or flavor of spices such as pepper, clove, cinnamon, mint, etc.

Structure: an array of flavors within a wine presented in a sequence which indicates complexity and balance.

"Sturdy": a term to describe full-bodied, robust wine with excellent flavor.

"Supple": a term often used to describe young red wines with decent character.

Sur lie: a procedure in which wine is left on its yeast sediments for a period after fermentation and before bottling. This sometimes adds complexity and an appealing, fresh quality.

Sweet: an overall taste impression of wines that carry at least two percent residual sugar.

Tafelwein: table wine. The lowest classification of German wines.

Tannin: chemicals present in red wines (mostly from grape skins) which prevent them from oxidizing, allow them to age for several years, and provide the astringent taste in young wines.

"Tart": a term used to describe a wine with considerable acid content.

"Thin": a term to describe wine lacking flavor and body.

Tinto: Spanish word for red.

"Tired": a term to describe an old wine that has passed its peak of development.

Total Acidity (T.A.): fixed and volatile acidity combined.

Transfer method: a technique for making Champagne in which the wine is taken from the fermentation bottle, put in a tank to remove the sediment, and rebottled.

Trockenbeerenauslese: a heavy-bodied, white, German dessert wine that is sweet and honeylike with considerable complexity.

Vanilla: a scent imparted by aging wine in oak which contains vanillin.

Varietal: a wine whose label carries the name of the major grape variety used to produce it (e.g., Chardonnay, Petite Sirah, Vignoles).

Vinifera: the European grape species to which most great wine varieties belong. The genus is *Vitis*.

Vin ordinaire: a French term for ordinary or everyday wine.

Vino de mesa: Spanish for table wine.

Vintage: the year in which a grape crop is grown. Not to be confused with the year in which the wine may be released.

Vintner: a person who makes wine. After making great wine, a vintner becomes an enologist.

Viticulture: the science and art of growing grapes.

Volatile Acidity (V.A.): that part of acidity attibuted to acetic acid, which can contribute some benefit at very low levels but gives an impression of vinegar at higher levels.

"**Watery**": a term for thin wine that lacks body and flavor.

"**Weedy**": a term for wine that has aromas or flavors reminiscent of hay or grasses.

Wine Thief: a glass tube used by vintners to remove samples from barrels for tasting. In France, a *chantepleure*.

"**Yeasty**": a term for wines that undergo secondary fermentation, which imparts aromas of yeast.

"**Young**": a term for a relatively new wine. Considered a positive attribute in many whites, Rosés, and light-bodied reds, this indicates immaturity in full-bodied reds.

Winery Index

252

254

257

About the Authors

The authors, Alan R. Putnam, Ph.D., and Sandra L. Putnam, M.B.O.,[1] (more commonly known as Al and Sandi, Sal and Andi, or the Putts) might be considered unique in that they are a reincarnated couple. They mysteriously appeared in their present form (slightly overweight) on the lawn of Preston Vineyards near Healdsburg, California, in the spring of 1990. Each was pleased to find a bottle of robust red wine in hand. After immediately stocking their vehicle with exquisite wines from the Dry Creek Valley, they motored to Gallatin Canyon, Montana, where they witnessed a magnificent mayfly hatch on the Gallatin River and set about erecting a log home. They still reside in Gallatin Gateway.

In their former lives, both worked at Michigan State University (MSU). Al was a professor of Horticulture; he performed research (some involving viticulture) and taught undergraduate and graduate classes. Sandi managed the office of the Department of Microbiology and Public Health. In January 1990 both succumbed to a mysterious illness which doctors finally diagnosed as *acute academia anemia*.

Over the past twenty-five years, the Putts have traveled to most of the wine producing areas of the U.S. and abroad. They spent six-month leaves from MSU at Cornell University and the University of California-Davis where they studied the New York and California wine industries in depth. They've grown their own grapes and made their own wine. More importantly, they've consumed over ten thousand bottles of wine and tasted countless thousands of other samples. They've talked with many vintners and have read everything they can on the subject. Recently, they've become interested in research on wine's health benefits.

While at MSU, Al published over two hundred scientific and popular articles, wrote twelve book chapters, and co-edited a science reference book. Sandi is expert at editorial aspects (getting the ideas into lucid form). As you'll soon learn from reading this book, both of these reincarnates are wine advocates.

---

[1] Must be obeyed.

To order additional copies of *Wine Magic*....

...Simply fill out this form and send it to:

Salandi Enterprises
P. O. Box 369
Gallatin Gateway, MT 59730

Name:_____

Address: _____

City: _____ State: _____ Zip: _____

Please enclose check or money order for $14.95 + $2.05 shipping and handling ($17 total) per book. Volume discounts available; please inquire.

— —

Make check or money order payable to Salandi Enterprises.

We welcome any suggestions you have for the next edition.

_____

_____

_____

_____

_____

_____